Westward Expansion
Primary Sources

Westward Expansion Primary Sources

Tom Pendergast
and Sara Pendergast
Christine Slovey, Editor

U·X·L

AN IMPRINT OF THE GALE GROUP
DETROIT · SAN FRANCISCO · LONDON
BOSTON · WOODBRIDGE, CT

11/00

Tom Pendergast and Sara Pendergast

Staff

Christine Slovey, *U•X•L Senior Editor*
Carol DeKane Nagel, *U•X•L Managing Editor*
Tom Romig, *U•X•L Publisher*

Rita Wimberley, *Senior Buyer*
Dorothy Maki, *Manufacturing Manager*
Evi Seoud, *Assistant Production Manager*
Mary Beth Trimper, *Production Director*

Shalice Shah-Caldwell, *Permissions Specialist*

Michelle DiMercurio, *Cover Art Director*
Pamela A. E. Galbreath, *Page Art Director*
Kenn Zorn, *Product Design Manager*

Kelly A. Quin, *Image Editor*
Pamela A. Reed, *Imaging Coordinator*
Robert Duncan and Dan Newell, *Imaging Specialists*
Randy Bassett, *Image Database Supervisor*
Barbara J. Yarrow, *Graphic Services Supervisor*

Marco Di Vita, Graphix Group, *Typesetting*

Library of Congress Card Number: 00–107861

ISBN 0–7876–4864–7

Printed in the United States of America

10 9 8 7 6 5 4 3 2 1

Contents

Settling the West. *(Archive Photos, Inc. Reproduced by permission.)*

Nat Love. *(Courtesy of the Denver Public Library.)*

A frontier town. *(Photograph by Kennett. Courtesy of the National Archives and Records Administration.)*

Reader's Guide

The westward expansion of the United States, which took place between 1763 and 1890, is at once one of the most romantic sagas of human accomplishment and one of the bleakest tragedies of human cruelty. In just over one century, American settlers, soldiers, and diplomats helped the United States expand from a mere thirteen British colonies clinging to the eastern seaboard, to a sprawling nation stretching 3,000 miles from the Atlantic to the Pacific Oceans.

Westward Expansion: Primary Sources tells the story of westward expansion in the words of the people who lived it. Seventeen full or excerpted documents provide a wide range of perspectives on this period in history. Included are excerpts from the journals of early pioneers and memoirs of mountain men, cowboys, a woman who grew up on a Texas ranch, and a Native American warrior who fought at the Battle of Little Bighorn. Also included are excerpts from publications, such as *The American Settler's Guide,* that helped settlers make their way in the West. Reprinted in full is the Indian Removal Act of 1830 and the congressional testimony of John S. Smith, witness to the Sand Creek Massacre.

Format

The excerpts in *Westward Expansion: Primary Sources* are divided into six chapters. Each of the chapters focuses on a specific theme: Exploring the West; Indian Wars; Settling the West; The Cowboy Life; The Gold Rush; and Closing the Frontier. Every chapter opens with a historical overview, followed by reprinted documents.

Each excerpt has seven sections:

- **Introductory material** places the document and its author in a historical context.

- **Things to remember while reading** offers important background information about the featured text.

- **Excerpt** presents the document in its original spelling and format.

- **What happened next...** discusses the impact of the document and/or relevant historical events following the date of the document.

- **Did you know...** provides interesting facts about the document and its author.

- **Consider the following...** poses questions about the material for the reader to consider.

- **For More Information** offers resources for further study of the document and its author as well as sources used by the authors in writing the material.

Additionally, the chapters contain numerous sidebar boxes, some focusing on the author of the featured document, others highlighting interesting, related information. More than sixty black-and-white photos and maps illustrate the text. Each excerpt is accompanied by a glossary running in the margin alongside the reprinted document that defines terms, people, and ideas. Each volume begins with a timeline of events and a "Words to Know" section. The volume concludes with a subject index so students can easily find the people, places, and events discussed throughout *Westward Expansion: Primary Sources*.

Dedication

To our children, Conrad and Louisa, who have journeyed with us on our own westward trek.

Special Thanks

Special thanks are due to Lynne E. Heckman, teacher of American history at Valley View Middle School in Snohomish, Washington, for helping us understand the needs and interests of middle school students and teachers, and to the many historians and writers whose work on the West we filtered through our minds as we prepared this collection.

Comments and Suggestions

We welcome your comments on *Westward Expansion: Primary Sources* and suggestions for other topics in history to consider. Please write: Editors, *Westward Expansion: Primary Sources,* U•X•L, 27500 Drake Rd., Farmington Hills, Michigan 48331-3535; call toll-free: 1-800-877-4253; fax to (248) 414-5043; or send e-mail via http://www.galegroup.com.

Timeline of Events in Westward Expansion

1622   Indian chief Powhatan's younger brother, Ope-chanough, starts the first Indian war by attacking colonists in Jamestown, Virginia, to protest white use of Indian land.

1754   The French defeat George Washington and American colonists fighting for the British at the Battle of Fort Necessity on July 3–4, beginning the French and Indian War.

1763   The first Treaty of Paris is signed, ending the French and Indian War. Under the treaty, France relinquishes its claim to Canada and the Ohio Valley to England

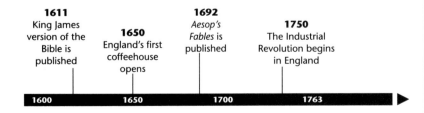

1611 King James version of the Bible is published

1650 England's first coffeehouse opens

1692 *Aesop's Fables* is published

1750 The Industrial Revolution begins in England

| 1600 | 1650 | 1700 | 1763 |

and hands over its holdings west of the Mississippi River to Spain.

1763 Hoping to end Indian attacks in the Ohio Valley, the British issue the Proclamation of 1763, which recalls all settlers from west of the Appalachian crest and forbids further emigration into the area.

1769 Catholic missionary Father Junipero Serra and the Spanish army establish the first of twenty-one missions along the coast of California. Serra directs soldiers to round up the Native North Americans and bring them, by force if necessary, to the missions.

1776 The Revolutionary War begins. Among the many factors contributing to the war are clashes between colonists and the British over access to land west of the Appalachians.

1783 The Revolutionary War ends. The second Treaty of Paris grants the newly formed United States of America its independence. The United States gains all of the territory from the Great Lakes south to the Gulf of Mexico and from the Appalachian Mountains west to the Mississippi River.

1783 To raise funds, the newly formed U.S. government claims all of the Indian lands east of the Mississippi River (consisting of present-day Indiana, Kentucky, Ohio, and Tennessee) to sell to settlers. The Chippewa, Delaware, Kickapoo, Miami, Ottawa, Potawatomi, Shawnee, and Wyandot nations and some Iroquois warriors join together to oppose the invasion of U.S. settlers into their territory.

1803 The United States purchases from France more than 800,000 acres of land west of the Mississippi River for $15 million. The Louisiana Purchase doubles the size

A native Californian, c. 1852. ©Corbis. Reproduced by permission.)

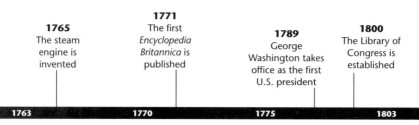

1765
The steam engine is invented

1771
The first *Encyclopedia Britannica* is published

1789
George Washington takes office as the first U.S. president

1800
The Library of Congress is established

1763   1770   1775   1803

of the United States. This territory today makes up the states of Arkansas, Iowa, Kansas, Louisiana, Missouri, Montana, Nebraska, North Dakota, Oklahoma, and South Dakota and parts of Colorado, Minnesota, and Wyoming.

1804 Meriwether Lewis, William Clark, and their entourage set out from St. Louis, Missouri, on May 14 to determine whether the Gulf of Mexico and the Pacific Ocean are linked by a river system. Finding no such water connection, they pioneer an overland route across the Rocky Mountains.

1806 The Lewis and Clark expedition returns to St. Louis on September 23 after nearly twenty-eight months of exploration. The expedition had been given up for lost, and its return is celebrated throughout the country.

1808 John Jacob Astor charters the American Fur Company; it becomes the largest U.S. fur trading company by 1827.

1810 Several British fur traders set up companies in the Northwest. In response, John Jacob Astor organizes the Pacific Fur Company to claim the territory west of the Rocky Mountains and establishes a fort at present-day Astoria, Oregon. Already well-established east of the Rockies, Astor hopes to gain control over the entire American fur trade with his western enterprise.

1812 The War of 1812 begins. In a war that is often called the Second War for Independence, Americans seek to finally eliminate the British presence in the Old Northwest and to end British attacks on American ships carrying goods to France.

1814 The Treaty of Ghent ends the War of 1812. The British agree that all the territory south of the Great Lakes to

Native Americans greeting the Lewis and Clark expedition. *(Corbis-Bettmann. Reproduced by permission.)*

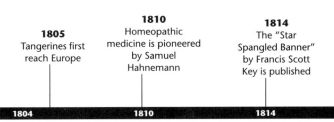

1805 Tangerines first reach Europe

1810 Homeopathic medicine is pioneered by Samuel Hahnemann

1814 The "Star Spangled Banner" by Francis Scott Key is published

1804　　1810　　1814　　1819

the Gulf of Mexico belongs to the United States. The British also agree not to give any help to their Indian allies in this territory.

1820   The U.S. Congress approves the Missouri Compromise, which outlaws slavery within the Louisiana Purchase territory north of 36°30′ latitude. Missouri enters the Union as a slave state, while Maine enters as a free state.

1821   Mexico gains its independence from Spain and opens its borders with the United States.

1823   William Ashley begins the annual mountain man Rendezvous for American fur trappers in the Rocky Mountains. Trappers gather at the annual Rendezvous to sell their pelts and gather a year's worth of supplies.

1829   Gold is discovered on Cherokee land in present-day Georgia. Gold seekers arrive in overwhelming numbers and lawlessness begins. Georgia increases its efforts to relocate the Cherokee to lands west of the Mississippi River.

1830   The U.S. Congress votes in favor of the Indian Removal Act on May 28. The act calls for the removal—voluntary or forced—of all Indians to lands west of the Mississippi River.

1831   Zenas Leonard begins his trapping career with the Gantt and Blackwell Company.

1834   Congress establishes Indian Territory, which covers parts of the present-day states of Oklahoma, Nebraska, and Kansas, far smaller than the "all lands west of the Mississippi" that whites had once promised.

1835   A small group of Cherokee signs the Treaty of New Echota on December 29, selling all remaining Chero-

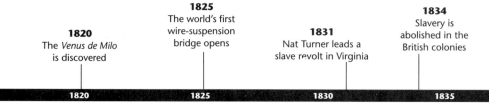

1820
The *Venus de Milo* is discovered

1825
The world's first wire-suspension bridge opens

1831
Nat Turner leads a slave revolt in Virginia

1834
Slavery is abolished in the British colonies

1820   1825   1830   1835

kee land east of the Mississippi River to the United States. The majority of Cherokee oppose the treaty.

1835–42 The Seminole Wars begin in the winter of 1835. After Seminole Indians refuse to leave their land in Florida, they are led by war chief Osceola in a fight against U.S. Army troops in the swamps of Florida. The war costs the U.S. government more than $20 million and the lives of fifteen hundred troops. Osceola is captured during a truce and dies in prison in 1838. The war continues until 1842, at which time most Seminole are moved west of the Mississippi River.

1836 On April 21, Mexican president Antonio López de Santa Anna and a large army lay siege to a band of Texans holed up at the Alamo Mission. After a ten-day battle, every American man is killed. "Remember the Alamo" becomes the battle cry of Texans who fight back against Santa Anna and win independence for the Republic of Texas on May 14, 1836.

1836 The Republic of Texas claims all land between the Rio Grande and Nueces Rivers. Sam Houston is sworn in as president on October 22.

1836 Narcissa Prentiss Whitman and Eliza Spalding, two Protestant missionaries, become the first white women to cross the Rocky Mountains when they travel westward with their husbands.

1838 The U.S. Army forms the Corps of Topographical Engineers to look at western lands with an eye toward settlement. The Corps of Engineers makes maps and surveys of the frontier until the 1860s.

1838–39 The removal of the Cherokee Indians from Georgia to Indian Territory (present-day Oklahoma) begins in October. General Winfield Scott and seven thou-

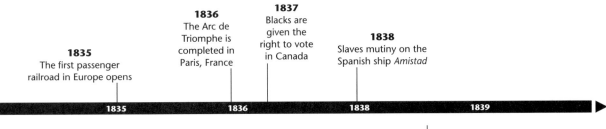

1835
The first passenger railroad in Europe opens

1836
The Arc de Triomphe is completed in Paris, France

1837
Blacks are given the right to vote in Canada

1838
Slaves mutiny on the Spanish ship *Amistad*

1835   1836   1838   1839

sand federal troops are sent to the Cherokee's homeland to insist that the Cherokee leave. Scott's troops imprison any Cherokee who resist and burn their homes and crops. The Cherokee remember the trek as the "Trail Where They Cried," while U.S. historians call it the "Trail of Tears." More than four thousand Cherokee die on the forced march before they reach their destination in March 1839.

1840 The U.S. fur-trapping system deteriorates due to beaver depletion and shifts in fashion toward silk hats.

1842 John C. Frémont leads his first expedition to the West to explore the country between the Missouri River and the Rocky Mountains from May to October.

1843 The Oregon Trail is opened from Idaho to the Grande Ronde Valley in Oregon. The Great Migration, the name given to the first major exodus of emigrants westward, draws one thousand settlers onto the Oregon Trail.

1844–45 The U.S. Congress passes laws to build military posts to protect settlers moving from the East to California and Oregon. These forts cause conflict with Indian tribes along the route.

1845 John C. Frémont's *Report of the Exploring Expedition to the Rocky Mountains* is published.

1845 In March, President John Tyler signs a resolution to bring Texas into the Union. Because the border of Texas is still contested, Tyler's action angers the Mexican government and it breaks off diplomatic relations with the United States.

1845 As war with Mexico looms, John L. O'Sullivan, editor of *The United States Magazine and Democratic Review,*

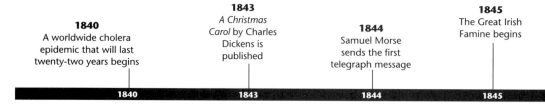

1840
A worldwide cholera epidemic that will last twenty-two years begins

1843
A Christmas Carol by Charles Dickens is published

1844
Samuel Morse sends the first telegraph message

1845
The Great Irish Famine begins

1840   1843   1844   1845

defines American's faith in the expansion of their nation as their "manifest destiny." The idea of manifest destiny implies that Americans have the God-given right to acquire and populate the territories stretching west to the Pacific.

1846   The Mexican-American War officially begins on May 11. The United States and Mexico go to war to settle their disagreement over the southern border of Texas. Texas and the United States claim the Rio Grande as the southern border. Mexico argues that the Nueces River is the actual border.

1846   California's Bear Flag Revolt begins on June 14 when settlers claim their independence from Mexico and raise a flag at Sonoma bearing a black bear and a star.

1846   The Oregon Treaty is signed with Britain on June 15 giving territory south of the forty-ninth parallel to the United States. Though the British had occupied the area since 1818, the American population of Oregon Country has grown to 5,000 by 1845 while the British claim only 750 inhabitants.

1847   Elise Amalie Wærenskold settles in Texas.

1848   James Marshall discovers gold at Sutter's Mill in California on January 24, thus beginning the California Gold Rush.

1848   The Treaty of Guadalupe Hidalgo is signed on February 2 ending the Mexican-American War. The treaty grants the United States all or part of the present-day states of Arizona, California, Colorado, New Mexico, Utah, and Wyoming. It is a territorial addition second only to the Louisiana Purchase and virtually doubles the size of the country.

1846
The Smithsonian Institution is founded in Washington, D.C.

1847
The first U.S. postage stamps are sold to the public

1848
The first women's rights convention is organized

1846   1847   1848

1848 In April, Edward Kemble, editor of the *California Star* newspaper, joins the first party to leave San Francisco for the gold mines.

1849 Elisha Douglass Perkins and five traveling companions begin their overland journey to California in hopes of striking it rich in the gold rush. An estimated thirty-two thousand people travel to California in 1849, most hoping to discover a gold mine.

1850 The U.S. Congress passes a series of laws to address the growing divisions over the slavery issue and disputes over the land acquired in the Mexican-American War. The famous Compromise of 1850 addresses the problem of slavery in the new territories of New Mexico and California. It outlaws the slave trade in Washington, D.C., but allows it everywhere else throughout the South. In addition, California is admitted to the Union as a free state, and a new and tougher fugitive slave law replaces the poorly enforced Fugitive Slave Act of 1793.

1851 Tensions between the army and the Navajo Indians escalate quickly after the army constructs Fort Defiance in present-day eastern Arizona.

1861–72 The Apache Wars begin in southern Arizona in 1861 when Apache chief Cochise escapes from an army post in Arizona with hostages. In 1871 Cochise opposes efforts to relocate his people to a reservation in New Mexico. In 1872 he finally agrees not to attack the U.S. Army in exchange for reservation land in eastern Arizona.

1862 The Homestead Act of 1862 is passed by the U.S. Congress. Nearly 470,000 homesteaders apply for homesteads in the next eighteen years.

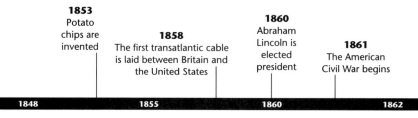

1853 Potato chips are invented

1858 The first transatlantic cable is laid between Britain and the United States

1860 Abraham Lincoln is elected president

1861 The American Civil War begins

| 1848 | 1855 | 1860 | 1862 |

1864 On November 29, Colonel John M. Chivington leads a force from Colorado in an unprovoked attack on a Southern Cheyenne and Arapaho camp at Sand Creek, killing an estimated five hundred men, women, and children. The Sand Creek Massacre is one of the first Indian battles to attract significant attention in the East.

1864 The "Long Walk" of the Navajo begins. Forces led by Christopher "Kit" Carson trap a huge number of Navajo in Canyon de Chelly in present-day Arizona, a steep-sided canyon in which the Navajo had traditionally taken refuge. The Navajo are marched southeast to Bosque Redondo, with many dying along the way.

1864 Fanny Kelly's wagon train is attacked in July and she is taken prisoner by Sioux Indians. She lives among the Sioux for five months until the Native Americans hand her over to U.S. troops.

1865 Congress opens a formal investigation of the actions of U.S. Army forces under the command of Colonel Chivington at Sand Creek. An army judge labels the Sand Creek Massacre "a cowardly and cold-blooded slaughter, sufficient to cover its perpetrators with indelible infamy, and the face of every American with shame and indignation."

Crow warriors in custody of the U.S. Army. *(©Corbis. Reproduced by permission.)*

1866 The first of the great cattle drives begins in Texas. Cowboys round up cattle and drive them northward to rail lines that reach into Kansas. In the years to come some eight million longhorn cattle travel the trails north to Kansas from ranches across Texas and throughout the Great Plains.

1867 Joseph McCoy, an Illinois livestock dealer, founds the town of Abilene, Kansas, as a gathering point for cat-

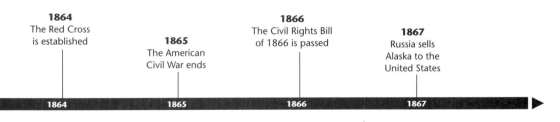

1864
The Red Cross
is established

1865
The American
Civil War ends

1866
The Civil Rights Bill
of 1866 is passed

1867
Russia sells
Alaska to the
United States

1864   1865   1866   1867

Dodge City, Kansas in the 1880s. *(Corbis-Bettmann. Reproduced by permission.)*

tle drives from Texas. Rail lines stretching eastward from Abilene deliver cattle to eastern markets.

1868   U.S. military authorities force Navajo chiefs to sign a treaty, agreeing to live on reservations and cease opposition to whites. The treaty establishes a 3.5 million-acre reservation within the Navajo nation's old domains (a small portion of the original Navajo territory).

1869   The completion of the first transcontinental United States railroad is celebrated with the Golden Spike ceremony on May 10. The railroads joining the Atlantic and Pacific coasts are linked at Promontory Point, Utah, north of the Great Salt Lake.

1870   The U.S. Supreme Court, in the case of *McKay v. Campbell,* decides that Indians arc not U.S. citizens since their allegiance is to their tribe, not to the United States. Because of this ruling Indians are denied protections guaranteed by the U.S. Constitution.

1871   The famous cattle town of Dodge City, Kansas, is founded. Within a year the settlement boasts of a general store, three dance halls, and six saloons, and soon becomes a gathering place for cowboys fresh off the range.

1871   The U.S. Congress stops the practice of making treaties with Indians. Congress allows "agreements," which do not recognize tribes as independent nations. At the end of the treaty era, American Indian tribes still control one-tenth of the forty-eight states, or about one-fourth of the land between the Mississippi River and the Rocky Mountains. By the early 1900s much of this land is owned by the U.S. government.

1874   An expedition led by George Armstrong Custer discovers gold in the Black Hills of South Dakota, sacred

1869
The Suez Canal is opened to traffic

1870
The Franco-Prussian War begins

1871
The Second German Reich is proclaimed at Versailles

1872
Susan B. Anthony and others are arrested for trying to vote

1868   1870   1872   1874

land for the Lakota Sioux, Cheyenne, and other tribes. In violation of the Fort Laramie Treaty, gold miners flood the Black Hills. Soon Indian and U.S. Army forces are fighting over this land.

1875   U.S. president Ulysses Grant vetoes a bill that would protect the buffalo from extinction.

1876   At the Battle of Little Bighorn on June 25 forces led by Custer are defeated by combined Native American forces. The Indians' victory is their last major triumph against the whites.

1877   After the Battle of Little Bighorn, all of the Nez Percé Indians are ordered to report to reservations. Chief Joseph of the Nez Percé leads a band of his people on a long, torturous journey to elude army forces, but they are eventually captured just forty miles from the Canadian border.

1880   Cattle drives up the Chisholm Trail reach their peak.

1883–84   The Fence Cutter's War begins when a drought in Texas makes good grazing land scarce. Small ranchers and homesteaders pressure lawmakers to ban the fencing of public lands. When they receive no assistance, they band together in small groups with names like the Owls, Javelinas, or Blue Devils and, under the cover of night, tear down the offending fences.

1884   Josiah Gregg's book *Commerce of the Prairies* records the arduous task of overland travel and paints an optimistic picture of emigrant trains forging across the prairies to claim the continent. Many use the book as a reference as they prepare for their own journey.

1885   The cowboy era ends. Increased settlement of Kansas leads to the closing of the cattle towns, and expanding

Cowboys at night awakening the relief watch. *(Corbis-Bettmann. Reproduced by permission.)*

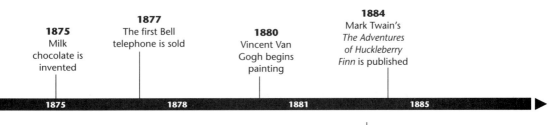

1875
Milk chocolate is invented

1877
The first Bell telephone is sold

1880
Vincent Van Gogh begins painting

1884
Mark Twain's *The Adventures of Huckleberry Finn* is published

| 1875 | 1878 | 1881 | 1885 |

railroad lines mean that ranchers no longer have to drive cattle to railheads. Huge blizzards that strike the plains in 1886 and 1887 kill off cattle by the thousands, proving that cattle can't be left to fend for themselves. Finally, farmers claim increasing amounts of western land, and ranchers are forced to purchase and fence land for their cattle. Men who were once cowboys now become mere farmhands—but the legend of the cowboy lives on.

1890 The Battle of Wounded Knee takes place on December 29, ending the last major Indian resistance to white settlement in America. Nearly 500 well-armed troopers of the U.S. 7th Cavalry massacre an estimated 300 (out of 350) Sioux men, women, and children in a South Dakota encampment. The Army takes only 35 casualties.

1890 The Superintendent of the Census for 1890 declares that there is no longer a frontier in America. The census report's conclusion about the closing of the frontier later encourages President Theodore Roosevelt to begin setting aside public lands as national parks.

1892 The eighteenth edition of Henry N. Copp's *The American Settler's Guide* is published.

1893 Historian Frederick Jackson Turner delivers an address at the Columbian Exposition in Chicago that changes the way Americans think about the conquest of the West and its affect on the American character.

1907 Nat Love's memoirs, *The Life and Adventures of Nat Love, Better Known in the Cattle Country as "Deadwood Dick"* are published.

1931 Wooden Leg, a warrior who fought against George Armstrong Custer's troops in the Battle of Little Bighorn, narrates his dramatic autobiography to Thomas Marquis.

1900
Jazz music originates in New Orleans

1912
The *Titanic* hits an iceberg and sinks

1917
V. I. Lenin leads communist takeover of Russia

1929
Great Depression begin

1890   1905   1920   1931

Words to Know

C

Californios: Descendants of the original Spanish settlers in California.

Cattle drive: Moving a herd of cattle from the open range to a railroad line. Cattle drives were led by bands of cowboys who tended the cattle.

Cholera: An acute intestinal infection. Cholera causes violent vomiting, fever, chills, and diarrhea. This infection killed hundreds of emigrants making their way west.

Colonies: Regions under the political control of a distant country.

E

Emigrants: People who leave one region to move to another. Those who moved from the East to settle in the West during westward expansion were known as emigrants.

F

French and Indian War: A war between the British and combined French and Indian forces from 1755 to 1763 over control of the fur trading regions of the American interior.

Frontier: A term used by whites to refer to lands that lay beyond white settlements, including lands that were already occupied by Indians and Mexicans. In the United States the frontier existed until 1890 when Americans had settled the entire area between the Atlantic and Pacific Oceans.

G

Ghost Dance: A religious movement that was adopted by some Plains Indians in the 1880s and 1890s. The religion predicted that magical powers would allow the Indians to gain back all their land from the whites.

Great Migration: The mass movement of emigrants westward on the Oregon Trail that began in 1843 and eventually carried some 350,000 settlers to the West.

Great Plains: The vast area of rolling grasslands between the Mississippi River and the Rocky Mountains.

H

Homestead Act of 1862: An act passed by Congress that gave settlers up to 160 acres of free land if they settled on it and made improvements over a five-year span. This act was responsible for bringing thousands of settlers into the west.

I

Indian Removal Act of 1830: An act passed by Congress calling for the removal—voluntary or forced—of all Indians to lands west of the Mississippi.

L

Louisiana Territory: Over 800,000 acres of land west of the Mississippi that was acquired from France for $15 million by President Thomas Jefferson in the Louisiana Purchase of 1803.

M

Manifest Destiny: The belief that by acquiring and populating the territories stretching from the Atlantic Ocean west to the Pacific Ocean, Americans were fulfilling a destiny ordained by God. This idea has been criticized as an excuse for the bold land grabs and the slaughter of Indians that characterized westward expansion, but those who believed in it thought they were demonstrating the virtues of a nation founded on political liberty, individual economic opportunity, and Christian civilization.

Mexican-American War: This war between the United States and Mexico, fought between 1846 and 1848, began as a battle over the southern border of Texas but soon expanded as the United States sought to acquire the territory that now includes Arizona, California, Colorado, Nevada, New Mexico, Utah, and Wyoming.

Missionaries: Proponents of a religion who travel into unexplored territories to try to convert the indigenous peoples to the missionaries' religion. Spanish missionaries had an important influence in California; Protestant missionaries in Oregon and Washington; and Catholic missionaries throughout the French-influenced areas of the East.

N

Northwest Passage: A mythical water route that linked the Atlantic Ocean to the Pacific Ocean; this passage was long sought by explorers of North America.

O

Old Northwest: The area of land surrounding the Great Lakes and between the Ohio River and the Mississippi River; it included the present-day states of Ohio, Indiana, Illinois, Michigan, Wisconsin, and part of Minnesota.

Oregon Country: The name given to a vast expanse of land west of the Rocky Mountains and north of the Spanish territory containing the present-day states of Washington, Oregon, Idaho, and western Montana. This territory was jointly occupied by the British and the United States until 1846, when England ceded the territory to the United States.

Oregon Trail: A 2,000-mile trail that led from St. Joseph, Missouri, to the mouth of the Columbia River in Oregon. Thousands of settlers traveled on the trail from the 1830s to the 1890s. A major branch of the trail, the California Trail, led settlers to the gold fields of California.

R

Rendezvous: A gathering or meeting. The annual mountain man Rendezvous was a gathering of trappers and traders in the Rocky Mountain region. At the Rendezvous, fur trappers sold the furs and bought the goods that would allow them to survive through the next year. The mountain men entertained themselves during the Rendezvous with drinking, singing, dancing, and sporting contests.

S

South Pass: A low mountain pass over the Continental Divide located in present-day Wyoming; this pass was a major milestone on the Oregon Trail.

T

Territory: The name given to a region before it became a state. The Northwest Ordinance paved the way for the orderly admission of territories into the Union.

Trans-Appalachian West: The area of land that stretched west from the crest of the Appalachian Mountains to the Mississippi River.

Treaty of Guadalupe Hidalgo: This treaty with Mexico, signed on February 2, 1848, ended the Mexican-American War and granted to the United States territory including all or part of the present-day states of Arizona, California, Colorado, Nevada, New Mexico, Utah, and Wyoming.

V

Vaqueros: Hispanic men who worked on the ranches of Spaniards who settled in southern California and Mexico. Vaqueros were the first cowboys.

W

War of 1812: A war fought between England and the United States from 1812 to 1814 that was aimed at settling control of the trans-Appalachian west and shipping disputes between the two countries. Many Indian tribes sided with the English. The American victory established complete American control of the area.

Westward Expansion
Primary Sources

Exploring the West

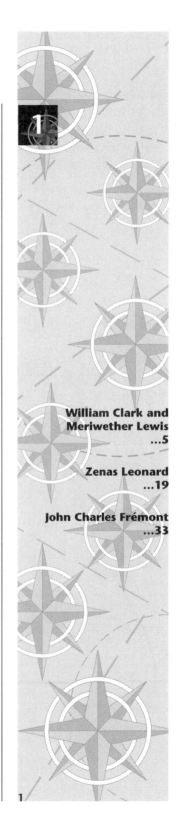

As the British colonies on the eastern seaboard became more populated in the mid-1700s, colonists began to look beyond the Appalachian Mountains and contemplate westward expansion. Looking westward, they could only imagine the incredible riches the continent would offer to them. Not much information was known about the territory west of the Appalachians. A 1795 map did offer a fairly accurate picture of the western region of North America, but it mistakenly depicted several inland lakes as being considerably larger than the Great Salt Lake. The map's cartographers probably drew these lakes from vague reports they had received from Indians. In 1806 John Cary produced a map that accurately depicted the Pacific coastline, but he did not include inland details—which resulted in a map that left blank almost the entire region west of the Mississippi River.

Curious to know more specifically what the western region had to offer, President Thomas Jefferson (1743–1826) commissioned Meriwether Lewis (1774–1809) and William Clark (1770–1838) in 1803 to find a navigable water route from the Missouri River to the Pacific Ocean. In addition,

Lewis and Clark were asked to report as many inland details as they could.

When Jefferson first started organizing the Lewis and Clark expedition, the territory that he wanted them to explore did not fall within U.S. boundaries. France controlled the area west of the Mississippi River up to the Rocky Mountains; the area was called the Louisiana Territory. Great Britain, Spain, Russia, and the United States claimed the Pacific Northwest. In April 1803, before the expedition would get underway, the United States negotiated with France to purchase the Louisiana Territory for around $15 million, thus making a large portion of the territory they were about to explore part of the United States.

The Lewis and Clark expedition left St. Louis on May 14, 1804. From 1804 to 1806 Lewis and Clark kept detailed journals of their travels. *The Journals of Lewis and Clark* describe a country with abundant natural resources that could strengthen the economic stature of the United States. Lewis and Clark were the first to describe what really lay west of the Mississippi River. They also produced a map, although it was not very accurate. Nevertheless, Lewis and Clark's expedition encouraged many people to venture across the Mississippi River.

Those who first followed Lewis and Clark's lead were fur trappers and eager merchants. The stories the fur trappers and adventurers told—of the fertile Willamette Valley of the Oregon Territory, and the grassy plains of Texas and the Oklahoma and Kansas Territories—thrilled and shocked the incredulous but curious easterners. *Adventures of Zenas Leonard Fur Trader* tells of the real difficulties encountered in such primitive western areas and how to earn a living as a trapper. Stories like Zenas Leonard's later inspired the American government to send more explorers across the Mississippi River to create accurate maps of the unknown reaches of the country.

In 1837 Captain Benjamin Louis Eulalie de Bonneville compiled a map that accurately depicted the waterways of the region west of the Rocky Mountains. Bonneville's map was the most accurate available until Charles Preuss completed his map of the John C. Frémont expeditions in the 1840s. Though Frémont was not the most skilled explorer, he hired talented, knowledgeable scouts and trappers to help keep his parties on track. Despite his lack of technical skills, Frémont was a masterful promoter of the West. His glamorous representations of the western frontier influenced many Americans' decision to go west and offered accurate descriptions to travelers on their way west. ***The Life of Col. John Charles Frémont and His Narrative of Explorations and Adventures in Kansas, Oregon and California*** provides vivid detail of the land and of the experiences of early explorers.

William Clark and Meriwether Lewis

Excerpts from **The Journals of Lewis and Clark**
Edited by Bernard DeVoto
Published in 1953

By 1800 Europeans and Americans understood the basic geography of most of the world's continents, with the exception of the western two-thirds of North America, the interior of Africa, the Arctic, and Antarctica. France, England, Russia, Spain, and the United States were very interested in the region beyond the Mississippi River in North America for its commercial potential but had not yet explored it extensively. Even Native American communities knew only their immediate areas—the land that they hunted or cultivated regularly. They too lacked a continental perspective.

Thomas Jefferson, obsessed with cartography (mapmaking) and natural history, understood the necessity of exploring and mapping the vast region west of the Mississippi River. When Jefferson commissioned Lewis and Clark to explore the western region of the continent, he believed that the Blue Ridge Mountains of Virginia were the tallest peaks in North America; that the woolly mammoth and other prehistoric creatures might still roam the Dakotas; that the Great Plains featured volcanoes and a mountain of pure salt; that the Rio Grande, Missouri, and Columbia Rivers all rose from a single source; and

Meriwether Lewis.
(Corbis-Bettmann. Reproduced by permission.)

that a navigable water route connected the Atlantic and Pacific Oceans.

On January 18, 1803, Jefferson asked Congress for authorization to send a military expedition to explore along the Missouri River to its source in the Rocky Mountains, and then down the nearest westward-flowing river to the Pacific Ocean. The president also asked for an appropriation (an amount of public funds set aside for a specific purpose) of twenty-five hundred dollars to fund the expedition. Jefferson had two purposes for the proposed mission: to prepare the way for the extension of the American fur trade throughout the area to be explored; and to advance geographical knowledge of the continent.

To command the expedition, Jefferson chose his private secretary, Captain Meriwether Lewis (1774–1809). With the president's permission, Lewis then invited his old friend William Clark (1770–1838) to be the coleader of the expedition. The exploratory group included twenty-seven young, unmarried soldiers; George Drouillard, a man of mixed Native American and European heritage, who was a hunter and an interpreter; and Clark's African American slave, York. In addition, a corporal and five privates as well as several French boatmen were to accompany the expedition during the first season and then return with its records and scientific specimens. The Corps of Discovery began its historic journey on May 14, 1804. The journals of Lewis and Clark were the first eyewitness account of the West and its resources and native inhabitants.

Things to remember while reading the excerpts from *The Journals of Lewis and Clark*:

- In April 1803, shortly after the Lewis and Clark expedition was commissioned, the United States acquired the

Louisiana Territory, approximately 800,000 acres of land stretching west from the Mississippi River to the Rocky Mountains. The Louisiana Purchase doubled the size of the United States.

• At the time no one knew precisely how large the Louisiana Territory was or what its resources were. Today, the Louisiana Purchase is considered Jefferson's greatest achievement in his first term as president.

• Before the Louisiana Purchase, the half-million American settlers living west of the Appalachian Mountains relied on treaties with the Spanish (who owned the Louisiana Territory before ceding it to France in 1800) to transport their goods to market via the Mississippi River and New Orleans.

• The selected journal entries provide a glimpse into the trip west in 1804 as well as the return home in 1806.

William Clark.
(Courtesy of the Library of Congress.)

• Though both Lewis and Clark were educated men, they did not adhere to any conventions of grammar or spelling in their journals. You can make sense of many of the oddly spelled words by sounding them out. Capital letters appear throughout the text, but not necessarily at the beginning of sentences. Large spaces between words sometimes signify the separation of sentences without periods. Don't let the unusual appearance of this text keep you from enjoying Lewis and Clark's sense of wonder with the new land and the people they encountered.

• Non-italicized words are those that were added to the text by the original editor of the Lewis and Clark journals, Nicholas Biddle, based on explanations provided by George Shannon, one of the members of the expedition.

Excerpts from The Journals of Lewis and Clark

JUNE 17TH SUNDAY 1804

we Set out early and proceeded on one mile & came too to make oars, & repair our cable & toe rope &c. &c. which was necessary for the Boat & **Perogues,** *Sent out Sjt. Pryor and Some men to get ash timber for ores, and Set some men to make a Toe Rope out of the Cords of a Cable which had been provided by Capt. Lewis at Pittsburg for the Cable of the boat. George Drewyer our hunter and one man came in with 2 Deer & a Bear, also a young Horse, they had found in the Prarie, this horse has been in the Prarie a long time and is fat, I Suppose, he has been left by Some war party against the* **Osage,** *This is a Crossing place for the war parties against that nation from the Saukees, Aiaouez, [Iowas] & Souix. The party is much afflicted with* **Boils,** *and Several have the* **Deassentary,** *which I contribute to the water The Countrey about this place is butifull on the river rich & well timbered on the* **S.S.** *about two miles back a Prarie coms which is rich and interspursed with groves of timber, the count[r]y rises at 7 or 8 miles Still further back and is rolling. on the* **L. S.** *the high lands & Prarie coms. in the bank of the river and continus back, well watered and abounds in Deer Elk & Bear. The Ticks & Musquiters are verry troublesome.*

14TH August TUESDAY 1804—

The men Sent to the Mahar Town last evining has not returned we Conclude to send a Spye to Know the Cause of their delay, at about 12 oClock the Party returned and informd. us that they Could not find the Indians, nor any fresh Sign, those people have not returned from their Buffalow hunt. Those people having no houses no Corn or anything more than the graves of their ansesters to attach them to the old Village. Continue in **purseute** *of the Buffalow longer than others who has greater attachments to their native village. The ravages of the Small Pox (which Swept off 400 men & Womin & children) has reduced this nation not exceeding 300 men and left them to the insults of their weaker neighbours, which before was glad to be on friendly turms with them. I am told when this fatal* **malady** *was among them they*

&c.: Etc.

Perogue: Spelled *pirogue;* a canoe made out of a hollowed tree trunk.

Osage: American Indian tribe in Missouri.

Boil: A painful, pus-filled inflammation of the skin usually caused by an infection.

Deassentary: Spelled *dysentery;* an infection causing pain, fever, and severe diarrhea.

S.S.: Starboard side; the right side of the boat.

L.S.: Larboard side; Misspelling of the left side of the boat.

Purseute: Pursuit.

Malady: Illness.

Franzey: Spelled *frenzy;* agitation.

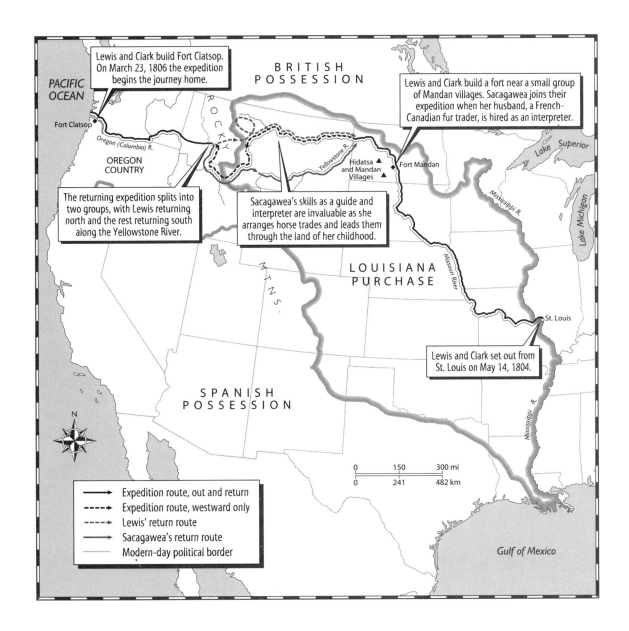

Lewis and Clark build Fort Clatsop. On March 23, 1806 the expedition begins the journey home.

BRITISH POSSESSION

PACIFIC OCEAN

Lewis and Clark build a fort near a small group of Mandan villages. Sacagawea joins their expedition when her husband, a French-Canadian fur trader, is hired as an interpreter.

Fort Clatsop

R O C K Y

Oregon (Columbia) R.

OREGON COUNTRY

Yellowstone R.

Hidatsa and Mandan Villages

Fort Mandan

Lake Superior

The returning expedition splits into two groups, with Lewis returning north and the rest returning south along the Yellowstone River.

Sacagawea's skills as a guide and interpreter are invaluable as she arranges horse trades and leads them through the land of her childhood.

MTNS.

LOUISIANA PURCHASE

Missouri River

Mississippi R.

Lake Michigan

SPANISH POSSESSION

St. Louis

Lewis and Clark set out from St. Louis on May 14, 1804.

Mississippi R.

N

0   150   300 mi
0   241   482 km

Expedition route, out and return
Expedition route, westward only
Lewis' return route
Sacagawea's return route
Modern-day political border

Gulf of Mexico

Carried their **franzey** to verry extroadinary length, not only of burning their Village, but they put their wives & children to Death with a view of their all going together to some better Countrey. they burry their Dead on the top of high hills and rais Mounds on the top of them. The cause or way those people took the Small Pox is uncertain, the most Probable, from Some other nation by means of a warparty.

The Lewis and Clark expedition left St. Louis, Missouri, in May 1804 and arrived on the coast of Oregon Territory in the winter of 1805. *(Map by XNR Productions, Inc. Reproduced by permission of The Gale Group.)*

[Clark]   25TH August SATTURDAY 1804.—

A cloudy morning Capt. Lewis & Myself concluded to go and See the Mound which was Viewed with Such **turror** by all the different Nations in this quarter, we Selected [nine men to go along] from the top of this High land the Countrey is leavel & open as far as can be Seen, except Some few rises at a great Distance, and the Mound which the Indians Call Mountain of little people or Spirits, *at 4 miles we Crossed the Creek 23 yards wide in an extensive Valley and* **Contined** *on at two miles further our Dog was so Heeted and fatigued we was obliged [to] Send him back to the Creek, at 12 oClock we arrived at the hill Capt. Lewis much fatigued from heat the day it being verry hot & he being in a debilitated State from the Precautions he was obliged to take to prevent the effects of the Cobalt, &* **Minl** *Substance which had like to have poisoned him two days ago his want of water, and Several of the men complaining of Great thirst, determined us to make for the first water. We proceeded on to the Place we Campd last night and Stayed all night.*

The reagular form of this hill would in Some measure justify a belief that it owed its orrigin to the hand of man; but as the earth and loos pebbles and other substances of which it was Composed, bore an exact resemblance to the Steep Ground which border on the Creek in its neighbourhood we concluded it was most probably the production of nature.

The only remarkable Charactoristic of this hill admiting it to be a natural production is that it is insulated or Seperated a considerable distance from any other, which is verry unusial in the natural order or disposition of the hills. [Clark is describing Spirit Mound near Vermillion, South Dakota.]

[Clark]   25TH SEPT.—

all well, raised a Flag Staff & made a **orning** or Shade on a Sand bar in the mouth of Teton River, for the purpose of Speeking with the Indians under, the Boat Crew on board at 70 yards Distance from the bar The 5 Indians which we met last night Continued, about 11 OClock the **It** & 2d Chief Came we gave them Some of our Provisions to eat, they gave us great Quantitis of Meet Some of which was Spoiled we feel much at a loss for the want of an interpeter the one we have can Speck but little.

Met in Council at 12 oClock and after Smokeing, **agreeable to the useal Custom,** Cap. Lewis proceeded to Deliver a Speech which we [were] oblige[d] to **Curtail** for want of a good interpeter all our

Turror: Misspelling of terror.

Contined: Misspelling of continued.

Minl: Mineral.

Orning: Misspelling of awning.

It: First.

Agreeable to the useal Custom: As is customary, or usually done.

Curtail: To cut short.

Cloake: Spelled *cloak;* disguise or cover.

party paraded. gave a Medal to the Grand Chief Calld. in Indian Un
ton gar Sar bar *in French* Beeffe nure *Black Buffalow....*

*Envited those Cheifs on board to Show them our boat and such
Curiossities as was Strange to them, we gave them 1/4 a glass of
whiskey which they appeared to be verry fond of, Sucked the bottle
after it was out & Soon began to be troublesome, one the 2d Cheif
assumeing Drunkness, as a* **Cloake** *for his rascally intentions I went*

The Lewis and Clark
expedition greeting a group
of Native Americans.
*(Corbis-Bettmann. Reproduced
by permission.)*

Seased: Spelled *seized;* took.

Insolent: Rude or disrespectful.

Justures: Misspelling of gestures.

Suffered: Allowed.

Musick: Musical instruments.

By as they Said the particular request of the Chiefs of that Village: The men said that the chiefs had requested music for dancing.

Thro jelloucy and mortification as to our treatment towards them: The Indians were not happy with how they had been treated.

Gross Ventres: Spelled *Gros Ventre;* a Great Plains American Indian tribe.

Chinnooks: Spelled *Chinook;* a Native American group originally inhabiting western Washington and Oregon.

Clatsops: American Indian tribe within the Chinook Nation.

Squars: Spelled *squaws;* a disparaging (offensive) term for a Native American woman.

Abhor: Hate, or regard with disgust.

with those Cheifs (in one of the Perogues with 5 men— 3 & 2 Inds.) (which left the boat with great reluctance) to Shore with a view of reconsileing those men to us, as Soon as I landed the Perogue three of their young Men **Seased** the Cable of the Perogue, (in which we had Pressents &c) the Chiefs Soldr. Huged the mast, and the 2d Chief was verry **insolent** both in words & **justures** (pretended Drunkenness & staggered up against me) declareing I should not go on, Stateing he had not receved presents sufficent from us, his justures were of Such a personal nature I felt My self Compeled to Draw my Sward (and Made a Signal to the boat to prepare for action)....

TUESDAY JANUARY THE 1ST 1805—

The Day was ushered in by the Descharge of two Cannon, we **Suffered** 16 men with their **Musick** to visit the 1st Village for the purpose of Danceing, **by as they Said the particular request of the Chiefs of that Village,** about 11 oClock I with an inturpeter & two men walked up to the Village, (my views were to alay Some little Miss understanding which had taken place **thro jelloucy and mortification as to our treatment towards them** I found them much pleased at the Danceing of our men, I ordered my black Servent to Dance which amused the Croud Verry much, and Somewhat astonished them, that So large a man should be active &c. &c. a Chief returnd from a Mission on which they had been Sent to meet a large party (150) of **Gross Ventres** who were on their way down from their Camps 10 Miles above to revenge on the Shoe tribe an injury which they had received by a Shoe man Steeling a Gros Ventres Girl, those Chiefs gave the pipe [and] turned the party back, after Delivering up the Girl, which the Shoe Chief had taken and given to them for that purpose. I returned in the evening....

THURSDAY NOVEMBER 21sT 1805

A cloudy morning most of the **Chinnooks** leave our camp and return home, the Wind blew hard from the S. E. which with the addition of the flood tide raised verry high waves which broke with great violence against the shore throwing water into our camp the forepart of this day Cloudy at 12 oClock it began to rain and continud all day moderately, Several Indians Visit us to day of different nations or Bands Some of the Chiltz Nation who reside on the Sea Coast near Point Lewis, Several of the **Clatsops** who reside on the Opposit Side of the Columbia imediately opposit to us, and a Cheif from the Grand rapid to whome we gave a Medal.

FORT CLATSOP 1805-06 WINTER QUARTERS OF LEWIS AND CLARK EXPEDITION

An old woman & Wife to a Cheif of the Chunnooks *came and made a Camp near ours. She brought with her 6 young **Squars** (her daughters & nieces) I believe for the purpose of Gratifying the passions of the men of our party and receving for those indulgiences Such Small [presents] as She (the old woman) thought proper to accept of.*

*Those people appear to View Sensuality as a Necessary evel, and do not appear to **abhor** it as a Crime in the unmarried State.*

Fort Clatsop, in northwestern Oregon, where the Lewis and Clark expedition spent the winter of 1805 before heading back to St. Louis, Missouri. *(Archive Photos, Inc. Reproduced by permission.)*

*The young females are fond of the attention of our men and appear to meet the sincere **approbation** of their friends and connections, for obtaining their favours, the Womin of the Chinnoook Nation have handsom faces low and badly made with large legs & thighs which are generally Swelled from a Stopage of the circulation in the feet (which are Small) by maney Strands of Beeds or curious Strings which are drawn tight around the leg above the ankle, their legs are also **picked** with defferent figures, I saw on the left arm of a Squar the following letters* J. Bowman, *all those are considered by the natives of this quarter as handsom deckerations, and a woman without those deckerations is Considered as among the lower Class....*

MONDAY (TUESDAY) JANUARY 7TH 1806.

*Last evening **Drewyer** visited his traps and caught a beaver and an otter; the beaver was large and fat we have therefore **fared sumptuously** today; this we consider a great prize for another reason, it being a full grown beaver was well supplied with the materials for making bate with which to catch others. To prepare beaver bate, the **castor** or bark stone is taken as the base, this is gently pressed out of the bladderlike bag which contains it, into a **phiol** of 4 ounces with a wide mouth; if you have them you will put from four to six stone in a phiol of that capacity, to this you will add half a nutmeg, a douzen or 15 grains of cloves and thirty grains of cinimon finely pulverized, stir them well together and then add as much ardent sperits to the composition as will reduce it the consistency [of] mustard prepared for the table; when thus prepared it resembles mustard precisely to all appearance. when you cannot procure a phiol a bottle made of horn or a tight earthen vessel will **answer**, in all cases it must be **excluded from the air** or it will soon **loose it's virtue**; it is fit for **uce** immediately it is prepared but becomes much stronger and better in about four or five days and will keep for months provided it be perfectly secluded from the air. when cloves are not to be had use double the quantity of Allspice, and when no spice can be obtained the bark of the root of **sausafras**. it appears to me that the principal uce of the spices is only to give a variety to the scent of the bark stone and if so the mace **vineller** and other sweet-smelling spices might be employed with equal advantage.*

[Lewis]   TUESDAY APRIL IST 1806.

We were visited by several canoes of natives in the course of the day;. most of whom were decending the river with their women and children. they informed us that they resided at the great rapids [the

Approbation: Approval.

Picked: Tattooed.

Drewyer: George Drewyer, a hunter and interpreter with the expedition.

Fared sumptuously: Had a good dinner.

Castor: Gland in a beaver that secretes castoreum, a strong-smelling oily substance used in perfumes and once thought to have medicinal purposes.

Phiol: Spelled *phial;* a vial, or small vessel.

Answer: Fill the need; will also work.

Excluded from the air: Kept in an airtight container.

Loose it's virtue: Spoil.

Uce: Misspelling of *use.*

Sausafras: Spelled *sassafras;* a type of tree bark that has a spicy flavor, like root beer.

Vineller: Misspelling of *Vanilla.*

Dalles] and that their relations at that place were much streightened at that place for want of food; that they had consumed their winter store of dryed fish and that those of the present season had not yet arrived. I could not learn wheather they took the sturgeon but presume if they do it is in but small quantities as they complained much of the scarcity of food among them. they informed us that the nations above them were in the same situation & that they did not expect the Salmon to arrive untill the full of the next moon which happens on the 2d of May. we did not doubt the **varacity** of these people who seemed to be on their way with their families and effects in surch of **subsistence** which they find it easy to procure in this fertile valley.

WEDNESDAY JUNE 25TH 1806

last evening the indians entertained us with setting the fir trees on fire. they have a great number of dry limbs near their bodies which when Set on fire create a very sudden and emmence blaize from bottom to top of those tall trees. they are a boutifull object in this situation at night. this exhibition remi[n]de[d] me of a display of firewo[r]ks. the nativs told us that their object in Setting those trees on fire was to bring fair weather for our journey. We collected our horses and set out at an early hour this morning. one of our guides complained of being unwell, a Symptom which I did not much like as such complaints with an indian is generally the **prelude** to his abandoning any enterprise with which he is not well pleased. we left 4 of those indians at our encampment they promised to pursue us in a fiew hours....

FRIDAY 22ND AUGUST 1806

as I was about to leave the cheifs [of the Chyennes] lodge he requested me to Send Some traders to them, that their country was full of beaver and they would then be encouraged to kill beaver, but now they had no use for them as they could get nothing for their skins and did not know well, how to catch beaver. if the white people would come amongst them they would become acquainted and they [the white people] would learn them how to take the beaver. I promised the Nation that I would inform their Great father the President of the U States, and he would have them Supplied with goods, and mentioned in what manner they would be Supplied &c. &c....

SUNDAY 21ST SEPTR. 1806

rose early this morning colected our men several of them had axcepted of the invitation of the citizens and visited their families. at half after 7 A. M we Set out. passed 12 canoes of **Kickapoos**

Varacity: Spelled *veracity;* truthfulness.

Subsistence: Goods to sustain life; in this case food.

Prelude: An action that occurs prior to some other action.

Kickapoos: A Native American tribe.

assending on a hunting expedition. Saw Several persons also stock of different kind on the bank which reviv'd the party very much. at 3 P M we met two large boats assending. at 4 P M we arived in Sight of St. Charles, the party rejoiced at the Sight of this hospita[b]l[e] village **plyed** *thear ores with great* **dexterity** *and we Soon arived opposit the Town this day being Sunday we observed a number of Gentlemen and ladies walking on the bank, we saluted the Village by three* **rounds** *from our* **blunder-buts** *and the Small arms of the party, and landed near the lower part of the town. we were met by great numbers of the inhabitants, we found them excessively polite. we received invitations from Several of those Gentlemen. Mr. Querie under took to Supply our party with* **provisions** *&c. the inhabitants of this village appear much delighted at our return and seem to* **vie** *with each other in their politeness to us all. we came only 48 miles to day. the banks of the river thinly settled &c. (some Settlements since we went up).* [DeVoto, pp. 8, 19, 23, 35–36, 75, 289–90, 303, 337, 409, 463, 477]

What happened next . . .

Lewis and Clark's expedition was only the first to chronicle the geography and nature of the West; other explorers soon followed. Between 1806 and 1807 Zebulon Pike (1779–1813) led an expedition west of the Mississippi River that extended into northern New Spain. Pike is most remembered for his widely circulated report on the Rio Grande, his description of the Great Plains as a desert, and his discovery of the mountain peak in present-day Colorado that now bears his name. From 1819 to 1820 Stephen Long's expedition led soldiers and scientists west across the central Plains to the Rocky Mountains, also exploring vast portions of the Mississippi and Missouri River valleys. Naturalists on this trip collected and reported new information about plants, animals, soil, climate, and geology. By the mid-1820s, Long's journey had prompted a series of books, maps, and scientific articles that aided the later investigations of men such as explorer John C. Frémont (see John C. Frémont entry in this chapter).

Plyed: Spelled *plied;* worked.

Dexterity: Skill.

Rounds: Shots.

Blunder buts: Spelled *blunderbuss;* a short musket of wide bore and flaring muzzle used to scatter shot at close range.

Provisions: Food and supplies needed for the next leg of the journey.

Vie: Compete.

Did you know . . .

- Eight or nine counterfeit (fake) editions of *The History of the Expedition Under the Commands of Captains Lewis and Clark* were published.

- The secretary of war granted William Clark a lieutenancy—not a captaincy as Jefferson had promised for the expedition. Nevertheless, Lewis demanded that he and Clark both serve as captains. None of those under their command questioned that Lewis and Clark had equal authority.

- After the expedition, Clark was appointed brigadier general of the militia and the agent of the United States for Indian Affairs. Lewis was appointed governor of the Louisiana Territory.

Consider the following . . .

- Did Lewis and Clark hold prejudices against the Indians?

- How would you characterize the meetings between Lewis and Clark and the Indians? Were they friendly, formal, respectful?

- Did Lewis and Clark believe that all Indians share the same culture?

- What difficulties did Lewis and Clark encounter?

For More Information

Cutright, Paul Russell. *A History of the Lewis and Clark Journals.* Norman: University of Oklahoma Press, 1976.

DeVoto, Bernard, ed. *The Journals of Lewis and Clark.* Boston: Houghton Mifflin Company, 1953.

Fifer, Barbara, and Vicky Soderberg. *Along the Trail with Lewis and Clark.* Great Falls: Montana Magazine, 1998.

Gilbert, Bil. *The Trailblazers.* New York: Time-Life Books, 1973.

Irving, W. *Astoria.* New York: The Century Co., 1909.

Jackson, Donald, ed. *Letters of the Lewis and Clark Expedition with Related Documents: 1783–1854.* Urbana: University of Illinois Press, 1962.

Kroll, Steven. *Lewis and Clark: Explorers of the American West.* New York: Holiday House, 1994.

Schanzer, Rosalyn. *How We Crossed the West: The Adventures of Lewis and Clark.* Washington, D.C.: National Geographic Society, 1997.

Thwaites, Reuben Gold, ed. *Original Journals of the Lewis and Clark Expedition.* 8 vols. New York: Dodd, Mead & Co., 1904–5.

Zenas Leonard

Excerpt from **Adventures of Zenas Leonard Fur Trader**
Edited by John C. Ewers
Published in 1959

More than anything else, the growing fur trade attracted white men across the Mississippi River into the interior of North America. Fur traders, also called mountain men, had traveled over the Appalachian Mountains, around the Great Lakes, over the Rocky Mountains, and into the southwestern deserts in search of beaver pelts long before white settlers started to carve farms out of the wilderness. In the early 1800s, with the fur supply between the Appalachians and the Mississippi River depleted and settlements filling up the wilderness land, European fur trappers looked to the land beyond the Mississippi River. The Spanish, French, and British dominated the fur trade in this region when the United States purchased the Louisiana Territory from France in 1803. After the Louisiana Purchase, Americans began to hope that expanding their involvement in the fur trade would be good for the American economy. Keeping the fur trade in mind as they searched for the Northwest Passage, Meriwether Lewis and William Clark reported on the abundance of beavers along the western rivers and their tributaries.

One of Lewis and Clark's traveling companions, John Colter (c. 1775–1813), became the first and one of the most famous American mountain men. Joining hunters Forest Hancock and Joseph Dickson as they explored the Rocky Mountains, Colter led a small American trapping party near present-day Yellowstone National Park. Later, in 1806, he led the first large fur-trading expedition to Yellowstone and became the first white man to see Jackson Hole, Wyoming, and the geysers and mudpots of Yellowstone National Park. Hundreds of trappers followed Colter as industrious Americans established new fur-trading companies. By 1810 Manuel Lisa, Andrew Henry, and Pierre Menard formed the Missouri Fur Company. Although Blackfoot Indians forced this company to abandon its efforts at the Three Forks of the Missouri River between the Jefferson and Madison Rivers, other trappers kept coming. In 1822 Andrew Henry and William H. Ashley established the Rocky Mountain Fur Company. The Rocky Mountain Fur Company's success in sending small parties of men to trap throughout the country and then gather once a year at a given place to sell pelts and buy supplies started the tradition of the yearly trappers' rendezvous (also sometimes called the mountain man rendezvous). The first rendezvous was held in 1825 on Henry's Fork of the Green River, where hundreds of trappers and friendly Indians gathered. Zenas Leonard left on his first trapping expedition in 1831. His narrative provides a glimpse into trappers' daily struggles and awesome adventures.

Things to remember while reading the excerpt from *Zenas Leonard Fur Trader*:

- The fur trade dominated commerce in St. Louis when the United States purchased the Louisiana Territory in 1803.

- In 1804 St. Louis had a population of about one thousand people.

- Zenas Leonard began his trapping career with the Gantt and Blackwell Company in 1831, but the company dissolved within a year. Leonard was a free trapper for a little more than a year before joining Captain Benjamin L. E. de Bonneville's group, which lasted until Leonard's return home in 1835.

Excerpt from Zenas Leonard Fur Trader

Of the adventures of a company of 70 men, who left St. Louis in the spring of 1831, on an expedition to the Rocky Mountains, for the purpose of trapping for furs, and trading with the Indians, by one of the company, MR. ZENAS LEONARD, of Clearfield County, Pa.—comprising a minute description of the incidents of the adventure, and a valuable history of this immense territory—not from maps and charts, but from personal observation.

The company under the command of Captains Gant and Blackwell, left St. Louis on the 24th of April, 1831. Each man was furnished with the necessary equipments for the expedition—such as traps, guns, &c.; also horses and goods of various descriptions, to

Illustration of the annual trappers' rendezvous, where trappers gathered to sell their pelts and buy supplies for the next season. *(Courtesy of the Library of Congress.)*

&c.: Etc.

trade with the Indians for furs and buffalo robes. We continued our journey in a western direction, in the state of Missouri, on the south side of the Missouri river, through a country thinly inhabited by the whites and friendly Indians, until we arrived at Fort Osage the extreme point of the white settlement. Here we remained several days and purchased and packed up **a sufficiency of provision,** as we then thought, for our **subsistence** through the wilderness to what is called the buffalo country; a distance of about two hundred miles. From thence we proceeded up the Missouri until we arrived at the mouth of the **Kanzas** river, where we again tarried two or three days, for the purpose of trading some goods to the Kanzas Indians for corn, moccasins, &c.

This tribe of Indians live in small huts, built of poles, covered with straw and dirt, and in shape similar to a potato hole. They cultivate the soil quite extensively, and raise very good corn, pumpkins, beans and other vegetables. The principal chief is called "White Ploom."—The nation is supposed to contain eight hundred warriors.

From **thence** we proceeded on our journey up the river. We found the country here beautiful indeed—abounding with the most delightful prairies, with here and there a small brook, winding its way to the river, the margins of which are adorned with the lofty pine and cedar tree. These prairies were completely covered with fine low grass, and decorated with beautiful flowers of various colors; and some of them are so extensive and clear of timber and brush that the eye might search in vain for an object to rest upon. I have seen beautiful and enchanting sceneries depicted by the artist, but never anything to equal the work of **rude** nature in those prairies. In the spring of the year when the grass is green and the blossoms fresh, they present an appearance, which for beauty and charms, is beyond the art of man to depict....

....Several scouting parties were sent out in search of beaver signs, who returned in a few days and reported that they had found beaver signs, &c. Captain Gant then gave orders to make preparations for trapping. Accordingly the company was divided into parties of fifteen to twenty men in each party, with their respective captains placed over them—and directed by Captain Gant in what direction to go. Captain Washburn ascended the Timber Fork; Captain Stephens the Laramies; Captain Gant the Sweet Water—all of which empty into the river Platte near the same place. Each of these companies were directed to ascend these rivers until they found beaver sufficiently plenty for trapping, or till the snow and cold weather

A sufficiency of provision: Enough supplies.

Subsistence: Survival.

Kanzas: Misspelling of Kansas.

Thence: There.

Rude: Robust or rugged.

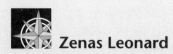

Zenas Leonard

Born March 19, 1809, at the mouth of Clearfield Creek in Pennsylvania, Zenas Leonard had the genes of an adventurer. His grandfather had immigrated to the British colonies from Ireland before the Revolutionary War. Trading with the Native Americans for a time to earn his living, he later settled into farming. Zenas's father, Abraham, carved out a farm on the frontier for his nine children and his wife Elizabeth. Zenas Leonard was uninterested in making his living "picking stones"—as he described farming—and decided to see what the city could offer. Leonard left his family's home in Clearfield County, Pennsylvania, and walked to Pittsburgh in the spring of 1830, where he worked for a time as a clerk in his uncle's store. In the city, he heard stories of the fur trade. Leonard soon left for St. Louis, the central point of the fur trade, to try his luck in that adventurous industry. As a clerk for Gantt and Blackwell, a trapping company with aspirations of competing with the Rocky Mountain Fur Company and the American Fur Company, Leonard got his first taste of the fur trade. He left on his first expedition on April 24, 1831. His narrative describes his adventurous four years in the Rocky Mountains as a clerk and trapper.

When Leonard returned to his family's home nearly five years after leaving, his friends and neighbors couldn't hear enough about his adventures in the West. Leonard found himself telling his story over and over. Finally, he decided to write it down for one and all to read. Though much of the narrative was written from memory and from the diaries of traveling companions, the first publisher of Leonard's narrative, D. W. Moore, noted his faith in the truthfulness of Leonard's account: "[I]ndeed, among the many who heard the narrative from his own lips, we have yet to hear the first one say they disbelieve it. At all events, in its perusal, the reader will encounter no *improbabilities,* much less *impossibilities:*—hence it is but reasonable to suppose that in traversing such a wilderness as lays west of the Rocky Mountains, such hardships, privations and dangers as those described by Mr. Leonard, must necessarily be encountered." Published in 1839, Moore's testimony highlights this narrative's usefulness to those interested in exploring or settling the West.

*compelled them to stop; at which event they were to return to the mouth of the Laramies River, to pass the winter together. While at this place, **engaged in secreting our merchandise,** which we did by digging a hole in the ground sufficiently large to contain them, and covering them over so that the Indians might not discover them—*

Engaged in secreting our merchandise: Busy hiding their supplies.

four men (three whites and one Indian) came to our tent. This as-tonished us not a little, for a white man was the last of living beings that we expected to visit us in this vast wilderness—where nothing was heard from dark to daylight but the fierce and terrifying growls of wild beasts, and the more shrill cries of the **merciless savages**. *The* **principal** *of these men was a Mr. Fitzpatrick, who had been en-gaged in trapping along the Columbia River, on the west side of the Rocky Mountains, and was then on his way to St. Louis. He was an old hand at the business and we expected to obtain some useful in-formation from him, but we were disappointed. The selfishness of man is often disgraceful to human nature; and I never saw more striking evidence of this fact, than was presented in the conduct of this man Fitzpatrick.* **Notwithstanding** *we had treated him with great friendship and hospitality, merely because we were to engage in the same business with him, which he knew* **we never could ex-haust or even impair**—*he refused to give us any information what-ever, and appeared disposed to treat us as intruders. On the 3d of September, Captain Blackwell, with two others, joined Fitzpatrick, and started back to the state of Missouri, for an additional supply of merchandise, and were to return in the summer of 1832....*

On New Years Day, notwithstanding our horses were nearly all dead, as being fully satisfied that the few that were yet living must die soon, we concluded to have a feast in our best style; for which purpose we made preparation by sending out four of our best hunters, to get a choice piece of meat for the occasion. These men killed ten buffalo, from which they selected one of the fattest humps they could find and brought in, and after roasting it handsomely be-fore the fire, we all seated ourselves upon the ground, encircling, what we there called a splendid **repast** *to dine upon. Feasting sump-tuously, cracking a few jokes, taking a few rounds with our rifles, and wishing heartily for some liquor, having none at that place, we spent the day....*

....In the meantime, Smith, Fully, and myself were busily en-gaged in trapping on the tributary streams of the river Platte. We encountered much difficulty and danger in this excursion, from wild beasts and hostile Indians. One circumstance with a bear I must re-late:—On a pleasant summer evening, when nothing seemed dis-posed to disturb the tranquility of our forest home, we built a fire under the cliff of a large rock, on the bank of a small creek, to roast some buffalo meat. After having cooked and eat our evening repast, I was standing close to the rock, apart from the other men ten or

Merciless savages: Leonard is referring negatively to Native Americans.

Principal: Leader.

Notwithstanding: Although.

We never could exhaust or even impair: They couldn't use up all of the beaver; Leonard is saying there were enough beaver for all the trappers.

Repast: Meal.

twelve feet—all at once one of them jumped up and ran off, ex-claiming "the bear," "the bear!" I instantly cast my eyes to the top of the **precipice**, where they encountered this hideous monster seat-ed on the rock with his mouth wide open, and his eyes sparkling like fire. My whole frame shook with agitation. I knew that to attempt to run would be certain death. My gun was standing against a tree within my reach, and after calling for the aid of my companions, I raised my rifle to my face and taking deliberate aim at the most fatal spot, fired—which brought **Sir Bruin** to the ground. In the meantime Smith and Fully came to my assistance, and also discharged the con-tents of their rifles into his head.

In a few days afterwards we were joined by the rest of the com-pany, who, having **secreted** the fur, &c., at the mouth of the Laramies River, had come in search of us. We now, for the first time, got a knowledge of the conduct of Stephens relative to our fur. The men informed us of the contract between them and Stephens. [Stephens had earlier guaranteed these men an equal share of the furs caught by Smith, Fully, and Leonard.] We answered that

Fur traders were among the first whites to venture into the western territories. Native Americans sometimes resented the trappers intruding on their land.
(© CORBIS. Reproduced by permission.)

Precipice: A steep mass of rock, such as the face of a cliff.

Sir Bruin: The bear; bruin is another word for bear.

Secreted: Hidden.

White fur traders visiting a Native American settlement; some early traders established peaceful relationships with various Indian tribes.
(© Bettmann/Corbis. Reproduced by permission.)

we could agree to no such contract—that the fur belonged to us, and that we intended to keep it. They then devised other means to secure their share of 150 beaver skins (the whole number we had caught). Stephens then told the men that he would not be accountable for any of the fur, and the only way to obtain any of it, was to take it by force. Seeing the folly of further resistance—18 against 3—we were obliged to surrender our earnings, which they took and divided equally among themselves. The next day we left this compa-

ny at whose hands we had received such ill treatment, and returned to the mouth of the Laramies, with the expectation of meeting Captain Gant—but we were sadly mistaken—on our arrival there no traces of Capt. G.'s company could be discovered....

*....After traveling a few miles this morning, some of the men, in taking a view of the country before us, discovered something like people upon horses, who appeared to be coming toward us. After continuing in the same direction for some time we came in view with the naked eye, when we halted. They advanced towards us displaying a British flag. This we could not comprehend; but on coming closer discovered them to be hostile Indians. We immediately **despatched** a messenger back to the **rendezvous** for reinforcements and prepared ourselves for defense. The Indians commenced building a fort in the timber on the bank of the river; but at the time we were not aware of what they were doing. After waiting here a few hours we were reinforced by two hundred whites, two hundred Flatheads, and three hundred Nez Perces Indians. The Indians with the British flag, on seeing such a number of people galloping down the plain at full speed, immediately retreated within their fort, whither they were hotly pursued. The friendly Indians soon discovered them to belong to the Blackfeet tribe, who are decidedly the most numerous and warlike tribe in the mountains, and for this reason are not disposed to have any friendly **intercourse** with any other nation of an inferior number, unless they are good warriors and well armed with guns, &c. We thought we could rush right on them and drive them out of the brush into the plain and have a decisive battle at once. We advanced with all possible speed, and a full determination of success, until we discovered their fort by **receiving a most destructive fire from the enclosure**. This threw our ranks into complete confusion, and we all retreated into the plain, with the loss of five whites, eight Flatheads and ten Nez Perces Indians killed, besides a large number of whites and Indians wounded. The formation of their fort astonished all hands. We had been within a few hundred yards of them all day and did not discover that they were building it. It was large enough to contain five hundred warriors; and built strong enough to resist almost any attempt we might make to **force it**. After dressing the wounded, and having **reconnoitered** their fort, our forces were divided into several **detachments**, and sent in different directions with the intention of surrounding the fort and making them prisoners. This was done under the **superintendence** of Fitzpatrick, who acted as commander-in-chief.*

Despatched: Spelled *dispatched;* sent with a specific purpose.

Rendezvous: Designated meeting place.

Intercourse: Communication.

Receiving a most destructive fire from the enclosure: They were being shot at by Blackfeet who were in the fort.

Force it: Penetrate the fort.

Reconnoitered: Inspected; gained more information about.

Detachments: Units or divisions.

Superintendence: Supervision, direction, or authority.

Fashion Spurs Exploration

The hunt for beaver pelts that drew so many mountain men onto the western frontier was driven primarily by the demands of the fashion industry. The beavers' underfur was prized for making waterproof felt hats. In the 1820s and 1830s, the height of the beaver pelt trade in North America, hatters would pay between $6.00 and $9.00 per pelt, while on the frontier the pelts themselves were exchanged as currency.

By the 1840s, however, overtrapping of beaver and changes in fashion put the fur trade in jeopardy; the industry was no longer profitable. Many ex-trappers remained in the western territories they knew so well, establishing farms or general trading posts in the Rocky Mountains, or helping settlers make the journey westward.

Estimation: Opinion.

Electioneering: Campaigning.

Circuitous: Roundabout.

Breastwork: Temporary fort.

Balls: Bullets.

Approbation: Approval.

Pretext: Professed purpose, excuse.

A continual fire was kept up: Both sides continued shooting at each other.

*In a case of this kind any man not evincing the greatest degree of courage and every symptom of bravery, is treated as a coward; and the person who advances first, furthest and fastest, and makes the greatest display of animal courage, soon rises in the **estimation** of his companions. Accordingly with the hope of gaining a little glory while an opportunity offered, though not for any **electioneering** purpose, as a politician in the States would do—I started into the brush, in company with two acquaintances (Smith and Kean) and two Indians. We made a **circuitous** route and came towards the fort from a direction which we thought we would be least expected. We advanced closer and closer, crawling upon our hands and knees, with the intention of giving them a select shot; and when within about forty yards of their **breastwork**, one of our Indians was shot dead. At this we all lay still for some time, but Smith's foot happening to shake the weeds as he was laying on his belly, was shot through. I advanced a little further, but finding the **balls** to pass too quick and close, concluded to retreat. When I turned, I found that my companions had deserted me. In passing by, Smith asked me to carry him out, which met my **approbation** precisely, for I was glad to get out of this unpleasant situation under any **pretext**—provided my reputation for courage would not be questioned. After getting him on my back, still crawling on my hands and knees, I came across Kean, lying near where the first Indian fell, who was mortally wounded and died soon after. I carried Smith to a place of safety and then returned to the siege. **A continual fire was kept up**, doing more or less execution on both sides until late in the afternoon, when we advanced to close quarters, having nothing but the thickness of their breastwork between us, and having them completely surrounded on all sides to prevent any escaping. This position we maintained until sunset, in the meantime having made preparations to set fire to the fort, which was built principally of old dry logs, as soon as night would set in, and stationed men at the point where we thought they would be most likely* *to make the first break, for the purpose of taking them on the wing, in their flight. Having made all these preparations, which were to put an end to all further **molestation** on the part of the Blackfeet, our whole scheme and contemplated victory was frustrated by a most ingenious and well executed device of the enemy. A few minutes before the torch was to be applied, our captives commenced the most tremendous yells and shouts of triumph, and menaces of defiance, which seemed to move heaven and earth. Quick as thought a report spread through all quarters, that the plain was covered with Blackfeet Indians coming to reinforce the **besieged.** So complete was the **consternation** in our ranks, created by this **stratagem**, that in five minutes afterward there was not a single white man, Flathead, or Nez Perces Indian within a hundred yards of the fort. Every man thought only of his own security and run for life without ever looking round, which would at once have convinced him of his folly. In a short time it was **ascertained** that it was only a stratagem, and our men began to collect together where our baggage was. I never shall forget the scene here exhibited. The rage of some was unbounded, and approached to madness. For my own part, although I felt much regret at the result after so much toil and danger, yet I could not but give the savages credit for the skill they displayed in preserving their lives, at the very moment when desperation, as we thought, had seized the mind of each of them.*

*By the time we were **made sensible of** the full extent of our needless alarm, it had began to get dark; and on ascertaining the extent of the injury which we received (having lost 32 killed, principally Indians), it was determined not to again attempt to surround the fort, which was a sore disappointment to some of the men who were keen for **chastising** the Indians for their trick....*

April 10th. Beaver we found in abundance—catching more or less every day, and everything seemed to promise a profitable business ...

... About the 10th of June we suspended our trapping and returned to Wind River, where we found Captain Bonneville and his men waiting for us according to appointment, at the mouth of Popoasia Creek.

*Here we encamped for a few days, until we could collect our **peltries** together and make a divide—having sent some of our men to bring our merchandise, &c., from the place where we had deposited it, who succeeded without any difficulty.... We now set about packing and sorting our furs, &c., and making arrangements for the ensuing year—such as paying off hands, hiring them for another term, and apportioning the different companies. Captain Walker, with*

Molestation: Attack.

Besieged: Those surrounded by hostile forces.

Consternation: Confusion.

Stratagem: A military maneuver designed to deceive or surprise an enemy.

Ascertained: Learned or discovered.

Made sensible of: Understood.

Chastising: Punishing.

Peltries: Animal Skins.

fifty-nine men, was to continue trapping in this country for one year from this time, and Captain Bonneville, with the remainder, taking all the peltries we had collected, and which were packed upon horses and mules, was to go to the States and return in the summer of 1836, with as strong a force as he could collect, and a large supply of merchandise, and meet Captain Walker in this neighborhood.

On parting this time, many of the men were at a loss to know what to do. Many were anxious to return to the States, but feared to do so, lest the offended law might hold them responsible for misdemeanors committed previous to their embarking in the trapping business, and others could not be persuaded to do so for any price—declaring that a civilized life had no charms for them. Although I intended to return to the mountains again, I was particularly anxious to first visit the States lest I should also forget the blessings of civilized society, and was very thankful when I found myself in Captain Bonneville's company, on the march towards the rising sun. As we traveled along we killed all the game we could, this being necessary, as provision is very scarce on the course we intended to pursue between the village of the Pawnee Indians and the white settlements. About the 25th of July we arrived on the Platte River, which we followed down until we arrived at the Pawnee Village, situated about one hundred and fifty miles from where the Platte River empties into the Missouri. After trading with these Indians for some corn, we left them and traveled rapidly every day until we arrived in Independence (Mo.), which is the extreme western white settlement, on the 29th of August, 1835—after being absent four years, four months, and five days. [Ewers, pp. 3–4, 8–9, 14, 27–28, 42–45, 58, 160–61]

What happened next . . .

By 1831 large numbers of free trappers as well as the American Fur Company competed for a share of the mountain fur trade. So many trappers combed the western rivers by 1839 that the scarcity of beavers made the mountain trappers' yearly rendezvous unprofitable. Within a few decades the American fur-trading industry had ended. Although the furs could no longer be found in sufficient abundance, the trappers' stories about the western regions continued to filter throughout

the country. The U.S. government became curious about the potential for spreading settlements across the West and perhaps finding other natural sources of revenue. With their expert knowledge of the otherwise unknown reaches of the country, many of the trappers went on to act as guides for explorers who mapped the West or to lead overland wagon trains that began traveling across the Mississippi River.

The mountain men's stories had sparked the imaginations of many curious and adventurous people, but the reports of government-sponsored explorers made the seemingly impossible real. The vivid descriptions of distant places enticed many to risk leaving the security of civilization to strike out on their own.

Did you know . . .

- In 1807 Manuel Lisa constructed the first U.S. trading post on the Upper Missouri River at Fort Raymond in Montana.

- The rendezvous, a gathering at which trappers and Indians sold their goods and bought supplies, was the most important social and business event of the American fur trade from the 1820s to the 1830s.

- The annual American fur trade with China surpassed $5 million in 1806.

- John Jacob Astor chartered the American Fur Company in 1808. It became the largest U.S. fur-trading company in 1827.

- In 1840 the U.S. fur trapping industry deteriorated due to beaver depletion and shifts in fashion toward silk hats.

Consider the following . . .

- Did Leonard find trapping a profitable business?

- What were Leonard's experiences with Native Americans?

- Did Leonard find the frontier an easy place to live?

- Was there camaraderie between trappers?

- How did Leonard account for his bravery during the battle with the Blackfeet?

For More Information

Chittenden, Hiram Martin. *The American Fur Trade of the Far West.* 3 vols. New York: F. P. Harper, 1902.

Ferris, Warren Angus. *Life in the Rocky Mountains; a Diary of Wanderings on the Sources of the Rivers Missouri, Columbia, and Colorado from February, 1830, to November, 1835.* Edited by Paul C. Phillips. Denver: F. A. Rosenstock, Old West Pub. Co., 1940.

Leonard, Zenas. *Adventures of Zenas Leonard Fur Trader.* Edited by John C. Ewers. Norman: University of Oklahoma Press, 1959.

Leonard, Zenas. *Narrative of the Adventures of Zenas Leonard, a Native of Clearfield County, Pa. Who Spent Five Years in Trappin for Furs, Trading with the Indians, &c., &c., of the Rocky Mountains: Written by Himself.* Clearfield, PA: D.W. Moore, 1839.

O'Neil, Paul. *The Frontiersmen.* Alexandria, VA: Time-Life Books, 1977.

John C. Frémont

Excerpt from **The Life of Col. John Charles Frémont,
and His Narrative of Explorations and Adventures
in Kansas, Nebraska, Oregon and California**
By Samuel M. Smucker
Published in 1856

In 1842 John C. Frémont (1813–1890), known as "The Path-finder," led an expedition between the Missouri River and the Rocky Mountains. In 1843 he led another from Independence, Missouri, along the Kansas River, across the Rocky Mountains, and over the Laramie Plain through South Pass. Frémont's description of the Salt Lake Valley inspired Brigham Young and his Mormon followers to settle there a decade later. Frémont's party eventually reached the Columbia River north of what he called the Great Basin. From there Frémont followed the Sierra Nevada range south into California. The expedition endured a brutal winter season before finally arriving at Sutter's ranch, a site that in 1849 would be overwhelmed by prospective gold seekers.

Like most military explorers, Frémont was motivated by the potential for increasing American territory. However, his findings proved significant for subsequent geographical explorations. With the aid of Charles Preuss, a Prussian cartographer, Frémont produced the first accurate map of the overall trans-Mississippi west as well as a special emigrant map of the Oregon and California trails with precise informa-

tion on distances, landmarks, and river crossings. His exuberant writings encouraged many to migrate to the West. The following narrative is an excerpt from Frémont's expedition into the country between the Missouri River and the Rocky Mountains from May to October of 1842.

Things to remember while reading the excerpt from *The Life of Col. John Charles Frémont*:

- In 1843 the first major migration of emigrants staked out claims to land west of the Rocky Mountains after traveling more than two thousand miles along the Oregon Trail.

- Frémont's nickname was not entirely accurate since he generally followed routes that had already been discovered earlier by other explorers, trappers, and traders. However, it was his accurate surveys and exciting reports that encouraged large numbers of people to settle the American West.

- Frémont's wife, Jessie—the daughter of influential Missouri senator Thomas Hart Benton—helped him write his reports.

- Frémont's reports inspired great popular interest in the West and garnered political support for territorial expansion. More than ten thousand copies of his first report were sold.

- In 1842 Frémont hired Kit Carson (1809–1868) as guide and hunter at one hundred dollars a month. Carson would guide three of Frémont's expeditions.

- Frémont's accounts of his expeditions included dynamic descriptions of his guide, which brought Kit Carson fame as a hero of the West. In his first report, Frémont wrote that "mounted on a fine horse, without a saddle, and scouring

John C. Frémont was also known as "The Pathfinder." His nickname wasn't entirely accurate since Frémont generally followed trails discovered by earlier explorers.
(Courtesy of the Library of Congress.)

bareheaded over the prairies, Kit was one of the finest pictures of a horseman I have ever seen."

- During his first expedition, Frémont climbed Frémont Peak in the Wind River Range of Wyoming, which he thought (at the time) was the highest peak in the Rocky Mountains.

Excerpt from The Life of Col. John Charles Frémont

A Narrative of Adventures and Explorations, in the Country Lying between the Missouri River and the Rocky Mountains

Frémont's wife, Jessie was an accomplished writer who helped organize Frémont's notes into an interesting narrative.
(Archive Photos, Inc. Reproduced by permission.)

[The third month of the journey: July 1842] *To the south, along our line of march to-day, the main chain of the Black or Laramie hills rises* **precipitously.** *Time did not permit me to visit them; but, from comparative information, the ridge is composed of the coarse sandstone or* **conglomerate** *hereafter described. It appears to enter the region of clouds, which are arrested in their course, and lie in masses along the summits. An inverted cone of black cloud (cumulus) rested during all the* **forenoon** *on the lofty peak of Laramie mountain, which I estimated to be about two thousand feet above the fort, or six thousand five hundred above the sea. We halted to noon on the* Fourche Amere, *so called from being timbered principally with the* liard amere, *(a species of poplar,) with which the valley of the little stream is tolerably well wooded, and which, with large expansive summits, grows to the height of sixty or seventy feet.*

The bed of the creek is sand and gravel, the water dispersed over the broad bed in several shallow streams. We found here, on the right bank, in the shade of the trees, a fine spring of very cold water. It will be remarked that I do not mention, in this portion of

Precipitously: Quite steeply.

Conglomerate: A type of rock that is made up of pebbles, stones, and other hard materials cemented together.

Forenoon: The hours between sunrise and noon.

Meridian: Imaginary lines that run north and south along the Earth's surface from the North Pole to the South Pole; used to locate one's place on the Earth; measured as longitude.

Verdure: Abundant green plant life.

Vicinity: Nearness.

Sterile: Unable to produce life; Frémont is noting that the landscape has become less lush.

Usurped: Overtaken.

Artemisia: Any of various aromatic plants having green or grayish foliage and numerous small flowers, including mugwort, sagebrush, tarragon, and wormweed.

Odoriferous: Aromatic, fragrant.

Ford: A shallow place in a river or stream where one can cross.

Transient: Short-lived.

Circuits: A path that circles around.

---

the journey, the temperature of the air, sand, springs, &c.—an omission which will be explained in the course of the narrative. In my search for plants, I was well rewarded at this place.

*With the change in the geological formation on leaving Fort Laramie, the whole face of the country has entirely altered its appearance. Eastward of that **meridian**, the principal objects which strike the eye of a traveler are the absence of timber, and the immense expanse of prairie, covered with the **verdure** of rich grasses, and highly adapted for pasturage. Wherever they are not disturbed by the **vicinity** of man, large herds of buffalo give animation to this country. Westward of Laramie river, the region is sandy, and apparently **sterile;** and the place of the grass is **usurped** by the **artemisia** and other **odoriferous** plants, to whose growth the sandy soil and dry air of this elevated region seem highly favorable.*

One of the prominent characteristics in the face of the country is the extraordinary abundance of the artemisias. They grow everywhere—on hills, and over the river bottoms, in tough, twisted, wiry clumps; and, wherever the beaten track was left, they rendered the progress of the carts rough and slow....

*[July] 28th.—In two miles from our encampment, we reached the place where the regular road crosses the Platte. There was two hundred feet breadth of water at this time in the bed, which has a variable width of eight to fifteen hundred feet. The channels were generally three feet deep, and there were large angular rocks on the bottom, which made the **ford** in some places a little difficult. Even at its low stages, this river cannot be crossed at random, and this has always been used as the best ford. The low stage of the water the present year had made it fordable in almost any part of its course, where access could be had to its bed....*

*The road which is now generally followed through this region is therefore a very good one, without any difficult ascents to overcome. The principal obstructions are near the river, where the **transient** waters of heavy rains had made deep ravines with steep banks, which render frequent **circuits** necessary. It will be remembered that wagons pass this road only once or twice a year, which is by no means sufficient to break down the stubborn roots of the innumerable artemisia bushes. A partial absence of these is often the only indication of the track; and the roughness produced by their roots in many places gives the road the character of one newly opened in a wooded country. This is usually considered the worst part of the road east of the mountains; and, as it passes through an open prairie re-*

gion, may be much improved, so as to avoid the greater part of the inequalities it now presents.

From the mouth of the Kansas to the Green River valley, west of the mountains, there is no such thing as a mountain road on the line of communication....

[August] 24th.—We started before sunrise, intending to break-fast at Goat Island. I had directed the land party, in charge of **Bernier,** to proceed to this place, where they were to remain, should they find no note to **apprize** them of our having passed. In the event of receiving this information, they were to continue their route, pass-ing by certain places which had been designated. Mr. Preuss accom-panied me, and with us were five of my best men, **viz.:** C. Lambert, Basil Lajeuneese, Honore Ayot, Benoist, and Descoteaux. Here ap-peared no scarcity of water, and we took on board, with various in-struments and baggage, provisions for ten or twelve days. We pad-dled down the river rapidly, for our little craft was light as a duck on the water; and the sun had been some time risen, when we heard

John C. Frémont was encouraged to romanticize his explorations of the West in order to encourage Americans to settle the region.
(Reproduced from the Collections of the Library of Congress.)

Bernier: Bernard Bernier, one of Frémont's most trusted men. Bernier was in charge of the land party.

Apprize: Spelled *apprise;* to inform.

Viz.: Namely.

Kit Carson worked as a guide and hunter for three Frémont expeditions.
(Archive Photos, Inc. Reproduced by permission.)

Velocity: Swiftness, speed of motion.

Reconnoiter: Inspect.

Cataract: A large or high waterfall.

before us a hollow roar, which we supposed to be that of a fall, of which we had heard a vague rumor, but whose exact locality no one had been able to describe to us. We were approaching a ridge, through which the river passes by a place called "canon," (pronounced kanyon,*)—a Spanish word, signifying a piece of artillery, the barrel of a gun, or any kind of tube; and which, in this country, has been adopted to describe the passage of a river between perpendicular rocks of great height, which frequently approach each other so closely overhead as to form a kind of tunnel over the stream, which foams along below, half choked up by fallen fragments. Between the mouth of the Sweet Water and Goat island, there is probably a fall of three hundred feet, and that was principally made in the canons before us; as, without them, the water was comparatively smooth. As we neared the ridge, the river made a sudden turn, and swept squarely down against one of the walls of the canon, with great* **velocity,** *and so steep a descent that it had, to the eye, the appearance of an inclined plane. When we launched into this, the men jumped overboard, to check the velocity of our boat; but were soon in water up to their necks, and our boat ran on. But we succeeded in bringing her to a small point of rocks on the right, at the mouth of the canon. Here was a kind of elevated sand-beach, not many yards square, backed by the rocks on the right, and around the point the river swept at a right angle. Trunks of trees deposited on jutting points, twenty to thirty feet above, and other marks, showed that the water here frequently rose to a considerable height. The ridge was of the same decomposing granite already mentioned, and the water had worked the surface, in many places, into a wavy surface of ridges and holes. We ascended the rocks to* **reconnoiter** *the ground, and from the summit the passage appeared to be a continued* **cataract,** *foaming over many obstructions, and broken by a number of small falls. We saw nowhere a fall answering to that which had been described to us as having twenty or twenty-five feet; but still concluded this to be the place in question, as, in the season of floods, the rush of the river against the wall* *would produce a great rise; and the waters, reflected squarely off, would descend through the passage in a sheet of foam, having every appearance of a large fall. Eighteen years previous to this time, as I have subsequently learned from himself, Mr. Fitzpatrick, somewhere above the river, had embarked with a valuable cargo of beaver. Unacquainted with the stream, which he believed would conduct him safely to the Missouri, he came unexpectedly into this canon, where he was wrecked, with the total loss of his furs. It would have been a work of great time and labor to pack our baggage across the ridge, and I determined to run the canon. We all again embarked, and at first attempted to check the way of the boat; but the water swept through with so much violence that we narrowly escaped being swamped, and were obliged to let her go in the full force of the current, and trust to the skill of the boatmen. The dangerous places in this canon were where huge rocks had fallen from above, and hemmed in the already narrow pass of the river to an open space of three or four and five feet. These obstructions raised the water considerably above, which was sometimes precipitated over in a fall; and at the other places, where this dam was too high, rushed through the contracted opening with tremendous violence. Had our boat been made of wood, in passing the narrows she would have been staved; but her elasticity preserved her unhurt from every shock, and she seemed fairly to leap over the falls.*

In this way we passed three cataracts in succession, where perhaps 100 feet of smooth water intervened; and, finally, with a shout of pleasure at our success, issued from out tunnel into the open day beyond. We were so delighted with the performance of our boat, and so confident in her powers, that we would not have hesitated to leap a fall of ten feet with her. [Smucker, pp. 134–35, 140–41, 174–76]

What happened next . . .

Mapping and explorations of the North American continent continued. During the Mexican-American War (1846–1848) and as hostilities increased between the federal government and Plains Indians, the U.S. Army explored and mapped large portions of the West for reconnaissance purposes. In other words, scouts produced maps that identified the locations of water holes and mountain passes. These maps were then used to deduce enemy movements. In 1854 G. K. Warren compiled all known research from the previous half-century to produce an exhaustive map of the United States from the Mississippi to the Pacific. Geographers agree that Warren's publication marked the official end of geographic exploration and the beginning of a new research stage: the detailed survey, which John Wesley Powell pioneered in the 1870s.

Following the Treaty of Guadalupe Hidalgo, which ended the Mexican-American War and established the official border between the United States and Mexico, the U.S. Topographical Corps surveyed the length of the Rio Grande, producing studies that proved valuable in later railroad development. At individual military posts, army surgeons wrote descriptive reports of the local terrain and flora and fauna as well as detailed accounts of health and sanitation levels of the troops and neighboring civilian communities. Government employees—engineers, soldiers, and topographers—also prospected for water, mapped rivers and harbors, built dams, and supervised road construction. These early efforts represented an alliance between science and government that continues to the present day.

Did you know . . .

- Frémont's report of his first two expeditions contradicted Zebulon Pike's view that the Plains were the "Great American Desert." Instead Frémont described the possibilities of this region. His report attracted many pioneers westward.

- Frémont's survey of the northern shores of the Great Salt Lake in 1843 encouraged the Mormons under Brigham Young to settle there four years later.

- Frémont's excursion into California from 1845 to 1846 played a major role in the U.S. taking control of that territory from Mexico. Frémont led a group of American settlers in California in their revolt against Mexico and set up California as an independent republic. California Territory became part of the United States after the Mexican-American War.

- Frémont became territorial governor of California, but his authority was quickly revoked by a regular army force

under General Stephen Kearny. When Frémont refused to give up his post, he was arrested and sent back east as a prisoner. There he was found guilty of mutiny and disobedience at a court-martial and dismissed from the army, but President James K. Polk remitted the sentence. Frémont, however, was furious at his treatment and quit the army anyway.

- After Frémont quit the army, he made a fortune in the California gold rush.

- Frémont briefly served as a U.S. senator from California and unsuccessfully ran for president as the first candidate of the newly established Republican Party in 1856.

- During the Civil War, Frémont briefly commanded all Union forces in the West. President Lincoln dismissed Frémont when Frémont overstepped his authority by issuing an order freeing all slaves in Missouri. Frémont lost his fortune in several ill-fated railroad schemes. President

Frémont's accounts of his adventures—such as climbing high mountains and navigating white-water rapids—enticed many to venture into the Far West. *(Sally A. Morgan; Ecoscene/ Corbis. Reproduced by permission.)*

Rutherford B. Hayes (1822–1893) appointed Frémont governor of the Arizona Territory in 1878.

Consider the following . . .

- Why did Frémont decide to run the rapids of the river?

- How did Frémont describe the prairies?

- What was the major difference between the landscape of the prairies and the land farther west?

- What aspects of Frémont's reports would inspire someone to travel west?

For More Information

Frémont, John C. *Report of the Exploring Expedition to the Rocky Mountains.* Washington D.C.: United States government, 1845.

Harris, Edward D. *John Charles Frémont and the Great Western Reconnaissance.* New York: Chelsea House, 1990.

Preuss, Charles. *Exploring with Frémont.* Edited by Erwin G. and Elizabeth K. Gudde. Norman: University of Oklahoma Press, 1958.

Sanford, William R., and Carl R. Green. *John C. Frémont: Soldier and Pathfinder.* Springfield, New Jersey: Enslow Publishers, 1996.

Smucker, Samuel M. *The Life of Col. John Charles Frémont, and His Narrative of Explorations and Adventures in Kansas, Nebraska, Oregon and California.* New York: Miller, Orton and Mulligan, 1856.

Indian Wars

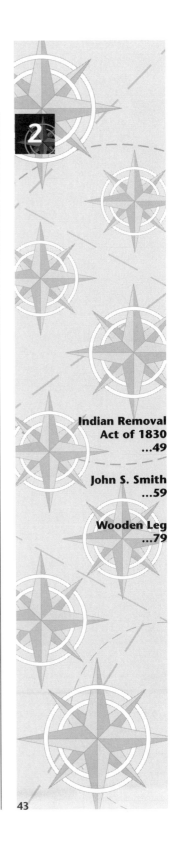

For more than three hundred years, white men battled Native Americans for control of the North American continent. Beginning shortly after European settlers landed on the shores of the present-day United States in the early seventeenth century and continuing until the dawn of the twentieth century, white settlers and soldiers waged an unrelenting war to claim the lands that Native Americans, or Indians, had long considered their own. Though the underlying cause of the wars was the white settlers' craving for land, the tensions were heightened by the huge cultural differences that separated the two peoples. Whites and Native Americans had very different ideas about how to use land, the meaning and importance of promises, and how to wage war. These cultural differences added to the tragedy of the Indian Wars.

From the beginning, the white conquerors had tremendous advantages. They possessed superior weapons, larger numbers, and a strong sense of purpose—to claim the land from coast to coast. Soon after the United States declared its independence from England, Americans began to pour into the trans-Appalachian West, the area between the

Appalachian Mountains and the Mississippi River. Though they met with resistance from the many Native American tribes who lived in the region, the settlers believed that they had a right to possess the land—and the American military agreed and provided military support. Most Americans believed that they would make the best use of the land by developing it into farms, towns, and cities that would help strengthen the United States. They believed that Native Americans were not making productive use of the land and used this idea to justify their claims to the land.

When the War of 1812 (1812–14) broke out between the Americans and the British over control of the territory known as the Old Northwest (the land north of the Ohio River up to the Canadian border and west of Pennsylvania up to the Mississippi River), Native Americans allied themselves with the British in hopes of slowing the flood of American settlers into their territory. The United States defeated the British and Indian forces in the War of 1812; the victory and the subsequent "improvements" made in the territory strengthened the American commitment to rid the United States of the Native Americans.

In 1830, after years of fighting, negotiating, and making and breaking treaties, the U.S. government decided to move all Native Americans, by force if necessary, to lands west of the Mississippi River. The **Indian Removal Act of 1830**, the first primary source in this chapter, defines the terms by which Indians would be forced from their land. Most Americans believed that this would permanently solve the problems between Native Americans and whites; it would remove Indians from the territory that whites wanted to settle and give Indians what seemed to the whites to be a fair amount of land to live on. And, at the time, whites couldn't foresee ever wanting the territory that they were giving the Indians.

Though the Indian Removal Act of 1830 was intended as a permanent solution to the nation's struggle with the American Indian population, a number of factors spurred further conflicts. Beginning in the 1830s the nation began to embrace the idea of manifest destiny, which held that the United States was divinely ordained to control all the land stretching from the Atlantic Ocean to the Pacific Ocean. A flood of emigrants began moving west along the Oregon and Santa Fe

Trails, heading for Texas, New Mexico, California, and Oregon Territory. In the late 1840s many of them were heading toward California and the gold rush. Whites again found themselves coming into conflict with Indians as they passed through Indian Territory on their way west. The backers of manifest destiny—including the most powerful political and military leaders of the United States—contended that their goals would not be met until all Indian tribes were firmly under U.S. control and confined safely to reservations.

Beginning in the late 1840s, after the Mexican-American War (1846–48), the U.S. military began a concerted effort to control the West. It took nearly twenty years for Americans to defeat the Navajo and Apache tribes in the Southwest. By the 1860s the military turned its attention to the last vast area under Indian control: the Great Plains. The Great Plains—which included the present-day states of Nebraska, Kansas, Oklahoma, North and South Dakota, Montana, Wyoming, and parts of Colorado and Idaho—was a land of

American settlers in the West believed that they had a right to possess the land the Native Americans had been living on for thousands of years. *(Archive Photos, Inc. Reproduced by permission.)*

Native Americans reenact the Battle of Little Bighorn, the greatest Indian victory in the long and bloody war for the Plains.
(© Brian Vikander/Corbis. Reproduced by permission.)

dry rolling prairies and harsh winters; moreover, the region was crossed over by many but settled by very few. It was, up until the 1850s, populated almost entirely by Indian tribes like the Sioux and Cheyenne, who had been there for centuries, living off the land, especially the buffalo that roamed the plains. These tribes were seminomadic, following the herds of buffalo that provided their sustenance. When Americans discovered deposits of gold in Colorado and Montana, and as settlers committed themselves to farming and ranching in the area once known as the Great American Desert, the peaceful life of the Plains Indians changed. For thirty years, they fought to defend their way of life. In the end they were defeated.

In 1864, whites and Indians clashed at Sand Creek in Colorado. Though its perpetrators called the battle a great victory, unbiased accounts revealed it to be one of the worst atrocities committed by white troops against the Indian people. In the second primary source in this chapter, **Congressional**

Testimony of John S. Smith, Eyewitness to the Sand Creek Massacre, John Smith, an Indian interpreter and agent, provides his account of the battle before a congressional committee appointed to examine the calamity that became known as the Sand Creek Massacre.

The Battle of Little Bighorn was the greatest Indian victory in the long and bloody war for the Plains. Frustrated at their inability to defeat the many tribes scattered across the northern Plains, U.S. military forces planned a major assault in the spring of 1876. On June 25, 1876, General George A. Custer attempted to surprise the Indians but instead found his forces overwhelmed by vast numbers of Indian warriors. Led by famous chiefs Sitting Bull, Lame White Man, and Crazy Horse, the Indian forces routed the army in one of their its defeats ever. *Wooden Leg: A Warrior Who Fought Custer* offers a young Cheyenne warrior's perspective on the battle. Wooden Leg's account highlights the bravery of the Indian warriors and the horror of battle.

Indian Removal Act of 1830

Legislation passed by the United States Congress in 1830

The War of 1812 marked the end of organized Indian resistance to white settlement of the area known as the Old Northwest (the area of land surrounding the Great Lakes and between the Ohio River and the Mississippi River; it included the present-day states of Ohio, Indiana, Illinois, Michigan, Wisconsin, and part of Minnesota). White pioneers poured into the trans-Appalachian West, settling in the area that now includes the states of Alabama, Mississippi, Louisiana, Illinois, Indiana, Missouri, and other Midwestern states. These settlers discovered, however, that many Indians hoped to remain on the lands that had been occupied by the Indians' ancestors. Though open warfare had ceased, whites and Indians continued to clash over who would occupy the fertile lands that the United States had claimed as the spoils of war. By 1830 many former territories had become states, and these states pushed for the removal of Indians from their land.

Andrew Jackson (1767–1845)—famed for his valor in the Battle of New Orleans in 1814 and renowned as a skilled Indian fighter—became president of the United States in 1829 and supervised a concerted effort to remove Indians

President Andrew Jackson led the effort to remove all American Indians to lands west of the Mississippi River. *(National Portrait Gallery/ Smithsonian Institution. Reproduced by permission.)*

from the lands east of the Mississippi River. In his first address to Congress as president, Jackson asked: "What good man would prefer a country covered with forests and ranged by a few thousand savages to our extensive Republic, studded with cities, towns, and prosperous farms, embellished with all the improvements which art can devise or industry execute, occupied by more than 12,000,000 happy people, and filled with all the blessings of liberty, civilization, and religion?" Pressured by the governments of frontier states that complained of the difficulties they faced in dealing with conflicts between Indian tribes and white settlers, Congress passed the Indian Removal Act of 1830. The Indian Removal Act called for the removal of all Indians to lands west of the Mississippi and voided all previous treaties regarding Indian land. The actual Indian Territory that was defined by Congress in 1834 was far smaller than the "all lands west of the Mississippi" that whites had once promised. The Indian Territory covered parts of the present-day states of Oklahoma, Nebraska, and Kansas. The Indian Removal Act, reprinted on the following

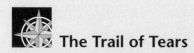

The Trail of Tears

By the late 1830s the Cherokee in Georgia, an educated and prosperous tribe, had done all they could to stay on their ancestral lands, including taking their case to the Supreme Court. Yet in 1838, Andrew Jackson's successor, Martin Van Buren (1782–1862), ordered U.S. troops and the Georgia state militia to remove the seventeen thousand Cherokee by whatever means necessary. According to Robert Utley and Wilcomb Washburn in *Indian Wars,* General Winfield Scott ordered that "every possible kindness . . . must be . . . shown by the troops." However, kindness is hardly the word to describe the horrors that were inflicted upon the Cherokee. As Utley and Washburn write: "Yet, on the sunny May morning when the soldiers set about their task, some of them raped, robbed, and murdered the Indians.... The army kept the Cherokees penned up in concentration camps throughout the stifling summer; many died, and many more fell ill. In the fall and early winter contingents started west, some in flatboats, some in wagons, some on foot."

The Cherokee were forced to march some twelve hundred miles. Dozens died every day on the journey, falling prey to disease, starvation, or exposure. Those who survived were robbed by marauding parties of white men along the way, who claimed Cherokee goods in exchange for wrongs done to them by other tribes. In all, four thousand Cherokee died before they reached their destination in March of 1839. The trek is remembered by the Cherokee as the Trail of Tears.

pages in its entirety, describes in cold, impersonal language, the removal of thousands of people from their homes. It also promises a number of things to the Indians.

Things to remember while reading the Indian Removal Act of 1830:

- Seven states—Alabama, Illinois, Indiana, Louisiana, Maine, Mississippi, Missouri—joined the United States in the years between 1812 and 1830. These states (except for Maine) pushed for the authority to remove Indians from state land.

- Andrew Jackson had gained a reputation as a fierce Indian fighter for his defeat of the Creek tribe in Georgia during the War of 1812 and for his battles against the powerful Seminole tribe in Florida in 1818 and 1819.

- Andrew Jackson served as teacher, lawyer, territorial governor, congressman, and war hero before becoming president. However, he was a crude and impulsive man with a hot temper. Thomas Jefferson once said of Jackson, "He is one of the most unfit men I know for such a place [as the White House]."

- Jackson is widely viewed as the first "people's president," for he welcomed all citizens into the political process and both respected and responded to the desires of the common people.

- The Indian Removal Act passed in the House of Representatives by a vote of 102 to 97.

Indian Removal Act of 1830
May 28, 1830

An Act to provide for an exchange of lands with the Indians residing in any of the states or territories, and for their removal west of the river Mississippi.

Be it enacted by the Senate and House of Representatives of the United States of America, in Congress assembled, *That it shall and may be lawful for the President of the United States to cause so much of any territory belonging to the United States, west of the river Mississippi, not included in any state or organized territory, and to which the Indian **title has been extinguished**, as he may judge necessary, to be divided into a suitable number of districts, for the reception of such tribes or nations of Indians as may choose to exchange the lands where they now reside, and remove there; and to cause each of said districts to be so described by natural or artificial marks, as to be easily distinguished from every other.*

And be it further enacted, *That it shall and may be lawful for the President to exchange any or all of such districts, so to be laid off and described, with any tribe or nation of Indians now residing within the limits of any of the states or territories, and with which the United States have existing treaties, for the whole or any part or portion of the territory claimed and occupied by such tribe or nation, within the bounds of any one or more of the states or territories,*

Title has been extinguished: Legal claim has ended.

NATIVE AMERICAN POLICY

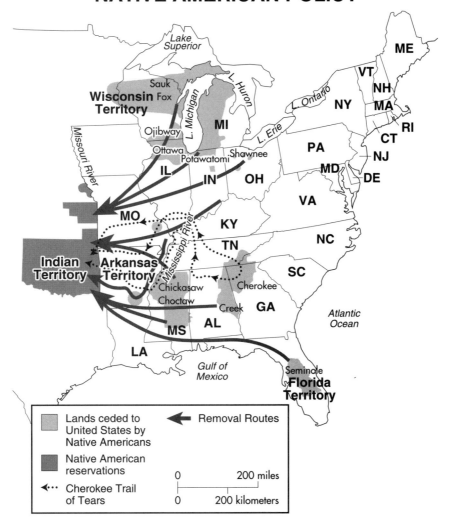

Map shows areas of the eastern United States that Native Americans were forced to leave and the routes they followed to Indian Territory.
(Reproduced by permission of The Gale Group.)

where the land claimed and occupied by the Indians, is owned by the United States, or the United States are bound to the state within which it lies to extinguish the Indian claim thereto.

And be it further enacted, *That in the making of any such exchange or exchanges, it shall and may be lawful for the President solemnly to assure the tribe or nation with which the exchange is made, that the United States will forever secure and guaranty to* them, and their heirs or successors, the country so exchanged with them; and if they prefer it, that the United States will cause a **patent or grant** to be made and executed to them for the same: Provided always, *That such lands shall revert to the United States, if the Indians become extinct, or abandon the same.*

And be it further enacted, *That if, upon any of the lands now occupied by the Indians, and to be exchanged for, there should be such **improvements** as add value to the land claimed by any individual or individuals of such tribes or nations, it shall and may be lawful for the President to cause such value to be **ascertained by appraisement or otherwise**, and to cause such ascertained value to be paid to the person or persons rightfully claiming such improvements. And upon the payment of such valuation, the improvements so valued and paid for, shall pass to the United States, and possession shall not afterwards be permitted to any of the same tribe.*

And be it further enacted, *That upon the making of any such exchange as is contemplated by this act, it shall and may be lawful for the President to cause such aid and assistance to be furnished to the emigrants as may be necessary and proper to enable them to remove to, and settle in, the country for which they may have exchanged; and also, to give them such aid and assistance as may be necessary for their support and subsistence for the first year after their removal.*

And be it further enacted, *That it shall and may be lawful for the President to cause such tribe or nation to be protected, at their new residence, against all interruption or disturbance from any other tribe or nation of Indians, or from any other person or persons whatever.*

And be it further enacted, *That it shall and may be lawful for the President to have the same superintendence and care over any tribe or nation in the country to which they may remove, as contemplated by this act, that he is now authorized to have over them at their present places of residence:* Provided, *That nothing in this act contained shall be construed as authorizing or directing the violation of any existing treaty between the United States and any of the Indian tribes.*

And be it further enacted, *That for the purpose of giving effect to the Provisions of this act, the sum of five hundred thousand dollars is hereby appropriated, to be paid out of any money in the treasury, not otherwise appropriated.*

Patent or grant: A legal promise that the land will always remain theirs.

Improvements: Any buildings, bridges, or roads built by Indians.

Ascertained by appraisement or otherwise: This phrase indicates that someone will determine what the improvements are worth.

What happened next . . .

As the process of Indian removal continued throughout the 1830s, native peoples were kicked off their land and directed to head west to Indian Territory, which was located in present-day Oklahoma. The Cherokee tribes of Georgia, realizing that armed warfare against the whites was futile, took their objections to Georgia's discriminatory laws to the U.S. Supreme Court. The Court actually ruled in favor of the Cherokee, stating that Indian tribes were "domestic dependent nations" that could conduct their own political processes and that they were afforded the protection of the federal government. But President Jackson ignored the ruling and supported Georgia's efforts to drive the Indians from the state. Some Indians left voluntarily, carrying their belongings to a new and unfamiliar land. Others resisted. Creek Indians in Alabama were dragged away in chains, and soldiers drove the Choctaw from Mississippi in the dead of winter. Many Indians died from the hardships they faced along the trail. All in all, thousands of Indians died as they were driven from their native lands.

Whites believed that Indian removal had ended the conflicts with Native Americans to everyone's satisfaction. Settlers would no longer be bothered by Indian attacks and the Indians would be able to pursue their lifestyle on lands of their own in the west. However, neither westward expansion nor the Indian wars would end with the removal of Indians west of the Mississippi River. With the great migration westward after the 1840s, white settlers again clashed with the Indian inhabitants of western lands. Ignoring earlier treaties, including those mentioned in the Indian Removal Act of 1830, the United States once again removed Indians from their land and sent them to reservations that became ever smaller in size. The Indian Removal Act, originally thought of as a final solution to the Indian problem, was thus just another step in the long process of removing nearly all Indian claims to land desired by the United States.

Did you know . . .

- Congressional debates over the Indian Removal Act of 1830 grew quite heated, with some powerful senators defending the rights of the Indians to remain on lands

The Seminole people in Florida resisted removal from their land in a war that lasted from 1835 to 1842. This etching depicts Native Americans being hunted with bloodhounds during the Seminole Wars.
(©Corbis. Reproduced by permission.)

granted them by earlier treaties. However, the head of the federal Indian Office, Thomas L. McKenney, believed that removing the Indians from contact with whites was the only way to preserve the Indian race.

- By 1840 the vast majority of Native Americans had been removed to lands west of the Mississippi.

- Florida's Seminole people resisted removal and fought American troops in a war that lasted from 1835 to 1842 and cost the United States $10 million and thousands of lives. The Seminole remained officially at war with the United States for more than a century.

Consider the following . . .
- Were Native Americans treated fairly? What promises did they have that the lands they were being moved to would not also be taken from them?

- We know that the Indian Removal Act of 1830 made the removal of Indians to lands west of the Mississippi legal, but did it make it right?

- How might supporters of the Indian Removal Act have argued for its passage? What benefits did they think it would bring?

- How might opponents of the Indian Removal Act have argued against its passage? Why do you think they did not win?

For More Information

Davis, Burke. *Old Hickory: A Life of Andrew Jackson.* New York: Dial Press, 1977.

Dunn, John M. *The Relocation of the North American Indian.* San Diego: Lucent Books, 1995.

Filler, Louis, and Allen Guttmann, eds. *The Removal of the Cherokee Nation: Manifest Destiny or National Dishonor?* Revised ed. Malabar, FL: Robert E. Krieger, 1988.

Horsman, Reginald. *Expansion and American Indian Policy, 1783–1812.* Norman: University of Oklahoma Press, 1992.

Indian Removal Act of 1830. *U.S. Statutes at Large.* Vol. 4, pp. 411–12.

Jacobs, Wilbur R. *Dispossessing the American Indian: Indians and Whites on the Colonial Frontier.* Norman: University of Oklahoma Press, 1985.

Judson, Karen. *Andrew Jackson.* Springfield, NJ: Enslow, 1997.

Mahon, John K. *History of the Second Seminole War, 1835–1842.* Revised ed. Gainesville: University Presses of Florida, 1967.

Osinski, Alice. *Andrew Jackson.* Chicago: Childrens Press, 1987.

Parlin, John. *Andrew Jackson: Pioneer and President.* New York: Chelsea Juniors, 1991.

Perdue, Theda, and Michael D. Green, eds. *The Cherokee Removal: A Brief History with Documents.* New York: St. Martin's Press, 1995.

Remini, Robert V. *Andrew Jackson and the Course of American Empire, 1767–1821.* New York: Harper and Row, 1977.

Stefoff, Rebecca. *Andrew Jackson: 7th President of the United States.* Ada, OK: Garrett Educational Corp., 1988.

Stephanson, Anders. *Manifest Destiny: American Expansion and the Empire of Right.* New York: Hill and Wang, 1995.

Utley, Robert M., and Wilcomb E. Washburn. *Indian Wars.* Boston: Houghton Mifflin, 1987.

Wallace, Anthony F. C. *The Long, Bitter Trail: Andrew Jackson and the Indians*. New York: Hill and Wang, 1993.

Weeks, Philip. *Farewell, My Nation: The American Indian and the United States, 1820–1890*. Arlington Heights, IL: Harlan Davidson, 1990.

Williams, Jeanne. *Trails of Tears: American Indians Driven from Their Lands*. New York: Putnam, 1972.

Wright, J. Leitch, Jr. *The Only Land They Knew: The Tragic Story of the American Indians in the Old South*. New York: The Free Press, 1981.

John S. Smith

Congressional Testimony of John S. Smith,
Eyewitness to the Sand Creek Massacre

Given on March 14, 1865
Joint Committee on the Conduct of the War,
Massacre of Cheyenne Indians, 38th Congress,
2nd Session, Washington, 1865

Soon after gold was discovered near Pikes Peak in Colorado in 1858, American legislators established the Colorado Territory. In order to encourage white settlement the government tried to negotiate a treaty that would place the Cheyenne and Arapaho tribes living throughout the territory on a small plot of land in southeastern Colorado. Many tribes either rejected or ignored the treaty and continued to roam the prairies and the foothills of the Rocky Mountains. Territorial governor John Evans (1814–1897) encouraged white citizens "to kill and destroy, as enemies of the country, wherever they may be found, all . . . Indians," according to Don Nardo in *The Indian Wars*. Evans also appointed a notorious Indian-hater, John M. Chivington, to lead the militia and drive the Indians out of Colorado.

Although many Indian groups continued to resist white advances in the region, one Indian leader, Black Kettle, believed that his tribe would do better to cooperate with the white men. Thus Black Kettle's Cheyenne obeyed Evans's order to report to the military base at Fort Lyon. After living there on government rations for a time, Black Kettle's people were relocated to a camp on Sand Creek where they could hunt for themselves. On November 29, 1864, a force of seven hundred armed soldiers approached the quiet Indian encampment along Sand Creek. Surprised that the army was nearing his camp, Black Kettle raised two flags: an American flag and a white flag of peace. Yet Chivington ordered his men to attack the camp, and they did so with a vengeance. The five hundred Indians in the camp—mostly women and children—defended themselves as best they could, but the soldiers massacred the inhabitants in a heartless and brutal manner. One member of Chivington's forces, quoted in Utley and Washburn's *Indian Wars,* remembered the battle: "They [the Indians] were scalped, their brains knocked out; the men used their knives, ripped open women, clubbed little children, knocked them in the head with their guns, beat their brains out, mutilated their bodies in every sense of the word." Approximately two hundred Cheyenne were killed, and Chivington's men, clutching Indian scalps, rode into Denver boasting of their victory.

Though Chivington and his supporters claimed they had won a great victory, others sensed that perhaps the Battle of Sand Creek had been merely an excuse for Chivington to exercise his hatred of Indians. Reports began to circulate that the battle was actually a slaughter of lightly armed and innocent Indians, perpetrated by drunken soldiers. Soon the U.S. secretary of war launched a formal investigation into the massacre. An army judge labeled the Sand Creek Massacre "a cowardly and cold-blooded slaughter, sufficient to cover its perpetrators with indelible infamy, and the face of every American with shame and indignation." The testimony reprinted below was submitted to Congress in 1865 and contributed to Chivington's court-martial (a trial in a military court; this punishment was ineffective, because Chivington had already left the military). Chivington withdrew from public life, and he was never held accountable for the deaths at Sand Creek.

Things to remember while reading the testimony of John S. Smith:
- Black Kettle, the leader of the Indians massacred at Sand Creek, wanted to cooperate with white authorities and

Some Native American tribes, such as Black Kettle's Cheyenne, attempted to cooperate with whites. Here they are shown coming into Fort Lyon as ordered by the U.S. Army. Despite their surrender, Black Kettle's tribe was massacred in their camp by U.S. troops. *(© Bettmann/Corbis. Reproduced by permission.)*

raised a white flag to signal his peaceful intentions to Chivington's forces.

- Chivington's defenders insist that he had evidence that proved that Black Kettle's Cheyenne tribe was involved in warfare against whites, and that the Cheyenne fought back quite fiercely against Chivington's attack. Chivington's critics insist that Black Kettle's people were completely peaceful and were mercilessly slaughtered.

- John S. Smith was an Indian agent and an interpreter who had been sent out to Black Kettle's camp to find out how many people were in the camp and to get a sense of the Indians' attitudes toward whites.

- Two examiners, Mr. Gooch and Mr. Buckalew, are questioning Smith.

Congressional Testimony of Mr. John S. Smith Washington, March 14, 1865

Joint Committee on the Conduct of the War, Massacre of Cheyenne Indians, 38th Congress, 2nd Session (Washington, 1865), pp. 56–9.

Mr. John S. Smith sworn and examined.

By Mr. Gooch:

Question. Where is your place of residence?

Answer. Fort Lyon, Colorado

Question. What is your occupation?

Answer. United States Indian interpreter and special Indian agent.

Question. Will you state to the committee all that you know in relation to the attack of Colonel Chivington upon the Cheyenne and Arapahoe Indians in November last?

*Answer. Major Anthony was in command at Fort Lyon at the time. Those Indians had been induced to remain in the vicinity of Fort Lyon, and were promised protection by the commanding officer at Fort Lyon. The commanding officer saw proper to keep them some thirty or forty miles distant from the fort, for fear of some conflict between them and the soldiers or the traveling population, for Fort Lyon is on a **great thoroughfare**. He advised them to go out on what is called Sand creek, about forty miles, a little east of north from Fort Lyon. Some days after they had left Fort Lyon when I had just recovered from a long spell of sickness, I was called on by Major S. G. Colley, who asked me if I was able and willing to go out and pay a visit to these Indians, **ascertain** their numbers, their general disposition toward the whites, and the points where other bands might be located in the interior.*

Great thoroughfare: A major roadway.

Ascertain: Determine precisely.

PACIFIC TELEGRAPH COMPANY.

NO. 1.]   TERMS AND CONDITIONS ON WHICH MESSAGES ARE RECEIVED BY THIS COMPANY FOR TRANSMISSION.

The public are notified that, in order to guard against mistakes in the transmission of messages, every message of importance ought to be repeated, by being sent back from the station at which it is to be received, to the station from which it is originally sent. Half the usual price for transmission will be charged for repeating the message; and while this Company will, as heretofore, use every precaution to ensure correctness, it will not be responsible for mistakes or delays in the transmission or delivery of repeated messages, beyond an amount exceeding five hundred times the amount paid for sending the message; nor will it be responsible for mistakes or delays in the transmission of unrepeated messages from whatever cause they may arise, nor for delays arising from interruptions in the working of its Telegraphs, nor for any mistake or omission of any other Company, over whose lines a message is to be sent to reach the place of destination. All messages will hereafter be received by this Company for transmission, subject to the above conditions.

E. CREIGHTON, Sup't, Omaha, N. T.   **J. H. WADE, Pres't, Cleveland, O.**

To Col Chivington   W Leavenworth   186

By Telegraph from   Oct 7   1864

Genl Blunt came on camp of Indians near Head of Pawnee September twenty fifth 25 Three or four thousand 4000 strong routed & pursued them several days Nine Indians killed our loss two 2 killed and seven 7 wounded The Indians went towards Head of Smoky These are probably the same Indians Col McKoops reports erroneously and unfortunately out of his command

S R Curtis
May Genl

58 N 605 pd

Question. What was the necessity for obtaining that information?

Answer. Because there were different bands which were supposed to be at war; in fact, we knew at the time that they were at war with the white population in that country; but this band had been in and left the post perfectly satisfied. I left to go to this village of Indians on the 26th of November last. I arrived there on the 27th and remained there the 28th. On the morning of the 29th, between daylight and sunrise—nearer sunrise than daybreak—a large number of troops were discovered from three-quarters of a mile to a mile below the village. The Indians, who discovered them, ran to my camp, called me out, and wanted to me to go and see what troops they were, and what they wanted. The head chief of the nation, Black Kettle, and head chief of the Cheyennes, was encamped there with us. Some years previous he had been presented with a fine American flag by Colonel Greenwood, a commissioner, who had been sent out there. Black Kettle ran this American flag up to the top of his lodge, with a small white flag tied right under it, as he had been advised to do in case he should meet with any troops out on

An 1864 telegram sent to Colonel Chivington prior to the events at Sand Creek, apprising the colonel of Indian activity in the area.
(© Corbis. Reproduced by permission.)

the prairies. I then left my own camp and started for that portion of the troops that was nearest the village, supposing I could go up to them. I did not know but they might be strange troops, and thought my presence and explanations could reconcile matters. Lieutenant Wilson was in command of the detachment to which I tried to make my approach; but they fired several volleys at me, and I returned back to my camp and entered my lodge.

Question. Did these troops know you to be a white man?

Answer. Yes, sir; and the troops that went there knew I was in the village.

Question. Did you see Lieutenant Wilson or were you seen by him?

Answer. I cannot say I was seen by him; but his troops were the first to fire at me.

Question. Did they know you to be a white man?

Answer. They could not help knowing it. I had on pants, a soldier's overcoat, and a hat such as I am wearing now. I was dressed differently from any Indian in the country. On my return I entered my lodge, not expecting to get out of it alive. I had two other men there with me: one was David Louderbach, a soldier, belonging to company G, lst Colorado cavalry; the other, a man by the name of Watson, who was a hired hand of **Mr. DD Coolly**, the son of **Major Coolly**, the agent.

After I had left my lodge to go out and see what was going on, Colonel Chivington rode up to within fifty or sixty yards of where I was camped; he recognized me at once. They all call me Uncle John in that country. He said, "Run here, Uncle John; you are all right." I went to him as fast as I could. He told me to get in between him and his troops, who were then coming up very fast; I did so; directly another officer who knew me—Lieutenant Baldwin, in command of a battery—tried to assist me to get a horse; but there was no loose horse there at the time. He said, "Catch hold of the **caisson**, and keep up with us."

By this time the Indians had fled; had scattered in every direction. The troops were some on one side of the river and some on the other, following up the Indians. We had been encamped on the north side of the river; I followed along, holding on the caisson, sometimes running, sometimes walking. Finally, about a mile above the village, the troops had got a parcel of the Indians **hemmed in**

Mr. DD Cooly: Probably misspelling of D. D. Colley.

Major Coolley: Probably a misspelling of Major Colley.

Caisson: A two-wheeled, horse-drawn vehicle used to hold ammunition.

Hemmed in: Surrounded.

under the bank of the river; as soon as the troops overtook them, they commenced firing on them; some troops had got above them, so that they were completely surrounded. There were probably a hundred Indians hemmed in there, men, women, and children; the most of the men in the village escaped.

By the time I got up with the **battery** to the place where these Indians were surrounded there had been some considerable firing. Four or five soldiers had been killed, some with arrows and some with bullets. The soldiers continued firing on these Indians, who numbered about a hundred, until they had almost completely destroyed them. I think I saw altogether some seventy dead bodies lying there; the greater portion women and children. There may have been thirty warriors, old and young; the rest were women and small children of different ages and sizes.

The troops at that time were very much scattered. There were not over two hundred troops in the main fight, engaged in killing this body of Indians under the bank. The balance of the troops were scattered in different directions, running after small parties of Indians who were trying to make their escape. I did not go [to] see how many they might have killed outside of this party under the bank of the river. Being still quite weak from my last sickness, I returned with the first body of troops that went back to the camp.

The Indians had left their lodges and property; everything they owned. I do not think more than one-half of the Indians left their lodges with their **arms**. I think there were between 800 and l,000 men in this command of United States troops. There was a part of three companies of the lst Colorado, and the balance were what were called 100 days men of the 3rd regiment. I am not able to say which party did the most execution on the Indians, because it was very much mixed up at the time.

We remained there that day after the fight. By 11 o'clock, I think, the entire number of soldiers had returned back to the camp where Colonel Chivington had returned. On their return, he ordered the soldiers to destroy all the Indian property there, which they did, with the exception of what **plunder** they took away with them, which was considerable.

Question. How many Indians were there there?

Answer. There were 100 families of Cheyennes, and some six or eight lodges of Arapahoes.

Battery: Where the artillery, or large guns, were placed.

Arms: Weapons.

Plunder: Property stolen by force.

Question. How many persons in all, should you say?

Answer. About 500 we estimate them at five to a lodge.

Question. 500 men, women and children?

Answer. Yes, sir.

Question. Do you know the reason for that attack on the Indians?

*Answer. I do not know any exact reason. I have heard a great many reasons given. I have heard that that whole Indian war had been brought on for selfish purposes. Colonel Chivington was running for Congress in Colorado, and there were other things of that kind; and last spring a year ago he was looking for an order to go to the front, and I understand he had this Indian war in view to retain himself and his troops in that country, to carry out his **electioneering** purposes.*

Question. In what way did this attack on the Indians further the purpose of Colonel Chivington?

Answer. It was said—I did not hear him say it myself, but it was said that he would do something; he had this regiment of three-months men, and did not want them to go out without doing some service. Now he had been told repeatedly by different persons—by myself, as well as others—where he could find the hostile bands.

*The same chiefs who were killed in this village of Cheyennes had been up to see Colonel Chivington in Denver but a short time previous to this attack. He himself told them that he had no power to **treat** with them; that he had received telegrams from General Curtis directing him to fight all Indians he met with in that country. Still he would advise them, if they wanted any assistance from the whites, to go to their nearest military post in their country, give up their arms and the stolen property, if they had any, and then they would receive directions in what way to act. This was told them by Colonel Chivington and by Governor Evans, of Colorado. I myself interpreted for them and for the Indians.*

Question. Did Colonel Chivington hold any communication with these Indians, or any of them, before making the attack upon them?

*Answer. No, sir, not then. He had some time previously held a council with them at Denver city. When we first recovered the white prisoners from the Indians, we invited some of the chiefs to go to Denver, inasmuch as they had **sued** for peace, and were willing to give up these white prisoners. We promised to take the chiefs to Denver, where*

Electioneering: Campaigning.

Treat: Discuss treaties.

Sued: Appealed.

they had an interview with men who had more power than Major Wynkoop had, who was the officer in command of the detachment that went out to recover these white prisoners. Governor Evans and Colonel Chivington were in Denver, and were present at this council. They told the Indians to return with Major Wynkoop, and whatever he agreed on doing with them would be recognized by them.

*I returned with the Indians to Fort Lyon. There we let them go out to their villages to bring in their families, as they had been invited through the proclamation or circular of the governor during the month of June, I think. They were gone some twelve or fifteen days from Fort Lyon, and then they returned with their families. Major Wynkoop had **made them one or two issues of provisions** previous to the arrival of Major Anthony there to assume command. Then Major Wynkoop, who is now in command at Fort Lyon, was ordered to Fort Leavenworth on some business with General Curtis, I think.*

*Then Major Anthony, through me, told the Indians that he did not have it in his power to issue rations to them, as Major Wynkoop had done. He said that he had assumed command at Fort Lyon, and his orders were positive from headquarters to fight the Indians in the vicinity of Fort Lyon, or at any other point in the Territory where they could find them. He said that he had understood that they had been behaving very badly. But on seeing Major Wynkoop and others there at Fort Lyon, he was happy to say that things were not as had been presented, and he could not pursue any other course than that of Major Wynkoop except the issuing rations to them. He then advised them to [go] out to some near point, where there was buffalo, not too far from Fort Lyon or they might meet with troops from the **Platte**, who would not know them from the hostile bands. This was the southern band of Cheyennes; there is another band called the northern band. They had no apprehensions in the world of any trouble with the whites at the time this attack was made.*

Question. Had there been, to your knowledge, any hostile act or demonstration on the part of these Indians or any of them?

*Answer. Not in this band. But the northern band, the band known by the name of Dog soldiers of Cheyennes, had committed many **depredations** on the Platte.*

Question. Do you know whether or not Colonel Chivington knew the friendly character of these Indians before he made the attack upon them?

Answer. It is my opinion that he did.

Made them one or two issues of provisions: Once or twice provided the Indians with supplies to live on.

Platte: The Platte River, to the north.

Depredations: Atrocious acts.

Question. On what is that opinion based?

*Answer. On this fact, that he stopped all persons from going on ahead of him. He stopped the mail, and would not allow any person to go on ahead of him at the time he was on his way from Denver city to Fort Lyon. He placed a guard around old Colonel Bent, the former agent there; he stopped a Mr. Hagues and many men who were on their way to Fort Lyon. He took the fort by surprise, and as soon as he got there he posted **pickets** all around the fort, and then left at 8 o'clock that night for this Indian camp.*

Question. Was that anything more than the exercise of ordinary precaution in following Indians?

Answer. Well, sir, he was told that there were no Indians in the vicinity of Fort Lyon, except Black Kettle's band of Cheyennes and Left Hand's band of Arapahoes.

Question. How do you know that?

Answer. I was told so.

By Mr. Buckalew:

Question. Do you know it of your own knowledge?

Answer. I cannot say I do.

Question. You did not talk with him about it before the attack?

Answer. No, sir.

By Mr. Gooch:

*Question. When you went out to him, you had no opportunity to hold **intercourse** with him?*

Answer. None whatever; he had just commenced his fire against the Indians.

Question. Did you have any communication with him at any time while there?

Answer. Yes, sir.

Question. What was it?

Answer. He asked me many questions about a son of mine, who was killed there afterwards. He asked me what Indians were there, what chiefs; and I told him as fully as I knew.

By Mr. Buckalew:

Question. When did you talk with him?

Pickets: Detachments of troops to act as lookouts.

Intercourse: Communication.

Answer. On the day of the attack. He asked me many questions about the chiefs who were there, and if I could recognize them if I saw them. I told him it was possible I might recollect the principal chiefs. They were terribly mutilated, lying there in the water and sand; most of them in the bed of the creek, dead and dying, making many struggles. They were so badly mutilated and covered with sand and water that it was very hard for me to tell one from another. However, I recognized some of them—among them the chief One Eye, who was employed by our government at $125 a month and rations to remain in the village as a spy. There was another called War Bonnet, who was here two years ago with me. There was another by the name of Standing-in-the-Water, and I supposed Black Kettle was among them, but it was not Black Kettle. There was one there of his size and dimensions in every way, but so tremendously mutilated that I was mistaken in him. I went out with Lieutenant Colonel Bowen, to see how many I could recognize.

By Mr. Gooch:

Question. Did you tell Colonel Chivington the character and disposition of these Indians at any time during your interviews on this day?

Answer. Yes, sir.

Question. What did he say in reply?

Answer. He said he could not help it; that his orders were positive to attack the Indians.

Question. From whom did he receive these orders?

Answer. I do not know; I presume from General Curtis.

Question. Did he tell you?

Answer. Not to my recollection.

Question. Were the women and children slaughtered indiscriminately, or only so far as they were with the warriors?

Answer. Indiscriminately.

Question. Were there any acts of barbarity perpetrated there that came under your own observation?

Answer. Yes, sir; I saw the bodies of those lying there cut all to pieces, worse mutilated than any I ever saw before; the women cut all to pieces.

By Mr. Buckalew:

Question. How cut?

Answer. With knives; scalped; their brains knocked out; children two or three months old; all ages lying there, from sucking infants up to warriors.

By Mr. Gooch:

Question. Did you see it done?

Answer. Yes, sir; I saw them fall.

Question. Fall when they were killed?

Answer. Yes, sir.

Question. Did you see them when they were mutilated?

Answer. Yes, sir.

Question. By whom were they mutilated?

Answer. By the United States troops.

Question. Do you know whether or not it was done by the direction or consent of any of the officers?

Answer. I do not; I hardly think it was.

By Mr. Buckalew:

Question. What was the date of that massacre?

Answer. On the 29th of November last.

Question. Did you speak of these barbarities to Colonel Chivington?

Answer. No sir; I had nothing at all to say about it, because at that time they were hostile towards me, from the fact of my being there. They probably supposed that I might be compromised with them in some way or other.

*Question. Who called on you to **designate** the bodies of those who were killed?*

Answer. Colonel Chivington himself asked me if I would ride out with Lieutenant Colonel Bowen, and see how many chiefs or principal men I could recognize.

Question. Can you state how many Indians were killed—how many women and how many children?

Answer. Perhaps one-half were men, and the balance were women and children. I do not think that I saw more than 70 lying dead then, as far as I went. But I saw parties of men scattered in every direction, pursuing little bands of Indians.

Designate: Identify.

Question. What time of day or night was this attack made?

Answer. The attack commenced about sunrise, and lasted until between 10 and 11 o'clock.

Question. How large a body of troops?

Answer. I think that probably there may have been about 60 or 70 warriors who were armed and stood their ground and fought. Those that were unarmed got out of the way as they best could.

Question. How many of our troops were killed and how many wounded?

Answer. There were ten killed on the ground, and thirty-eight wounded; four of the wounded died at Fort Lyon before I came on east.

Question. Were there any other **barbarities or atrocities** committed there other than those you have mentioned, that you saw?

Answer. Yes, sir; I had a half-breed son there, who gave himself up. He started at the time the Indians fled; being a half-breed he had but little hope of being spared, and seeing them fire at me, he ran away with the Indians for the distance of about a mile. During the fight up there he walked back to my camp and went into the lodge. It was surrounded by soldiers at the time. He came in quietly and sat down; he remained there that day, that night, and the next day in the afternoon; about four o'clock in the evening, as I was sitting inside the camp, a soldier came up outside of the lodge and called me by name. I got up and went out; he took me by the arm and walked towards Colonel Chivington's camp, which was about sixty yards from my camp. Said he, "I am sorry to tell you, but they are going to kill your son Jack." I knew the feeling towards the whole camp of Indians, and that there was no use to make any resistance. I said, "I can't help it." I then walked on towards where Colonel Chivington was standing by his camp-fire; when I had got within a few feet of him I heard a gun fired, and saw a crowd run to my lodge, and they told me that Jack was dead.

Question. What action did Colonel Chivington take in regard to that matter?

Answer. Major Anthony, who was present, told Colonel Chivington that he had heard some remarks made, indicating that they were desirous of killing Jack; and that he (Colonel Chivington) had it in his power to save him, and that by saving him he might make him a very useful man, as he was well acquainted with all the

Barbarities or atrocities:
Brutal and cruel acts.

Cheyenne and Arapahoe country, and he could be used as a guide or interpreter. Colonel Chivington replied to Major Anthony, as the Major himself told me, that he had no orders to receive and no advice to give. Major Anthony is now in this city.

By Mr. Buckalew:

Question. Did Chivington say anything to you, or you to him about the firing?

Answer. Nothing directly; there were a number of officers sitting around the fire, with the most of whom I was acquainted.

By Mr. Gooch:

Question. Were there any other Indians or half-breeds there at that time?

Answer. Yes, sir; Mr. Bent had three sons there; one employed as a guide for these troops at the time, and two others living there in the village with the Indians; and a Mr. Gerry had a son there.

Question. Were there any other murders after the first day's massacre?

Answer. There was none, except of my son.

Question. Were there any other atrocities which you have [not] mentioned?

Answer. None that I saw myself. There were two women that white men had families by; they were saved from the fact of being in my lodge at the time. One ran to my lodge; the other was taken prisoner by a soldier who knew her and brought her to my lodge for safety. They both had children. There were some small children, six or seven years old, who were taken prisoners near the camp. I think there were three of them taken to Denver with these troops.

Question. Were the women and children that were killed, killed during the fight with the Indians?

Answer. During the fight, or during the time of the attack.

Question. Did you see any women or children killed after the fight was over?

Answer. None.

Question. Did you see any Indians killed after the fight was over?

Answer. No, sir.

By Mr. Buckalew:

Question. Were the warriors and women and children all huddled together when they were attacked?

Answer. They started and left the village altogether, in a body, trying to escape.

By Mr. Gooch:

Question. Do you know anything as to the amount of property that those Indians had there?

Answer. Nothing more than their horses. They were supposed to own ten horses and mules to a lodge; that would make about a thousand head of horses and mules in that camp. The soldiers drove off about six hundred head.

Question. Had they any money?

Answer. I understood that some of the soldiers found some money, but I did not see it. Mr. D. D. Colley had some provisions and goods in the village at the time, and Mr. [Louderback] and Mr. Watson were employed by him to trade there. I was to interpret for them, direct them, and see that they were cared for in the village. They had traded for one hundred and four buffalo robes, one fine mule, and two horses. This was all taken away from them. Colonel Chivington came to me and told me that I might rest assured that he would see the goods paid for. He had confiscated these buffalo robes for the dead and wounded; and there was also some sugar and coffee and tea taken for the same purpose.

I would state that in his report Colonel Chivington states that after this raid on Sand creek against the Cheyenne and Arapahoe Indians he traveled northeast some eighty miles in the direction of some hostile bands of Sioux Indians. Now that is very incorrect, according to my knowledge of matters; I remained with Colonel Chivington's camp, and returned on his trail towards Fort Lyon from the camp where he made this raid. I went down with him to what is called the forks of the Sandy. He then took a due south course for the Arkansas river, and I went to Fort Lyon with the killed and wounded, and an escort to take us in. Colonel Chivington proceeded down the Arkansas river, and got within eleven miles of another band of Arapahoe Indians, but did not succeed in overtaking them. He then returned to Fort Lyon, re-equipped, and started immediately for Denver.

Question. Have you spent any considerable portion of your life with the Indians?

After the Sand Creek Massacre, Native Americans fought hard to keep their lands on the Great Plains. These captured Crow warriors fought until 1887. (© Corbis. Reproduced by permission.)

Answer. The most of it.

Question. How many years have you been with the Indians?

Answer. I have been twenty-seven successive years with the Cheyennes and Arapahoes. Before that I was in the country as a trapper and hunter in the Rocky mountains.

Question. For how long time have you acted as Indian interpreter?

Answer. For some fifteen or eighteen years.

Question. By whom have you been so employed?

Answer. By Major Fitzpatrick, Colonel Bent, Major Colley, Colonel J. W. Whitfield, and a great deal of the time for the military as guide and interpreter.

By Mr. Buckalew:

Question. How many warriors were estimated in Colonel Chivington's report as having been in this Indian camp?

Answer. About nine hundred.

Question. How many were there?

Answer. About two hundred warriors; they average about two warriors to a lodge, and there were about one hundred lodges. [Joint Committee on the Conduct of the War, pp. 4–12, 56–9, 101–8]

What happened next . . .

If Chivington's goal in launching the Sand Creek Massacre was to intimidate other Indian groups, it certainly backfired. Indian leaders who had counseled peace with the whites before Sand Creek largely abandoned their peaceful policies and joined with the more warlike tribes to commit themselves to total warfare. The Sand Creek Massacre convinced other Indian groups that they would have to work together to drive back the white advances, and encouraged these groups to engage in more systematic preparation for war. After Sand Creek, Indian warriors fought long and hard to retain their lands. The battle for the Great Plains lasted another twenty-six years. It ended with the slaughter of peaceful Indians at Wounded Knee and the relocation of the last native peoples to reservations in 1890.

Did you know . . .

• The Sand Creek Massacre was one of the first Indian battles to attract significant attention on the East Coast.

**Prisoners of Black Kettle's
tribe are marched through
the snow after a second
surprise attack by U.S. Army
forces led by George
Armstrong Custer on the
Washita River.**
*(Reproduced from the
Collections of the Library of
Congress.)*

Critics of government policy toward Indians cited the
massacre as proof that the United States was engaging in
atrocities against a peaceful people.

• After the massacre, Indian forces concentrated their defense of their land in the northern Plains region. The
massacre stiffened Indian resistance to white advances
and sparked twenty years of bitter war between the U.S.
Army and the Indians.

• In 1868 Black Kettle's tribe—diminished by the massacre
at Sand Creek—was again surprised by U.S. Army forces.
George Armstrong Custer led a surprise attack on the
tribe's encampment on the Washita River in Indian Territory, killing forty people, including Black Kettle and a
number of women and children.

• In 1999 the National Park Service began planning to
make the site of the Sand Creek Massacre a national
park—but they had difficulty locating the site.

Consider the following . . .

- How trustworthy did you find Smith's account of the Sand Creek Massacre? What evidence do you have to support your view?

- Does Smith find any justification for Chivington's attack?

- What is the attitude of Smith toward the death of his own son? How can you explain such an attitude?

- Smith doesn't level any direct accusations against Chivington, so how does he convey his opinion of the attack?

For More Information

Ballantine, Betty, and Ian Ballantine, eds. *The Native Americans: An Illustrated History.* Atlanta: Turner Publishing, 1993.

Joint Committee on the Conduct of the War. *Massacre of Cheyenne Indians,* 38th Congress, 2nd Session, 1865, pp. 4–12, 56–9, 101–8.

Nardo, Don. *The Indian Wars.* San Diego: Lucent Books, 1991.

Schultz, Duane P. *Month of the Freezing Moon: The Sand Creek Massacre, November 1864.* New York: St. Martin's Press, 1990.

Scott, Bob. *Blood at Sand Creek: The Massacre Revisited.* Caldwell, ID: Caxton Printers, 1994.

Utley, Robert M., and Wilcomb E. Washburn. *Indian Wars.* Boston: Houghton Mifflin, 1987.

Wooden Leg

Excerpt from Wooden Leg:
A Warrior Who Fought Custer
Interpreted by Thomas B. Marquis
Published in 1931

For years after the Sand Creek Massacre, U.S. soldiers and Indian warriors met in dozens of battles and skirmishes across the Plains region, with neither side gaining a decisive advantage. Eastern newspapers mocked the American forces for their inability to capture the relatively small bands of Indians who were causing so much trouble. The final conflict between these two forces came in the Black Hills of South Dakota. Sacred ground to many of the Plains tribes, the Black Hills had been protected by many treaties over the years. However, General George Armstrong Custer (1839–1876) led an expedition into the Black Hills in 1874 to protect white settlers who believed that there might be gold in the region. When gold was found, tens of thousands of fortune seekers and settlers moved into this sacred territory. The Indians had no choice but to respond.

In the winter of 1875, thousands of Indians from a number of different groups began to gather on the banks of the Little Bighorn River in southern Montana. There they planned their strategy for the defense of the Black Hills, unaware of (or ignoring) the army's threat to hunt down and kill any Indians found off their reservations. For its part, the U.S. Army planned a major attack on the tribes for the spring of 1876. Three contingents of men led by Generals George Crook, John Gibbon, and Alfred Terry and George Custer would storm the Indian camp and put an end to the Indian resistance.

As the U.S. troops approached the Indian camp at Little Bighorn, George Custer was eager to fight. Always impulsive, Custer ignored his orders to wait for all of the forces to be in place. He marched his force of some 675 men forward, hoping to take all of the glory if he and his men alone could defeat the Indians. Dividing his soldiers into three groups, Custer and his commanders attacked on the morning of June 25, 1876. The first group to meet the Indians, 280 men led by Major Marcus Reno, faced a vicious attack from Sitting Bull's Hunkpapa Sioux forces. Though they fought valiantly at first, the troops were soon overwhelmed and were forced to retreat. Digging into a nearby hill, Reno's men were reinforced with 125 troops led by Captain Frederick Benteen. Yet as they fought, they became aware that more and more Indians were heading off in another direction. Something was drawing the Indian attack away.

The Indian camp was being attacked from the other side, this time by a band of 267 men led by Custer himself. Three groups of Indians responded to this attack—the Cheyenne under Lame White Man, Hunkpapa Sioux under Gall, and the Oglala under Crazy Horse—and they soon surrounded Custer's men on all sides. According to *Indian Wars* author Don Nardo, "Thousands of Indians took part in the bloody assault, during which most of the soldiers dismounted and separated into small groups. Here, Crazy Horse's new battlefield strategy worked brilliantly. The Indians attacked in well-coordinated waves, overwhelming the troops. In the space of about forty-five minutes, Custer and all of his men were killed."

The Indians dispersed, preparing for battles to come. On the battlefield American soldiers discovered hundreds of dead comrades—268 in all—at the center of which lay a gathering of officers who had surrounded General Custer and fought to the bitter end. This final standoff, which ended in the death of all the soldiers, has become famous as Custer's Last Stand. The Indians had won their greatest victory ever over white forces. It was the high point for the Indian alliance, but it spurred a devastating army response. Within just a few years, army forces would track down and subdue all of the remaining Native American groups.

The following account of the Battle of Little Bighorn is excerpted from the autobiography of Wooden Leg, a Cheyenne warrior who fought in the battle when he was just eighteen years of age. Pay attention to how different Wooden Leg's account of battle is compared to what you would expect from an American soldier of similar age.

Things to remember while reading the excerpt from *Wooden Leg: A Warrior Who Fought Custer:*

- Wooden Leg's story offers rare insights from the Native American perspective. Several other Indians who fought in the battle reviewed his story and all agreed it was accurate.

- Prior to the Battle of Little Bighorn, Indian chiefs such as Red Cloud, Crazy Horse, and Sitting Bull began to teach their warriors more sophisticated methods of fighting. Rather than leaving battle actions entirely up to the individual warriors, as had traditionally been done, Indians began to coordinate their actions. They sent parties of decoys out to draw white forces in certain directions; then another group of Indians would attack the white forces from hiding places. Wooden Leg's account reflects some of these battle strategies.

- The Battle of Little Bighorn was Wooden Leg's first real experience fighting white soldiers; moreover, it represented his passage into manhood.

George Armstrong Custer led the battle against the northern Plains Indians at the Battle of Little Bighorn. *(Reproduced from the Collections of the Library of Congress.)*

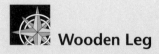

Wooden Leg

Little is known about the young warrior who provided such a dramatic account of the Indians' perspective on the Battle of Little Bighorn. Kummok'quiviokta, as he was known among the Cheyenne, was born along the Cheyenne River in present-day South Dakota in 1858. His people were routed in a battle with Colonel Joseph Reynolds in March 1876; a few months later, they joined their Sioux allies as they gathered along the Little Bighorn River. As his account illustrates, Wooden Leg took part in a number of skirmishes the day of the battle. By the spring of 1877, Wooden Leg surrendered to army soldiers and, with other members of his tribe, relocated to Indian Territory.

By the mid-1880s Wooden Leg had returned to Montana, where he found work as an army scout. He participated in the Ghost Dance religious movement that swept the Plains in 1890, but in 1908 he converted to Christianity. Wooden Leg died in 1940, nine years after he narrated his dramatic autobiography to Thomas Marquis.

Lariat: A rope used when tending horses.

Six shooter: A pistol that carries six bullets.

Picketed: Tied out or fenced in.

• Wooden Leg describes how army soldiers took their own lives rather than being captured by Indians. Why might soldiers have done this?

Excerpt from Wooden Leg: A Warrior Who Fought Custer

Chapter IX: The Coming of Custer

In my sleep I dreamed that a great crowd of people were making lots of noise. Something in the noise startled me. I found myself wide awake, sitting up and listening. My brother too awakened, and we both jumped to our feet. A great commotion was going on among the camps. We heard shooting. We hurried out from the trees so we might see as well as hear. The shooting was somewhere at the upper part of the camp circles. It looked as if all of the Indians there were running away toward the hills to the westward or down toward our end of the village. Women were screaming and men were letting out war cries. Through it all we could hear old men calling:

"Soldiers are here! Young men, go out and fight them."

*We ran to our camp and to our home lodge. Everybody there was excited. Women were hurriedly making up little packs for flight. Some were going off northward or across the river without any packs. Children were hunting for their mothers. Mothers were anxiously trying to find their children. I got my **lariat** and my **six shooter**. I hastened on down toward where had been our horse herd. I came across three of our herder boys. One of them was catching grasshoppers. The other two were cooking fish in the blaze of a little fire. I told them what was going on and asked them where were the horses. They jumped on their **picketed** ponies*

Cheyenne and Sioux warriors on the Great Plains, preparing for a reenactment of the Battle of Little Bighorn.
(© Brian Vikander/Corbis. Reproduced by permission.)

and dashed for the camp, without answering me. Just then I heard Bald Eagle calling out to hurry with the horses. Two other boys were driving them toward the camp circle. I was utterly winded from the running. I never was much for running. I could walk all day, but I could not run fast nor far. I walked on back to the home lodge.

My father had caught my favorite horse from the herd brought in by the boys and Bald Eagle. I quickly emptied out my war bag and set myself at getting ready to go into battle. I jerked off my ordinary clothing. I jerked on a pair of new breeches that had been given to me by an Uncpapa Sioux. I had a good cloth shirt, and I put it on. My old moccasins were kicked off and a pair of beaded moccasins substituted for them. My father strapped a blanket upon my horse and arranged the rawhide lariat into a bridle. He stood holding my mount.

"Hurry," he urged me.

I was hurrying, but I was not yet ready. I got my paints and my little mirror. The blue-black circle soon appeared around my face. The red and yellow colorings were applied on all of the skin inside *the circle. I combed my hair. It properly should have been oiled and braided neatly, but my father again was saying, "Hurry," so I just looped a buckskin **thong** about it and tied it close up against the back of my head, to float loose from there. My bullets, caps and powder horn put me into full readiness. In a moment afterward I was on my horse and was going as fast as it could run toward where all of the rest of the young men were going. My brother already had gone. He got his horse before I got mine, and his dressing was only a long buckskin shirt fringed with Crow Indian hair. The hair had been taken from a Crow at a past battle with them.*

The air was so full of dust I could not see where to go. But it was not needful that I see that far. I kept my horse headed in the direction of movement by the crowd of Indians on horseback. I was led out around and far beyond the Uncpapa camp circle. Many hundreds of Indians on horseback were dashing to and fro in front of a body of soldiers. The soldiers were on the level valley ground and were shooting with rifles. Not many bullets were being sent back at them, but thousands of arrows were falling among them. I went on with a throng of Sioux until we got beyond and behind the white men. By this time, though, they had mounted their horses and were hiding themselves in the timber. A band of Indians were with the soldiers. It appeared they were Crows or Shoshones. Most of these Indians had fled back up the valley. Some were across east of the river and were riding away over the hills beyond.

Our Indians crowded down toward the timber where were the soldiers. More and more of our people kept coming. Almost all of them were Sioux. There were only a few Cheyennes. Arrows were showered into the timber. Bullets whistled out toward the Sioux and Cheyennes. But we stayed far back while we extended our curved line farther and farther around the big grove of trees. Some dead soldiers had been left among the grass and sagebrush where first they had fought us. It seemed to me the remainder of them would not live many hours longer. Sioux were creeping forward to set fire to the timber.

Suddenly the hidden soldiers came tearing out on horseback, from the woods. I was around on that side where they came out. I whirled my horse and lashed it into a dash to escape from them. All others of my companions did the same. But soon we discovered they were not following us. They were running away from us. They were going as fast [as] their tired horses could carry them across an open valley space and toward the river. We stopped, looked a moment, and

Thong: A narrow strip of leather.

then we whipped our ponies into swift pursuit. A great throng of Sioux also were coming after them. My distant position put me among the leaders in the chase. The soldier [sic] horses moved slowly, as if they were very tired. Ours were lively. We gained rapidly on them.

I fired four shots with my six shooter. I do not know whether or not any of my bullets did harm. I saw a Sioux put an arrow into the back of a soldier's head. Another arrow went into his shoulder. He tumbled from his horse to the ground. Others fell dead either from arrows or from stabbings or jabbings or from blows by the stone war clubs of the Sioux. Horses limped or staggered or sprawled out dead or dying. Our war cries and war songs were mingled with many jeering calls, such as:

"You are only boys. You ought not to be fighting. We whipped you on the Rosebud. You should have brought more Crows or Shoshones with you to do your fighting."

Little Bird and I were after one certain soldier. Little Bird was wearing a trailing **warbonnet.** He was at the right and I was at the

The Battle of Little Bighorn with Chief Crazy Horse in spotted war paint in the center, drawn by Amos Badheart Bull, June 25, 1876. *(The Granger Collection, New York. Reproduced by permission.)*

Warbonnet: A headdress worn in battle.

left of the fleeing man. We were lashing him and his horse with our pony whips. It seemed not brave to shoot him. Besides, I did not want to waste my bullets. He pointed back his revolver, though, and sent a bullet into Little Bird's thigh. Immediately I whacked the white man fighter on his head with the heavy elk-horn handle of my pony whip. The blow dazed him. I seized the rifle strapped on his back. I wrenched it and dragged the looping strap over his head. As I was getting possession of this weapon he fell to the ground. I did not harm him further. I do not know what became of him. The jam of oncoming Indians swept me on. But I had now a good soldier rifle. Yet, I had not any cartridges for it....

I saw [soldiers] on distant hills down the river and on our same side of it. The news of them spread quickly among us. Indians began to ride in that direction. Some went along the hills, others went down to cross the river and follow the valley. I took this course. I guided my horse down the steep hillside and forded the river. Back again among the camps I rode on through them to our Cheyenne circle at the lower end of them. As I rode I could see lots of Indians out on the hills across on the east side of the river and fighting the other soldiers there. I do not know whether all of our warriors left the first soldiers or some of them stayed up there. I suppose, though, that all of them came away from there, as they would be afraid to stay if only a few remained.

Not many people were in the lodges of our camp. Most of the women and children and old Cheyennes were gone to the west side of the valley or to the hills at that side. A few were hurrying back and forth to take away packs. My father was the only person at our lodge. I told him of the fight up the valley. I told him of my having helped in the killing of the enemy Indian and some soldiers in the river. I gave to him the tobacco I had taken. I showed him my gun and all of the cartridges.

"You have been brave," he cheered me. "You have done enough for one day. Now you should rest."

"No, I want to go and fight the other soldiers," I said. "I can fight better now, with this gun."

"Your horse is too tired," he argued.

"Yes, but I want to ride the other one."

He turned loose my tired horse and roped my other one from the little herd being held inside the camp circle. He blanketed the new mount and arranged the lariat bridle. He applied the medicine treat-

ment for protecting my mount. As he was doing this I was making some improvements in my appearance, making the medicine for myself. I added my **sheathknife** to my stock of weapons. Then I looked a few moments at the battling Indians and soldiers across the river on the hills to the northeastward. More and more Indians were flocking from the camps to that direction. Some were yet coming along the hills from where the first soldiers had stopped. The soldiers now in view were spreading themselves into lines along a ridge. The Indians were on lower ridges in front of them, between them and the river, and were moving up a long **coulee** to get behind the white men.

"Remember, your older brother already is out there in the fight," my father said to me. "I think there will be plenty of warriors to beat the soldiers, so it is not needful that I send both of my sons. You have not your shield nor your eagle wing bone flute. Stay back as far as you can and shoot from a long distance. Let your brother go ahead of you."

Two other young men were near us. They had their horses and were otherwise ready, but they told me they had decided not to go. I showed them my captured gun and the cartridges. I told them of the tobacco and the clothing and other things we had taken from the soldiers up the valley. This changed their minds. They mounted their horses and accompanied me....

After the long time of the slow fighting, about forty of the soldiers came galloping from the east part of the ridge down toward the river, toward where most of the Cheyennes and many Ogallalas were hidden. The Indians ran back to a deep gulch. The soldiers stopped and got off their horses when they arrived at a low ridge where the Indians had been. Lame White Man, the Southern Cheyenne chief, came on his horse and called us to come back and fight. In a few minutes the warriors were all around these soldiers. Then Lame White Man called out:

"Come. We can kill all of them."

All around, the Indians began jumping up, running forward, dodging down, jumping up again, down again, all the time going toward the soldiers. Right away, all of the white men went crazy. Instead of shooting us, they turned their guns upon themselves. Almost before we could get to them, every one of them was dead. They killed themselves.

The Indians took the guns of these soldiers and used them for shooting at the soldiers on the high ridge. I went back and got my

Sheathknife: A knife held in a sheath, or sleeve.

Coulee: A deep gulch or ravine with sloping sides.

horse and rode around beyond the east end of the ridge. By the time I got there, all of the soldiers there were dead. The Indians told me that they had killed only a few of those men, that the men had shot each other and shot themselves. A Cheyenne told me that four soldiers from that part of the ridge had turned their horses and tried to escape by going back over the trail where they had come. Three of these men were killed quickly. The fourth one got across a gulch and over a ridge eastward before the pursuing group of Sioux got close to him. His horse was very tired, and the Sioux were gaining on him. He was moving his right arm as though whipping his horse to make it go faster. Suddenly his right hand went up to his head. With his revolver he shot himself and fell dead from his horse....

The shots quit coming from the soldiers. Warriors who had crept close to them began to call out that all of the white men were dead. All of the Indians then jumped up and rushed forward. All of the boys and old men on their horses came tearing into the crowd. The air was full of dust and smoke. Everybody was greatly excited. It looked like thousands of dogs might look if all of them were mixed together in a fight. All of the Indians were saying these soldiers also went crazy and killed themselves. I do not know. I could not see them. But I believe they did so.

Seven of these last soldiers broke away and went running down the coulee sloping toward the river from the west end of the ridge. I was on the side opposite from them, and there was much smoke and dust, and many Indians were in front of me, so I did not see these men running, but I learned of them from the talk afterward. They did not get far, because many Indians were all around them. It was said that these seven men, or some of them, killed themselves. I do not know, as I did not see them.

After the great throng of Indians had crowded upon the little space where had been the last band of fighting soldiers, a strange incident happened: It appeared that all of the white men were dead. But there was one of them who raised himself to a support on his left elbow. He turned and looked over his left shoulder, and then I got a good view of him. His expression was wild, as if his mind was all tangled up and he was wondering what was going on here. In his right hand he held his six-shooter. Many of the Indians near him were scared by what seemed to have been a return from death to life. But a Sioux warrior jumped forward, grabbed the six-shooter and wrenched it from the soldier's grasp. The gun was turned upon the white man, and he was shot through the

Westward Expansion: Primary Sources

head. Other Indians struck him or stabbed him. I think he must have been the last man killed in this great battle where not one of the enemy got away.

This last man had a big and strong body. His cheeks were plump. All over his face was a stubby black beard. His mustache was much longer than his other beard, and it was curled up at the ends. The spot where he was killed is just above the middle of the big group of white stone slabs now standing on the slope southwest from the big stone. I do not know whether he was a soldier chief or an ordinary soldier. I did not notice any metal piece nor any special marks on the shoulders of his clothing, it may be they were there. Some of the Cheyennes say now that he wore two white metal bars. But at that time we knew nothing about such things.

One of the dead soldier bodies attracted special attention. This was one who was said to have been wearing a buckskin suit. I had not seen any such soldier during the fighting. When I saw the body it had been stripped and the head was cut off and gone. Across the breast was some writing made by blue and red coloring into the skin. On each arm was a picture drawn with the same kind of blue and red paint. One of the pictures was of an eagle having its wings spread out. Indians told me that on the left arm had been strapped a leather packet having in it some white paper and a lot of the same kind of green picture-paper found on all of the soldier bodies. Some of the Indians guessed that he must have been the big chief of the soldiers, because of the buckskin clothing and because of the paint markings on breast and arms. But none of the Indians knew then who had been the big chief. They were guessing at it.

*The sun was just past the middle of the sky. The first soldiers, up the valley, had come about middle of the **forenoon**. The earlier part of the fighting against these second soldiers had been slow, all of the Indians staying back and approaching gradually. At each time of charging, though, the mixup lasted only a few minutes.*

Little Bighorn National Monument in Montana stands as a memorial to the soldiers who perished in the Battle of Little Bighorn.
(© Kevin R. Morris/Corbis. Reproduced by permission.)

Forenoon: The time between morning and noon.

I took one scalp. As I went walking and leading my horse among the dead I observed one face that interested me. The dead man had a long beard growing from both sides of his face and extending several inches below the chin. He had also a full mustache. All of the beard hair was of a light yellow color, as I now recall it. Most of the soldiers had beard growing, in different lengths, but this was the longest one I saw among them. I think the dead man may have been thirty or more years old. "Here is a new kind of scalp," I said to a companion. I skinned one side of the face and half of the chin, so as to keep the long beard yet on the part removed. I got an arrow shaft and tied the strange scalp to the end of it. This I carried in a hand as I went looking further....

I found a metal bottle, as I was walking among the dead men. It was about half full of some kind of liquid. I opened it and found that the liquid was not water. Soon afterward I got hold of another bottle of the same kind that had in it the same kind of liquid. I showed these to some other Indians. Different ones of them smelled and sniffed. Finally a Sioux said:

"Whisky."

Bottles of this kind were found by several other Indians. Some of them drank the contents. Others tried to drink, but had to spit out their mouthfuls. Bobtail Horse got sick and vomited soon after he had taken a big swallow of it. It became the talk that this whisky explained why the soldiers became crazy and shot each other and themselves instead of shooting us. One old Indian said, though, that there was not enough whisky gone from any of the bottles to make a white man soldier go crazy. We all agreed then that the foolish actions of the soldiers must have been caused by the prayers of our medicine men. I believed this was the true explanation. My belief became changed, though, in later years. I think now it was the whisky....

*[In the days after the battle the] Cheyenne warriors had a dance at this Greasy Grass camp. Charcoal Bear, our medicine chief, brought the buffalo skin from the sacred tepee and put it upon the top of a pole in the center of our camp circle. We danced around this pole. No women took part in the dancing. Many of them had sore legs from the **mourning cuts**. Our dance was not carried very far into the night. It was mostly a short telling of experiences, a counting of **coups**. My father told, in a few words, what his two sons had done. When he had ended the telling of my warrior acts, he said: "The name of this son of mine is Wooden Leg." Up to this time some*

Mourning cuts: The wives and daughters of killed warriors sliced their skin so that they would participate in the pain of the warrior's death.

Coups: Feats of bravery performed in battle, especially the touching of an enemy's body without causing injury.

people still used my boyhood name, Eats From His Hand. But now this old name was entirely gone. [Marquis, pp. 217–22, 226–8, 231–2, 237–41, 246, 274–5]

What happened next . . .

Following the Battle of Little Bighorn, the Indians separated into smaller units: Sitting Bull and his band escaped into Canada; and Crazy Horse was hounded by soldiers until 1877, when he finally surrendered and led his people onto a reservation. Other tribes were slowly rounded up and led to reservations. Their spirit had been broken by the never-ending pursuit of white soldiers and the continuing stream of white settlers who claimed Indian land as their own. By the 1880s there seemed to be no land left to them but the land on the reservations.

Wooden Leg was with his people when they surrendered, and he traveled to several reservations on the Plains before settling on a reservation near the Tongue River in Montana. "It is comfortable to live in peace on the reservation," Wooden Leg concluded his story. "It is pleasant to be situated where I can sleep soundly every night, without fear that my horses may be stolen or that myself or my friends may be crept upon and killed. But I like to think about the old times, when every man had to be brave. I wish I could live again through some of the past days when it was the first thought of every prospering Indian to send out the call: 'Hoh-oh-oh-oh, friends: Come. Come. Come. I have plenty of buffalo meat. I have coffee. I have sugar. I have tobacco. Come, friends, feast and smoke with me.'"

Did you know . . .

- The defeat of General Custer enraged many Americans and drew widespread support for the army's campaign to remove the "Indian menace" on the Plains.

- After the battle, Sitting Bull led his people in an exhausting winter journey north to Canada. Crazy Horse battled the forces of Brigadier General Nelson A. Miles during the winter, but on May 6 he led a band of three hundred Cheyenne and Oglala warriors to a defiant surrender at Fort Robinson, Nebraska.

- Crazy Horse remained a powerful leader among his people on the reservation. Fearful of Crazy Horse's influence, white authorities attempted to place him under guard. When he resisted, Crazy Horse was bayoneted to death by Indian soldiers.

Consider the following . . .

- What is Wooden Leg's attitude toward the white soldiers?

- What does Wooden Leg think of the behavior of the white soldiers in battle? What do they do that mystifies him and the other Indians?

- How does Wooden Leg decide what he should do in battle? Does he take commands from a leader? How might his account differ from the account of a white soldier following the orders of an army general?

- Did you find anything unexpected in this Indian account of the Battle of Little Bighorn?

For More Information

Halliburton, Warren J. *The Tragedy of Little Bighorn*. New York: F. Watts, 1989.

Henckel, Mark. *The Battle of the Little Bighorn*. Helena, MO: Falcon Press Publishing Co., 1992.

Krehbiel, Randy. *Little Bighorn*. New York: Twenty-First Century Books, 1997.

Nardo, Don. *Indian Wars*. San Diego: Lucent Books, 1991.

Rice, Earle, Jr. *The Battle of the Little Bighorn*. San Diego: Lucent Books, 1998.

Wills, Charles A. *The Battle of the Little Bighorn*. Englewood Cliffs, NJ: Silver Burdett Press, 1990.

Wooden Leg. *Wooden Leg: A Warrior Who Fought Custer*. Interpreted by Thomas B. Marquis. Lincoln: University of Nebraska Press, 1931.

Settling the West

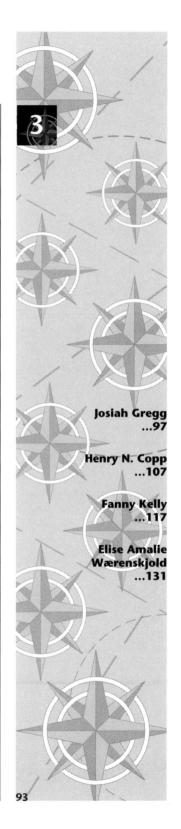

B etween 1800 and 1870, nearly half a million Americans set out across the frontier on the many trails that led westward. Using the Santa Fe Trail, the Oregon-California Trail, the Mormon Trail, or one of the many other trails, these trappers, traders, farmers, and families set out on a journey of discovery. For many the western frontier represented the opportunity of a lifetime: a chance to take control of their lives, to strike it rich, to make their own rules, or to claim their own land. Lured by promises—of gold, of lucrative trade, or of fertile farmland—pioneers endured weeks and even months of arduous travel in order to reach their destination and build the communities that defined the American West. The trails they blazed helped pave the way for the civilizing of the West.

The pioneers who journeyed west in the middle of the nineteenth century left their mark on the landscape and on the American character. Physical traces of the trails remain to this day: deep wagon wheel ruts are still visible in deserted stretches of the mountainous West, and many forts that are still standing attract curious tourists. As the pioneers reshaped the western landscape, they also created what is recognized as the American character. The hardships they endured to make a new life in the West left indelible marks on their temperaments, which came to embody the very spirit of America: brave, persistent, and tough.

The first pioneers to venture onto the frontier were guided only by a sense of adventure; those who followed were more cautious and pragmatic, hoping to make a life out West. Fortunately, the first western explorers and settlers offered advice on a variety of topics, from packing a wagon to meeting with Native Americans. Josiah Gregg (1806–1850) became one of the most respected authors to write about overland travel. In 1844 his book, **Commerce of the Prairies**, introduced readers to Indian groups, the flora and fauna of the prairies, and the new western way of life. The popularity of *Commerce of the Prairies* stemmed from Gregg's ability to bring "alive a world as unknown in that day as the back of the moon is to Americans today" and to give practical advice to the settler, according to David Freeman Hawke in the introduction to *Commerce of the Prairies*.

With the passage of the Homestead Act of 1862, many settlers were interested in claiming their own land. In addition to books like *Commerce of the Prairies* that would help them get to their destinations, people needed information that would help them claim the land the Homestead Act offered. To that end, Henry N. Copp's **The American Settler's Guide** was published in 1892. *The American Settler's Guide* clearly explained the public land system of the United States in great detail. Copp described the Homestead Act as legislation that made the United States a true land of opportunity. He explained every aspect of finding and claiming a plot of land, from gaining American citizenship and entering a claim to obtaining government relief for crop-devastating grasshopper infestations.

While guidebooks were popular reading in the middle of the century, letters from frontier settlers also attracted the interest of friends and family at home. The millions of letters from frontier settlers recounted their everyday existence and their new way of life, their struggles and successes on their own land, and their interest in creating supportive communities. Elise Amalie Wærenskjold, an emigrant from Norway, was one of the millions who wrote home. Her letters, translated and reprinted in **Land of Their Choice: The Immigrants**

Write Home, create a clear picture of life in Texas in the mid-1800s: her amusement with the many different religions, the common buildings on a Texas farm, and the daily challenges of breeding cattle and mowing hay.

Rarer than letters, testimonial books were first-person accounts of some of the most extraordinary experiences on the frontier. An Indian captive for five months, Fanny Kelly wrote an exciting tale of her adventure titled *Narrative of My Captivity Among the Sioux Indians.* Kelly's book provides rich insight into the terrible conflict between Indians and whites. Although her experience was unique, Kelly's descriptions highlight the dangers of overland travel and paint a vivid picture of how Indians responded to the encroaching mass of settlers.

A pioneer family's hopes are dashed when their horses collapse on the trail.
(Reproduced from the Collections of the Library of Congress.)

Josiah Gregg

Excerpt from Commerce of the Prairies: A Selection
Edited by David Freeman Hawke
Originally published in 1844

One thing that pioneers had in common was courage. For years, cautious observers in the East had warned against selling one's belongings, packing a wagon, and heading west. Newspaper editor Horace Greeley called it "palpable suicide" and statesman Daniel Webster warned that the West was a "region of savages and wild beasts."

By the 1840s, however, several events made the West more appealing to settlers: a long economic downturn that lasted from 1837 to 1842 encouraged many to seek their fortune in the West; Congress hinted that it would give land to Oregon settlers; Britain ceded the present-day states of Oregon and Washington to the United States in 1846; and the California gold rush attracted many people. The Great Migration, the name given to the first major departure of emigrants westward, drew one thousand settlers onto the Oregon Trail in 1843, and more came every year after that. The small trail soon became a well-traveled road stretching to the promised land. Many Americans felt that it was their "manifest destiny"—their right and duty to expand throughout the North American continent and secure these western lands.

A well-stocked wagon was as important as strength, endurance, and luck in making a successful trip west. Outfitters developed special wagons strong enough to endure the two thousand miles of rough trails, light enough to be pulled by a team of oxen or mules, and big enough to carry a family's possessions. The wagons were known as prairie schooners because their billowing canvas covers looked like sails from a distance.

The wagons could carry between 1,600 and 2,500 pounds of household goods. Food, of course, was essential. The early guidebooks recommended that each family have available 200 pounds of flour, 150 pounds of bacon, 10 pounds of coffee, 20 pounds of sugar, and 10 pounds of salt. (In addition to the food they carried, pioneers supplemented their diet with wild game, berries, and—if they had brought along a cow—fresh milk.) Cooking supplies and utensils were needed to prepare meals, but the cook had to be flexible and learn to cook over a campfire. Many families brought along furniture and heirlooms, though they often regretted the extra weight when the trail got rough. Barrels of water, rope, and wagon wheel grease also added weight to the wagon. Spare parts—including spokes, axles, and canvas roofs—could be carried under the wagon bed.

On an average day, a party of pioneers could expect to travel about fifteen miles; on some days they traveled more, and on others much less. Sometimes entire days would be spent just crossing a river. At the end of the day the wagons were pulled into a circle to provide a corral for the animals and to act as a defense against Indian attacks (which were quite rare). Evening campfires provided the members of the wagon train with the rare opportunity to relax. Campfires were made from whatever wood could be found or from buffalo chips (a polite name for dried buffalo dung). As the fires died, the settlers retired to makeshift sleeping arrangements: some slept inside the wagon, but most stretched out with a blanket on the ground. After a long day of travel, even the hard earth must have been a comfort. A few sentries stayed awake to ward off wild animals and look out for Indian thieves.

Josiah Gregg's *Commerce of the Prairies* has been hailed by some as the greatest book about the American West. Pub-

lished in 1844, Gregg's book recorded the difficult task of overland travel and painted an optimistic picture of emigrant trains forging across the prairies to claim western regions. Many people used the book as a reference as they prepared for their own journey.

A prairie schooner was one type of wagon commonly used by families moving to the West.
(© Bettmann/Corbis. Reproduced by permission.)

Things to remember while reading the excerpt from *Commerce of the Prairies*:

- Note that Gregg did not engage in violent conflict with Native Americans.

- Gregg recorded detailed notes about the various Indian cultures found on the prairies and in the Southwest.

- *Commerce of the Prairies* also included extensive descriptions of the geography of the prairies.

- *Commerce of the Prairies* is considered a classic account of how to organize caravans and how to handle mule trains.

Excerpt from Commerce of the Prairies
BOOK ONE

1. The Departure

As Independence is a point of convenient access (the Missouri river being navigable at all times from March till November), it has become the general 'port of embarkation' for every part of the great western and northern 'prairie ocean.' Besides the Santa Fe caravans, most of the Rocky Mountain traders and trappers, as well as emigrants to Oregon, take this town in their route. During the season of departure, therefore, it is a place of much bustle and active business.

*Among the **concourse** of travelers at this 'starting point,' besides traders and tourists, a number of pale-faced **invalids** are generally met with. The Prairies have, in fact, become very celebrated for their **sanative** effects—more justly so, no doubt, than the most fashionable **watering-places** of the North. Most chronic diseases, particularly liver complaints, **dyspepsias**, and similar **affections**, are often radically cured; owing, no doubt, to the peculiarities of diet, and the regular exercise **incident to prairie life**, as well as to the purity of the atmosphere of those elevated . . . regions. An invalid myself, I can answer for the efficacy of the remedy, at least in my own case.... Though I set out myself in a carriage, before the close of the first week I saddled my pony; and when we reached the buffalo range, I was not only as eager for the chase as the sturdiest of my companions, but I enjoyed far more exquisitely my share of the buffalo, than all the delicacies which were ever devised to provoke the most **fastidious** appetite.*

The ordinary supplies for each man's consumption during the journey, are about fifty pounds of flour, as many more of bacon, ten of coffee and twenty of sugar, and a little salt. Beans, crackers, and trifles of that description, are comfortable appendages, but being looked upon as dispensable luxuries, are seldom to be found in any of the stores on the road. The buffalo is chiefly depended upon for fresh meat, and great is the joy of the traveller when that noble animal first appears in sight....

*The supplies being at length **procured**, and all necessary preliminaries systematically gone through, the trader begins the difficult*

'Port of embarkation': Point of departure.

Concourse: Crowd.

Invalids: People afflicted with illnesses.

Sanative: Having the power to cure; healing or restorative.

Watering-places: Health resorts with mineral springs.

Dyspepsia: Disturbed digestion.

Affections: Afflictions.

Incident to prairie life: That are a part of prairie life.

Fastidious: Finicky.

Procured: Obtained.

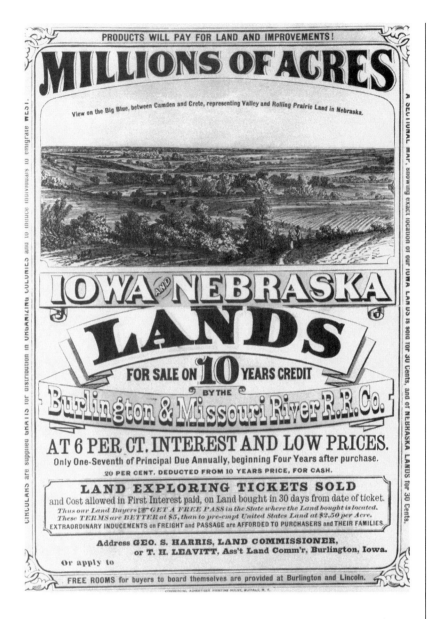

task of loading his wagons. Those who understand their business take every precaution so to stow away their packages that no jolting on the road can afterwards disturb the order in which they had been disposed. The ingenuity displayed on these occasions has frequently been such, that after a tedious journey of eight hundred miles, the goods have been found to have sustained much less injury, than they would have experienced on a turnpike-road, or from the ordinary handling of property upon our western steam-boats.

The next great difficulty the traders have to encounter is in training those animals that have never before been worked, which is frequently attended by an immensity of trouble....

*At last all are fairly launched upon the broad prairie—the miseries of preparation are over—the thousand anxieties occasioned by wearisome consultations and delays are felt no more. The charioteer, as he smacks his whip, feels a **bounding elasticity of soul** within him, which he finds it impossible to restrain;—even the mules prick up their ears with a peculiarly conceited air, as if in anticipation of that change of scene which will presently follow. Harmony and good feeling prevail everywhere. The hilarious song, the **bon mot** and the witty repartee, go round in quick succession; and before people have had leisure to take **cognizance** of the fact, the lovely village of Independence, with its multitude of associations, is already lost to the eye.*

*It was on the 15th of May, 1831, and one of the brightest and most lovely of all the days in the calendar, that our little party set out from Independence. The general **rendezvous** at Council Grove was our immediate destination. It is usual for the traders to travel thus far in detached parties, and to assemble there for the purpose of entering into some kind of organization, for mutual security and **defence** during the remainder of the journey. It was from thence that the formation of the Caravan was to be dated, and the chief interest of our journey to commence: therefore, to this point we all looked forward with great anxiety. The intermediate travel was marked by very few events of any interest. As the wagons had gone before us, and we were riding in a light carriage, we were able to reach the Round Grove, about thirty-five miles distant, on the first day, where we joined the rear division of the caravan, comprising about thirty wagons.*

*On the following day we had a foretaste of those **protracted**, drizzling spells of rain, which, at this season of the year, so much infest the frontier prairies. It began sprinkling about dark, and continued pouring **without let or [hindrance]** for forty-eight hours in succession; and as the rain was accompanied by a heavy **northwester**, and our camp was pitched in the open prairie, without a stick of available timber within a mile of us, it must be allowed **that the whole formed a prelude anything but flattering to [us]**. For my own part, finding the dearborn carriage in which I had a **berth** not exactly water-proof, I rolled myself in a blanket and lay snugly coiled upon a tier of boxes and bales, under cover of a wagon, and thus managed to escape a very severe drenching.*

Bounding elasticity of soul: A great sense of excitement.

Bon mot: Clever remarks.

Cognizance: Awareness, knowledge or recognition.

Rendezvous: Meeting place.

Defence: Spelled *defense.*

Protracted: Ongoing; lasting a long time.

Without let or [hindrance]: Without stopping.

Northwester: A violent storm that blows from the northwest.

That the whole formed a prelude anything but flattering to [us]: Gregg is saying that the storm was an awful way to begin the trip.

Berth: A place to sleep.

*The mischief of the storm did not exhaust itself, however, upon our persons. The loose animals sought shelter in the groves at a considerable distance from the encampment, and the wagoners being [loath] to turn out in search of them during the rain, not a few of course, when **applied for,** were missing. This, however, is no uncommon occurrence. Travellers generally experience far more annoyance from the straying of cattle during the first hundred miles, than at any time afterwards; because, apprehending no danger from the wild Indians (who rarely approach within two hundred miles of the border), they seldom keep any watch, although that is the very time when a cattle-guard is most needed. It is only after some weeks' travel that the animals begin to feel attached to the caravan, which they then consider about as much their home as the stock-yard of a dairy farm.*

*After leaving this spot the troubles and **vicissitudes** of our journey began in good earnest; for on reaching the narrow ridge which separates the Osage and Kansas waters (known as 'the Narrows'), we encountered a region of very troublesome **quagmires.** On such occasions it is quite common for a wagon to sink to the hubs in mud, while the surface of the soil all around would appear perfectly dry and smooth. To **extricate** each other's wagons we had frequently to employ double and triple teams, with 'all hands to the wheels' in addition—often led by the proprietors themselves up to the waist in mud and water....*

Early on the 26th of May we reached the long looked-for rendezvous of Council Grove, where we joined the main body of the caravan. Lest this imposing title suggest to the reader a snug thriving village, it should be observed, that, on the day of our departure from Independence, we passed the last human abode upon our route; therefore, from the borders of Missouri to those of New Mexico not even an Indian settlement greeted our eyes.

*This place is about a hundred and fifty miles from Independence, and consists of a continuous stripe of timber nearly half a mile in width, comprising the richest varieties of trees; such as oak, walnut, ash, elm, hickory, etc., and extending all along the valleys of a small stream known as 'Council Grove creek,' the principal branch of the Neosho river. This stream is bordered by the most fertile bottoms and beautiful upland prairies, well adapted to cultivation: such indeed is the general character of the country from thence to Independence. All who have traversed these delightful regions, look forward with anxiety to the day when the Indian **title** to the land shall be **extinguished,** and flourishing 'white' settlements dispel the gloom which at present prevails over this uninhabited region. Much of this prolific country now*

Applied for: Searched for.

Vicissitudes: Unexpected changes.

Quagmires: Land with a soft, muddy surface.

Extricate: Release; free from the mud.

Title: Claim.

Extinguished: Ended.

belongs to the Shawnees and other Indians of the border, though some portion of it has never been allotted to any tribe....

. . . Upon the calling of the roll, we were found to muster an efficient force of nearly two hundred men without counting invalids or other disabled bodies, who, as a matter of course, are exempt from duty. But no matter what the condition or employment of the individual may be, no one has the smallest chance of evading the 'common law of the prairies.' The amateur tourist and the listless loafer are precisely in the same wholesome predicament—they must all take their regular turn at the watch. . . . Even the invalid must be able to produce **unequivocal** *proofs of his inability, or it is a chance if the plea is admitted. For my own part, although I started on the 'sick list,' and though the prairie sentinel must stand fast and* **brook** *the severest storm (for then it is that the strictest watch is necessary), I do not remember ever having missed my post but once during the whole journey....*

The wild and motley aspect of the caravan **can be but imperfectly conceived** *without an idea of the costumes of its various members. The most 'fashionable' prairie dress is the fustian frock of the city-bred merchant furnished with a multitude of pockets capable of accommodating a variety of 'extra tackling.' Then there is the backwoodsman with his* **linsey** *or leather hunting-shirt—the farmer with his blue jean coat—the wagoner with his flannel-sleeve vest—besides an assortment of other costumes which go to fill up the picture.*

In the article of fire-arms there is also an equally interesting medley. The frontier hunter sticks to his rifle, as nothing could induce him to carry what he terms in derision 'the scatter-gun.' The sportsman from the interior flourishes his double-barrelled fowling-piece with equal confidence in its superiority. The latter is certainly the most convenient description of gun that can be carried on this journey; as a charge of buck-shot in night attacks (which are the most common), will of course be more likely to do execution than a single rifle-ball fired at random. The **'repeating' arms** *have lately been brought into use upon the Prairies, and they are certainly very formidable weapons, particularly when used against an* **ignorant savage foe**. *A great many were furnished beside with a bountiful supply of pistols and knives of every description, so that the party made altogether a very* **brigand-like** *appearance.* [Gregg, pp. 5–6, 7–9, 10, 11, 12–13]

Unequivocal: Undeniable.

Brook: Tolerate; stand up to.

Can be but imperfectly conceived: Cannot be pictured or imagined.

Linsey: Linsey-woolsey; a coarse fabric made of cotton or linen woven with wool.

"Repeating" arms: Revolvers; these guns that could hold more than one shot had just recently been invented.

Ignorant savage foe: Gregg is negatively referring to Native Americans.

Brigand-like: Like a band of criminals.

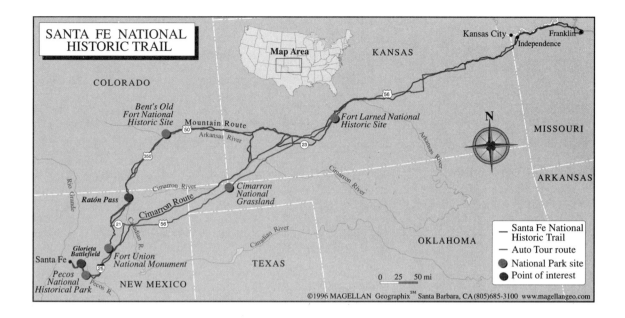

What happened next . . .

For the first several years after 1843 the vast majority of the travelers ended up in Oregon Country. However, by 1846 the trend began to change. Once word of gold in California spread eastward the number of travelers going south to California was four times the number venturing north into Oregon. Those going to Oregon had promises of vast acres of fertile farmland, but California had gold—and a warmer climate.

Along the Santa Fe Trail, many merchants had been reaping the benefits of trade in New Mexico since James Becknell and companions discovered profitable opportunities in Santa Fe in the 1820s. By 1846 it was estimated that the trade using the Santa Fe Trail had reached $1 million from a traffic flow of 363 wagons and 750 men; by 1860 trade topped $3.5 million. Such trade was conducted not only by American merchants but also by enterprising Mexican adventurers.

Did you know . . .

• Between 1843, the year of the Great Migration, and 1869, when the transcontinental railway was finished, the Oregon Trail carried an estimated 350,000 pioneers across two thousand miles of tortuous terrain.

The Santa Fe Trail.
(© Magellan Geographix/ Corbis. Reproduced by permission.)

- Even after the trains made transcontinental travel easier and cheaper, some pioneers continued to use the trails to cross the country as late as 1895.

- During the peak years, the Oregon- and California-trail was an essential link connecting the East and West.

- Gregg noted that "The wagons now most in use upon the Prairies are manufactured in Pittsburgh; and are usually drawn by eight mules or the same number of oxen. Of late years, however, I have seen much larger vehicles employed, with ten or twelve mules harnessed to each, and a cargo of goods of about five thousand pounds in weight."

- Botanists honored Josiah Gregg's botanical records by giving twenty-three plants the species name *greggi*.

Consider the following . . .

- Did Gregg consider the Indians' right to the land sacred?

- Did Gregg expect to meet hostile Indians?

- What job on the trail was shared by all?

- What effect did travel have on the health of settlers?

For More Information

Billington, Ray Allen. *Westward to the Pacific: An Overview of America's Westward Expansion.* St. Louis: Jefferson National Expansion Historical Association, 1979.

Gregg, Josiah. *Commerce of the Prairies: A Selection.* Edited by David Freeman Hawke. 1844. Reprint, Indianapolis: Bobbs-Merrill Company, 1970.

McNeese, Tim. *Western Wagon Trains.* New York: Crestwood House, 1993.

Penner, Lucille Recht. *Westward Ho!: The Story of the Pioneers.* New York: Random House, 1997.

Peters, Arthur King. *Seven Trails West.* New York: Abbeville Press, 1996.

Place, Marian T. *Westward on the Oregon Trail.* New York: American Heritage, 1962.

Roscoe, Gerald, and David Larkin. *Westward: The Epic Crossing of the American Landscape.* New York: The Monacelli Press, 1995.

Henry N. Copp

Excerpt from **The American Settler's Guide:
A Popular Exposition of the Public Land System
of the United States of America**
Published in 1892

The frontier was the wilderness beyond the borders of civilized towns, a mysterious region that offered people the opportunity to strike out on their own, to make their own successes. For European immigrants, the American frontier offered a dream never before imagined. In Europe, a serf could never think of leaving his allotted plot of land to rise from poverty; a shopkeeper's son could never hope to run his own store before his father's death. Yet in America, just outside of the newly formed towns, hardy souls could determine their own destiny in the unknown.

Securing Property

On the American frontier, as in few other places on earth, a man amounted to the sum of his skills and endurance. Without the established lines of ancestry and wealth that made up the social structure in Europe, the American frontier was open to anyone strong enough or courageous enough to master it and claim its riches. On the frontier, each person had the power to shape his or her own destiny. Never before had a society offered all its citizens the opportunity for success. In the American West, "all men were future 'gentlemen' and deserved this designation, all women were prospective 'ladies' and should be treated as such. 'With us,' one frontiersman stoutly maintained, 'a man's a man, whether he have a silk gown on him or not,'" writes Ray Allen Billington in *Westward to the Pacific*.

To encourage settlement on the frontier, the U.S. government created legislation that would give every person a chance to own land. Farming in the West was greatly encouraged by the Homestead Act of 1862, which gave settlers up to 160 acres of free land if they settled on it and made improvements over a five-year span. The Timber Culture Act of 1873 granted an additional 160 acres to farmers who agreed to plant a portion of their land with trees. Both acts served to attract many thousands of settlers to the wide-open spaces of the American West.

To help settlers understand the opportunities available to them in the West, Henry N. Copp edited *The American Settler's Guide*. This book explained the various implications of the Homestead Act and detailed how a settler actually secured a claim to a plot of land. As amendments were made to the Homestead Act, Copp published new editions of his guide to keep homesteaders abreast of any changes.

Things to remember while reading the excerpt from *The American Settler's Guide*:

- During the 1850s, Congress tried to pass homestead legislation, but southerners were opposed to the idea of "free land" because they could see no benefits for their region if the bill passed.

- One homestead legislation bill was passed by Congress in 1860, only to meet the veto of President James Buchanan (1791–1868).

- When Abraham Lincoln (1809–1865) was elected president in 1860, the South still controlled the Senate. But the secession of the Southern states and the absence of Southern congressmen made passage of homestead legislation possible. President Lincoln signed the bill in 1862.

• Eighteen editions of *The American Settler's Guide* were published by 1892.

Excerpt from The American Settler's Guide
Chapter III

Homesteads.

I. Homesteads in General.

*To the people of Europe, where the high price of real estate **confers** distinction upon its owner, it seems almost beyond belief that the United States should give away one hundred and sixty acres of land for nothing. Yet such is the fact; a compliance with the Homestead Law, and the payment of small fees and commissions to the local officers, **secure title** to a quarter-section of Government land. Laborers in other countries, who find it difficult to support their families, can here acquire wealth, social privileges, and political honors, by a few years of intelligent industry and patient **frugality**.*

All in the Atlantic States, who are discouraged with the slow, tedious methods of reaching independence, will find rich rewards awaiting settlers on the public lands, who have talent and energy, while the unfortunate in business and they who are burdened with debt, can, in the West and South, start anew in the race of life, for the Homestead Law expressly declares that "no land acquired under the provisions of this chapter (Homestead) shall in any event become liable to the satisfaction of any debt contracted prior to the issuing of the patent therefor."

*Citizens and those who have declared their intention to become citizens, who own no more than one hundred and sixty acres, may claim under the homestead laws, surveyed or unsurveyed lands, **not mineral in character**. This is conceded to the extent of one hundred and sixty acres .*

Chapter V.

Where to Settle.

The question "where to settle" is a serious one to the emigrant. The suggestions here offered are not in favor of any particular locali-

Confers: Bestows or gives.

Secure title: Give ownership.

Frugality: Thriftiness; not spending a lot of money.

Not mineral in character: This meant that settlers could claim land that is farmable, not land that the government would want mined for minerals such as gold or silver.

ty or community. They are such as must present themselves to every person who will give the subject serious consideration.

*The wonderful diversity of soil and climate, society and facilities for the several industries presented by the broad expanse of our country, offers to every man a **congenial** location and a happy home.*

*The advantages of migrating in companies of three to twenty families are many. An agent can be chosen to examine the region in which after full **inquiry, correspondence and reading,** it is decided to settle. Low rates can be obtained for **outfit,** traveling and other expenses, land in large quantities can be bought cheap, while the discomforts of going upon Government lands are materially lessened when friends go in colonies.*

Starting with the assumption that the emigrant is industrious, sober and intelligent, the points to be aimed at are—first and foremost, health and bodily comfort; second, mental and moral growth; third, financial success in the near future.

Health and Bodily Comfort

If the health of himself and family is good, a climate like the one he is leaving should be sought by the settler. Run no risk by going upon the low land when accustomed to the hills; to a humid atmosphere from a dry bracing one, or the reverse.

Consult the family physician, and gain all the information possible about the mean annual temperature, extremes of heat and cold, the amount of rainfall, chills and fever, etc., in the region decided upon.

*On the other hand, a change of climate often restores physical vigor. Many a **consumptive** from bleak New England has discovered fountains of health in the south and southwest.*

The surroundings, especially the state of society, have much to do with physical comfort. In a turbulent, irreligious community, where crime goes unpunished and the criminal is somewhat of a hero, a peace-loving family will be in a constant state of worry, that must eventually affect their general health. Let such regions be avoided as a pest-house is shunned.

*Political troubles prevent immigration, as they aid emigration or an exodus. No community that deprives any honest citizen of his political rights can expect to secure an intelligent class of immigrants, and may expect to lose those who are **disfranchised.***

The enterprising among them will find homes amidst a wiser people, and let the office-holders collect their salaries from waste land if

Congenial: Suited to one's needs or nature; agreeable.

Inquiry, correspondence and reading: Investigating.

Outfit: Supplies.

Consumptive: A person with consumption, another name for tuberculosis.

Disfranchised: Without political power or civil rights.

they can. There is no truer **axiom** than that in any neighborhood each man's gain is everybody's gain and each man's loss is everybody's loss.

MENTAL AND MORAL GROWTH

Seek a State or Territory whose officials appreciate churches and schools; where taxpayers perceive the fact that every dollar spent on education and religion is a saving of two dollars on the jail and penitentiary, where newspapers are numerous and libraries have been started, and literary, temperance and other societies are encouraged by the leading citizens. In sparsely settled regions in the Territories where society is not fully organized, much cannot be expected in the matter of education and religion, but the tone and sentiments of the people may be taken as a sure index of the future.

FINANCIAL SUCCESS

The settler must determine the kind of business he will pursue, then seek a locality best adapted to carrying it on. Farming is the most common and safest occupation in a new country. If he would

The Homestead Act of 1862 attracted thousands of settlers onto the American frontier.
(Archive Photos, Inc. Reproduced by permission.)

Axiom: A self-evident or universally recognized truth.

*make a specialty of live stock, fruit culture, wheat raising, or **aught** else, let the farmer consider all that tends to success.*

Railroad facilities, river and lake transportation, and nearness to markets, must be looked to; also the fence and other real estate laws, State and county debts, and the laws relative to municipal indebtedness, rates of taxation, character of officials, etc.; whether the school houses, churches and public buildings are already erected, and society fully organized. Homestead exemptions, cost of living and of building materials, nearness to stores, mills, etc., abundant water supply, Indians, droughts, grasshoppers, potato bugs, and everything else that can affect his success, should receive due attention.

Land near a railroad at $5.00 an acre, is cheaper than land at $1.25 several miles from transportation. Do not buy too much land simply because it is cheap. One hundred and sixty acres are all an ordinary man can attend to properly, and taxes on a large farm balance considerable profit.

Other things being equal, choose a settlement near mines and manufactures, or rapid streams likely to be used for manufactures; near the junction of rivers or valleys, where a valley crosses a river or ends at a lake.

Such locations always secure good markets for farm produce, and rapidly advance the price of land, becoming centers of business and sites for future cities, [sic]

The title which a settler acquires to lands in this country is in fee simple. *It is not a lease for any term of years, but perpetual ownership, whether he buys of the general Government, or a State, or of a corporation. The land becomes his property, to hold during life, and transmit to his heirs, or he may sell it at will. There is no landlord, no rent to pay, nor any church rates exacted. He is himself lord of the manor, and peer of his fellow-citizens of all classes.*

A RECOMMENDATION

The General Land Office issues free of cost circulars of instruction. A letter "To the Hon. Commissioner of the General Land Office, Washington, D.C.," and requesting a copy of the general instructions under the homestead and other laws, will secure a valuable document without charge. [Copp, 28, 120–1]

Aught: Anything.

What happened next . . .

Millions of people claimed land through the Homestead Act. Despite the relative ease with which settlers could gain ownership of large tracts of land, farming in the West proved to be quite difficult for some. Settlers could claim land without farming tools or any experience or special knowledge to aid their endeavor. While 160 acres was plenty of land to provide for a family in fertile regions of the country, in the desert and semiarid regions it was far too little. The expense of irrigation in the dryer regions and the cost of shipping goods to market on railroads forced many homesteaders into debt.

In addition to the difficulties of farming in the best circumstances, environmental catastrophes proved devastating to some homesteaders. Gale-force winds, hailstorms, tornadoes, and blizzards caused much damage in western regions. Droughts ruined many harvests. Prairie fires swallowed crops. From 1874 to 1877, swarms of locusts devoured farmers' crops as well as their best leather boots.

Main Street in a frontier town in Oklahoma Territory. Depending on where pioneers decided to settle, they may have found a small town that offered some comforts of civilization to the local population.
(Photograph by Kennett. Courtesy of the National Archives and Records Administration.)

An abandoned homestead in Bend National Park, Texas. Environmental catastrophes and plagues of insects drove many families from the prairies.
(Photograph by Robert J. Huffman/Field Mark Publications. Reproduced by permission.)

To alleviate some of these problems, amendments to the Homestead Act were incorporated over the years, including provisions for forest land and grazing land. In addition, the five-year residence requirement was changed to three years in 1912, and the maximum acreage tract (the land that the settler could acquire) was increased to 640 acres. Despite the difficulties, many homesteaders rose to the challenges of life on their land. The wooden-frame and brick houses, the windmills that harness the strong winds to pump water from the ground, and the rows and rows of crops across the western states stand as testament to the endurance and ingenuity of homesteaders.

Did you know . . .

- Democratic senator from Tennessee Andrew Johnson (1808–1875) led the fight for homestead legislation.

- The largest land claim, known as the Oklahoma land rush, occurred on April 22, 1889, when in a single day some fifty thousand settlers claimed lands that were just opened to settlement.

- European immigrants were encouraged to partake of the Homestead Act by railroad company propaganda. The railroads hoped to profit by providing transportation for farmers' goods to market.

Consider the following . . .

- How was ownership of property different in America than in Europe?

- What did a homesteader need to consider before selecting a plot of land?

For More Information

Billington, Ray Allen. *Westward to the Pacific: An Overview of America's Westward Expansion.* St. Louis: Jefferson National Expansion Historical Association, 1979.

Copp, Henry N. *The American Settler's Guide: A Popular Exposition of the Public Land System of the United States of America.* 18th edition. Washington D. C.: Henry N. Copp, 1892.

Penner, Lucille Recht. *Westward Ho!: The Story of the Pioneers.* New York: Random House, 1997.

Fanny Kelly

Excerpt from Narrative of My Captivity
Among the Sioux Indians

Originally published in 1872
Reprinted in *In Their Own Words: Warriors and Pioneers*
Edited by T. J. Stiles
Published in 1996

Although legend has it that wagon trains crossing the prairie were under constant attack from marauding bands of Indians, such attacks were relatively infrequent—except on a few trails such as the Bozeman Trail—and rarely led to death. Native Americans posed little real danger to the emigrants. Much of the contact between whites and Indians was peaceful, as Indians provided direction to emigrants passing through their lands, or as the emigrants traded their guns for Indian horses. Some of the native groups demanded that travelers pay a toll to cross their land. But there was also some open conflict between Native Americans and whites. Indians commonly slipped into camps at night and stole horses and other goods. In fact, the Pawnee gained a reputation for thievery. Other groups, such as the Crow and the Blackfeet, disliked the travelers crossing their tribal lands and raided the camps or caught and killed stragglers. In the end, though, few whites were killed by Indians on the Oregon-California Trail, the same trail on which Fanny Kelly traveled.

While Indians did not pose a grave danger to pioneers, life on the trail was certainly dangerous. Long days of traveling under a hot sun were difficult in themselves, and these problems were compounded by the sometimes back-breaking labor of fording streams and climbing steep mountain trails. Accidents cost many lives, especially those of children. It was not uncommon for a child to fall off a wagon and be crushed beneath the heavy wheels.

In addition, environmental catastrophes sometimes occurred, catching weary or unprepared travelers at a disadvantage. Many travelers of the Santa Fe Trail told harrowing tales of the horrors they encountered as they faced a shortage of water and severe dehydration. Equally daunting was the threat of prairie fires. Whether started by lightning or by a carelessly tended campfire, a prairie fire could sweep across the land with devastating speed, consuming everything in its path.

The most pressing danger to pioneers was disease. Pneumonia, whooping cough, measles, smallpox, and other sicknesses took many lives, but the biggest killer was cholera. An acute intestinal infection, cholera caused violent vomiting, fever, chills, and diarrhea. As the sickness swept through the camps it killed quickly, sometimes in a matter of hours. Those who survived were severely weakened. The disease was prevalent on the trail, especially in the 1840s. One pioneer described the road from Independence to Fort Laramie as a graveyard.

Despite these real dangers, many pioneers braved the unknown in hopes of building a better life. Fanny Kelly is one of many who traveled the overland trails. Her description of her capture by Indians as she traveled from Kansas across the Plains toward Idaho illustrates the real horror of the clash between Indian and white cultures as whites ventured onto the Plains. Her tale, which she wrote for publication aftef her release, describes the confusion of both cultures as they struggle to stake claims to the same land.

Things to remember while reading the excerpt from Fanny Kelly's narrative:

- Fanny Kelly regarded the Indians as savages when she was captured.

- General Sully's attack on the Oglala people was unprovoked.

- Fanny Kelly and her adopted daughter, Mary, were taken prisoner, but Fanny dropped Mary from her horse one night while traveling to a Native American camp. Fanny never saw Mary again, and there is no record that the girl survived.

- Fanny Kelly spent the majority of her captivity in Wyoming.

Pioneers being attacked by Comanches, 1857, engraving by Schoolcraft. Although legend has it that wagon trains crossing the prairie were under constant attack from marauding bands of Indians, such attacks were relatively infrequent on most of the trails, and whites were rarely killed.
(Bettmann. Reproduced by permission.)

Excerpt from Narrative of My Captivity Among the Sioux Indians

The years 1852 to 1856 witnessed, probably, the heaviest immigration the West has ever known in a corresponding length of time. Those who had gone before sent back to their friends such marvelous accounts of the fertility of the soil, the rapid development of the country, and the ease with which fortunes were made, the "Western fever" became almost epidemic. Whole towns in the old, Eastern States were almost depopulated. Old substantial farmers, surrounded apparently by all the comforts that the heart could wish, sacrificed the homes wherein their families had been reared for generations, and, with all their worldly possessions, turned their faces toward the setting sun. And with what high hopes! Alas! how few, comparatively, met their realization.

In 1856, my father, James Wiggins, joined a New York colony bound for Kansas. Being favorably impressed with the country and its people, they located the town of Geneva, and my father returned for his family. Reaching the Missouri River on our way to our new home, my father was attacked with cholera and died. In obedience to his dying instructions, my widowed mother, with her little family, continued on the way to our new home. But, oh! with what saddened hearts we entered into its possession....

Our family remained in this pleasant prairie home, where I was married to Josiah S. Kelly. My husband's health failing, he resolved upon a change of climate. Accordingly, on the 17th of May, 1864, a party of six persons, consisting of Mr. Gardner Wakefield, my husband, myself, our adopted daughter (my sister's child), and two colored servants [named Frank and Andy], started from Geneva, with high-wrought hopes and pleasant anticipations of a romantic and delightful journey across the plains, and a confident expectation of future prosperity among the golden hills of Idaho....

As a rule, the emigrants travel without tents, sleeping in and under wagons, without removing their clothing. Cooking among emigrants to the far West is a very primitive operation, a frying pan and perhaps a Dutch oven comprising the major part of the kitchen furniture. The scarcity of timber is a source of great inconvenience and discomfort, "buffalo chips" being the main substitute. At some of the stations, where opportunity offered, Mr. Kelly bought wood by the pound, as I had not yet been long enough inured to plains privations to relish food cooked over a fire made with "chips" of that kind. We crossed the Platte River by binding four wagon boxes together, then loaded the boat with goods, and were rowed across by about twenty men. We were several days in crossing. Our cattle and horses swam across. The air had been heavy and oppressively hot; now the sky began to darken suddenly, and just as we reached the

Buffalo chips: Dried buffalo dung.

Inured: Accustomed or used to.

opposite shore, a gleam of lightning, like a forked tongue of flame, shot out of the black clouds, blinding us by its flash, and followed by a frightful clash of thunder....

THE ATTACK AND THE CAPTURE

The day on which our doomed family were scattered and killed was the 12th of July, a warm and oppressive day. The burning sun poured forth its hottest rays upon the great Black Hills and the vast plains of Montana, and the great road was strewed with men, women, and children, and flocks of cattle, representing towns of adventurers....

We had no thought of danger or timid misgivings on the subject of savages, for our fears had been all dispersed by constantly received assurances of their friendliness. At the outposts and ranches, we heard nothing but ridicule of their pretensions to warfare, and at Fort Laramie, where information that should have been reliable was given us, we had renewed assurances of the safety of the road and friendliness of Indians.... We wended our way peacefully and cheerfully on, without a thought of the danger that was lying like a tiger in ambush in our path.

*Without a sound of preparation or a word of warning, the bluffs before us were covered with a party of two hundred and fifty Indians, painted and equipped for war, who uttered the wild war-whoop and fired a signal volley of guns and revolvers into the air. This terrible and unexpected **apparition** came upon us with such startling swiftness that we had no time to think before the main body halted and sent out a part of their force, which circled us round at regular intervals, but some distance from our wagons. Recovering from the shock, our men instantly resolved on defense and **corralled** the wagons. My husband was looked upon as leader, as he was principal owner of the train. Without regard to the insignificance of our numbers, Mr. Kelly was ready to stand his ground; but, with all the power I could command, I **entreated** him to **forbear** and only attempt **conciliation**. "If you fire one shot," I said, "I feel sure you will seal our fate, as they seem to outnumber us ten to one, and will at once massacre all of us." . . .*

My husband advanced to meet the chief and demand his intentions. The savage leader immediately came toward him, riding forward and uttering the words, "How! How!" which are understood to mean a friendly salutation. His name was Ottowa, and he was a war chief of the Oglala band of the Sioux nation. He struck himself on his breast, saying, "Good Indian, me," and pointing to those

Apparition: An unusual or unexpected sight.

Corralled: Pulled into a circle.

Entreated: Begged.

Forbear: To hold back.

Conciliation: Peaceful agreement.

around him, he continued, "Heap good Indian, hunt buffalo and deer." He assured us of his utmost friendship for the white people; then he shook hands, and his band followed his example, crowding around our wagons, shaking us all by the hand over and over again, until our arms ached, and grinning and nodding with every demonstration of good will....

*The chief at last **intimated** that he desired us to proceed on our way, promising that we should not be **molested**. We obeyed, without trusting them, and soon the train was again in motion, the Indians insisting on driving our herd, and growing **ominously** familiar. Soon my husband called a halt. He saw that we were approaching a rocky glen, **in whose gloomy depths he anticipated a murderous attack**, and from which escape would be utterly impossible. Our enemies urged us still forward, but we resolutely refused to stir, when they requested that we should prepare us supper, which they said they would share with us, and then go to the hills to sleep. The men of our party concluded it best to give them a feast. Mr. Kelly gave orders to our two colored servants to prepare at once to make a feast for the Indians....*

*Each man was busy preparing supper; Mr. Larimer and Frank were making the fire; Mr. Wakefield was getting provisions out of the wagon; Mr. Taylor was attending to his team; Mr. Kelly and Andy were out some distance gathering wood; Mr. Sharp was distributing sugar among the Indians; supper, that they asked for, was in rapid progress of preparation, when suddenly our terrible enemies **threw off their masks** and displayed their truly demonic natures. There was a simultaneous discharge of arms, and when the cloud of smoke cleared away, I could see the retreating form of Mr. Larimer and the slow motion of poor Mr. Wakefield, for he was mortally wounded.*

Mr. Kelly and Andy made a miraculous escape with their lives. Mr. Sharp was killed within a few feet of me. Mr. Taylor—I never can forget his face as I saw him shot through the forehead with a rifle ball. He looked at me as he fell backward to the ground a corpse. I was the last object that met his dying gaze. Our poor faithful Frank fell at my feet pierced by many arrows. I recall the scene with a sickening horror. I could not see my husband anywhere, and did not know his fate, but feared and trembled. With a glance at my surroundings, my senses seemed gone for a time, but I could only live and endure.

I had but little time for thought, for the Indians quickly sprang into our wagons, tearing off covers, breaking, crushing, and smash-

Intimated: Implied.

Molested: Attacked.

Ominously: Threateningly.

In whose gloomy depths he anticipated a murderous attack: He suspected the wagon train was being led into an ambush by Native Americans hiding in a valley ahead.

Threw off their masks: Kelly is speaking metaphorically, saying that the Native Americans stopped pretending to be friendly with them.

"The Attack and Capture of Our Train," an illustration from Fanny Kelly's narrative. (© *Corbis. Reproduced by permission.*)

ing all hindrances to plunder, breaking open locks, trunks, and boxes, and distributing or destroying our goods with great rapidity, using their tomahawks to pry open boxes, which they split up in savage recklessness.

Oh, what horrible sights met my view! Pen is powerless to portray the scenes occurring around me. They filled the air with the fearful war-whoops and hideous shouts. I endeavored to keep my *fears quiet as possible, knowing that an indiscreet act on my part might result in jeopardizing our lives, though I felt certain that we two helpless women would share death by their hands; but with as much of an air of indifference as I could command, I kept still, hoping to prolong our lives, even if but a few moments. I was not allowed this quiet but a moment, when two of the most savage-looking of the party rushed up into my wagon, with tomahawks drawn in their right hands, and with their left seized me by both hands and pulled me violently to the ground, injuring my limbs very severely, almost breaking them, from the effects of which I afterward suffered a great deal. I turned to my little* **Mary,** *who, with outstretched hands, was standing in the wagon, took her in my arms and helped her to the ground. I then turned to the chief, put my hand upon his arm, and implored his protection for my fellow prisoner and our children. At first he gave me no hope, but seemed utterly indifferent to my prayers. Partly in words and partly by signs, he ordered me to remain quiet, placing his hand upon his revolver, that hung in a belt at his side, as an argument to enforce obedience....*

BEGINNING OF MY CAPTIVITY

I was led a short distance from the wagon, with Mary, and told to remain quiet, and tried to submit; but oh, what a yearning sprang up in my heart to escape, as I hoped my husband had done! But many watchful eyes were upon me, and enemies on every side, and I realized that any effort then at escape would result in failure, and probably cause the death of all the prisoners....

[Kelly was then taken to a Native American camp; one night along the way to the camp she let Mary down from her horse and told her to run, hoping Mary would be found by other pioneers in the area or by U.S. Army troops. Fanny never saw Mary again. When the Indians arrived at the camp Fanny was led into the chief's lodge.] *Great crowds of curious Indians came flocking in to stare at me. The women brought their children. Some of them, whose fair complexion astonished me, I afterward learned were the offspring of fort marriages. One fair little boy, who with his mother had just returned from Fort Laramie, came close to me. Finding the squaw could speak a few words in English, I addressed her, and was told in reply to my questions that she had been the wife of a captain there, but that his white wife arriving from the East, his Indian wife was told to return to her people; she did so, taking her child with her....*

I was just beginning to rejoice in the dawning kindness that seemed to soften their swarthy faces, when a messenger from the

Mary: Kelly's adopted daughter.

war chief arrived, accompanied by a small party of young warriors sent to conduct me to the chief's presence. I did not at first comprehend the summons, and, as every fresh announcement only awakened new fears, I dreaded to comply, yet dared not refuse. Seeing my hesitation, the senior wife allowed a little daughter of the chief's, whose name was Yellow Bird, to accompany me, and I was then conducted to several feasts, at each of which I was received with kindness and promised good will and protection. It was here that the chief himself first **condescended** to speak kindly to me, and this and the companionship of the child Yellow Bird, who seemed to approach me with a trusting grace and freedom unlike the scared shyness of Indian children generally, inspired hope.

The chief here told me that henceforth I could call Yellow Bird my own, to take the place of my little girl that had been killed. I did not at once comprehend all of his meaning, still it gave me some hope of security....

[Kelly was invited to take part in a lengthy ceremony or meeting of the chief and other important members of the group. There was a celebration afterward that Kelly also attended.] *That night was spent in dancing. Wild and furious all seemed to me. I was led into the center of the circle, and assigned the painful duty of holding above my head human scalps fastened to a little pole. The dance was kept up until near morning, when all repaired to their respective lodges. The three kind sisters of the chief were there to convey me to mine.*

PREPARATIONS FOR BATTLE

The next morning the whole village was in motion. The warriors were going to battle against a white enemy, they said, and old men, women, and children were sent out in another direction to a place of safety, as designated by the chief. Everything was soon moving. With the rapidity of custom the tent poles were lowered and the tents rolled up. The cooking utensils were put together, and laid on crossbeams connecting the lower ends of the poles as they trail the ground from the horses' sides, to which they are attached. Dogs, too, are made useful in this exodus, and started off with smaller burdens dragging after them, in the same manner that horses are packed.

The whole village was in commotion, children screaming or laughing; dogs barking or growling under their heavy burdens; squaws running hither and thither, pulling down tepee poles, packing up everything, and leading horses and dogs with huge bur-

Condescended: Acted kindly to her even though he was considered superior to her.

dens.... The number and utility of these faithful dogs is sometimes astonishing, as they count hundreds, each bearing a portion of the general household goods....

This train was immensely large, nearly the whole Sioux nation having concentrated there for the purposes of war. The chief's sisters brought me a horse saddled, told me to mount, and accompany the already moving column that seemed to be spreading over the hills to the northward. We toiled on all day. Late in the afternoon we arrived at the ground of encampment, and rested for further orders from the warriors, who had gone to battle and would join us there.

I had no means of informing myself at that time with whom the war was raging, but afterward learned that General Sully's army was pursuing the Sioux, and that the engagement was with his men. In three days the Indians returned to camp, and entered on a course of feasting and rejoicing that caused me to believe that they had suffered very little loss in the affray. They passed their day of rest in this sort of entertainment; and here I first saw the scalp dance, which ceremonial did not increase my respect or confidence in the tender mercies of my captors. This performance is only gone through at night and by the light of torches, consequently its terrible characteristics are heightened by the fantastic gleams of the lighted brands. The women, too, took part in the dance, and I was forced to mingle in the fearful festivity, painted and dressed for the occasion, and holding a staff from the top of which hung several scalps....

The Indians felt that the **proximity** of the troops and their inroads through their best hunting-grounds would prove disastrous to them and their future hopes of prosperity, and soon again they were making preparations for battle; and again, on the 8th of August the warriors set forth on the warpath, and this time the action seemed to draw ominously near our encampment....

There seemed to be great commotion and great anxiety in the movements of the Indians, and presently I could hear the sound of battle; and the echoes, that came back to me from the **reports** of the guns in the distant hills, warned me of the near approach of my own people, and my heart became a prey to wildly conflicting emotions, as they hurried on in great desperation, and even forbid me turning my head and looking in the direction of battle.... **Panting** for rescue, yet fearing for its **accomplishment**, I passed the day. The smoke of action now rose over the hills beyond. The Indians now realized their danger, and hurried on in great **consternation.**

Proximity: Nearness.

Reports: Gunshots.

Panting: Eager.

Accomplishment: Being carried out or completed.

Consternation: Alarm.

*General Sully's soldiers appeared in close proximity, and I could see them charging on the Indians, who, according to their habits of warfare, **skulked** behind trees, sending their bullets and arrows vigorously forward into the enemy's ranks. I was kept in advance of the moving column of women and children, who were hurrying on, crying and famishing for water, trying to keep out of the line of firing....*

MOURNING FOR THE SLAIN

*As soon as we were safe, and General Sully pursued us no longer, the warriors returned home, and a scene of terrible mourning over the killed ensued among the women. Their cries are terribly wild and distressing on such occasions; and the near relations of the deceased indulge in frantic expressions of grief that cannot be described. Sometimes the practice of cutting the flesh is carried to a horrible and **barbarous** extent. They inflict gashes on their bodies and limbs an inch in length. Some cut off their hair, blacken their faces, and march through the village in procession, torturing their bodies to add vigor to their lamentations.*

*Hunger followed on the track of grief; all their food was gone, and there was no game in that portion of the country. In our flight they scattered everything, and the country through which we passed for the following two weeks did not yield enough to **arrest** starvation. The Indians were terribly enraged, and threatened me with death almost hourly, and in every form.*

I had so hoped for liberty when my friends were near; but alas! all my fond hopes were blasted. The Indians told me that the army was going in another direction.

They seemed to have sustained a greater loss than I had been made aware of, which made them feel very revengeful toward me. The next morning I could see that something unusual was about to happen....

Soon they sent an Indian to me, who asked me if I was ready to die—to be burned at the stake. I told him whenever Wakon-Tonka (The Great Spirit) was ready, he would call for me, and then I would be ready and willing to go. He said that he had been sent from the council to warn me, that it had become necessary to put me to death, on account of my white brothers killing so many of their young men recently. He repeated that they were not cruel for the pleasure of being so; necessity is their first law, and he and the wise chiefs, faithful to their hatred for the white race, were in haste to satisfy their thirst for vengeance; and further, that the interest of their nation required it.

Skulked: Lay in wait.

Barbarous: Barbaric; uncivilized.

Arrest: Put an end to.

"Jumping Bear points to the moon and swears to Fanny Kelly that he will deliver her letter to the white chief at Fort Sully," an illustration from Kelly's narrative. When Kelly's message was received at Fort Sully, General Sully demanded her return, and after some negotiations, the Sioux handed Kelly over to U.S. troops.
(© Corbis. Reproduced by permission.)

Assiniboines: Native American tribe from northeast Montana and parts of Canada.

As soon as the chiefs were assembled around the council fire, the pipe-carrier entered the circle, holding in his hand the pipe already lighted. Bowing to the four cardinal points, he uttered a short prayer, or invocation, and then presented the pipe to the old chief, Ottowa, but retained the bowl in his hand. When all the chiefs and men had smoked, one after the other, the pipe-bearer emptied the ashes into the fire, saying, "Chiefs of the great Dakota nation, Wakon-Tonka gives you wisdom, so that whatever be your determination, it may be comfortable to justice." Then, after bowing respectfully, he retired.

....At length one of the most aged of the chiefs, whose body was furrowed with the scars of innumerable wounds and who enjoyed among his people a reputation for great wisdom, arose.

Said he, "The pale faces, our eternal persecutors, pursue and harass us without intermission, forcing us to abandon to them, one by one, our best hunting grounds, and we are compelled to seek a refuge in the depths of these Bad Lands, like timid deer. Many of them even dare to come into prairies which belong to us, to trap beaver, and hunt elk and buffalo, which are our property. These faithless creatures, the outcasts of their own people, rob and kill us when they can. Is it just that we should suffer these wrongs without complaining? Shall we allow ourselves to be slaughtered like timid **Assiniboines**, without seeking to avenge ourselves? Does not the law of the Dakotas say, Justice to our own nation, and death to all pale faces? Let my brothers say if that is just," pointing to the stake that was being prepared for me.

"Vengeance is allowable," sententiously remarked Mahpeah (the Sky).

Another chief, Ottawa, arose and said, "It is the undoubted right of the weak and oppressed; and yet it ought to be proportioned to the injury received. Then why should we put this young, innocent woman to death? Has she not always been kind to us, smiled upon *us, and sang for us? Do not all our children love her as a tender sister? Why, then, should we put her to so cruel a death for the crimes of others, if they are of her nation? Why should we punish the innocent for the guilty?*

I looked to Heaven for mercy and protection, offering up those earnest prayers that are never offered in vain; and oh! how thankful I was when I knew their decision was to spare my life.... [Stiles, pp. 55, 56, 57, 58-60, 63, 65, 66, 75, 76, 77]

What happened next . . .

Shortly after the Oglala decided that Kelly should live, they handed her over to the Hunkpapa people with whom she quickly gained respect and the Indian name "Real Woman." While Kelly was living with the Hunkpapa, General Sully learned of her captivity and demanded her release. The Hunkpapa perceived Kelly to be unhappy in captivity and arranged for chiefs of the Blackfoot tribe to deliver her to Fort Sully. Five months after her capture, Kelly was free.

Kelly had witnessed the early part of the war with the Plains Indians. Provoked by the opening of the Bozeman Trail, which cut through the Indians' hunting ground, and started by General Alfred Sully's attack on the Sioux in 1863, the war with the Plains Indians would last for another twelve years.

Soon after gaining her freedom, Kelly rejoined her husband, Josiah, and returned to Ellsworth, Kansas, where they opened a hotel. They had three children before Josiah died of cholera in 1867. In 1870, Kelly moved to Washington, where she married again in 1880. Her book was published in 1872. She died in 1904.

Did you know . . .

• Of the 250,000 settlers who traveled the trails in the 1840s and 1850s, it is estimated that only 362 died at the hands of Indians.

- Though accurate death rates are not available, it is estimated that at least 20,000 of the 350,000 people who ventured forth on the Oregon-California Trail died on the way from various causes including illness, accidents, and injuries. That means that 1 in 17 of the pioneers did not reach his or her destination and that there was an average of ten graves per mile of the trail.

Consider the following . . .

- Did the Indians treat Fanny Kelly fairly?

- How were the perspectives of the Native Americans different from the whites' perspective?

For More Information

Kelly, Fanny. *Narrative of My Captivity Among the Sioux Indians*. Hartford, CT: Mutual Publishing Company, 1872.

Peters, Arthur King. *Seven Trails West*. New York: Abbeville Press, 1996.

Place, Marian T. *Westward on the Oregon Trail*. New York: American Heritage, 1962.

Roscoe, Gerald, and David Larkin. *Westward: The Epic Crossing of the American Landscape*. New York: The Monacelli Press, 1995.

Stiles, T. J., ed. *In Their Own Words: Warriors and Pioneers*. New York: Berkley Publishing Group, 1996.

Elise Amalie Wærenskjold

An excerpt from "A Lady Grows Old in Texas"
from Land of Their Choice: The Immigrants Write Home
Edited by Theodore C. Blegen
Published in 1955

Although many ventured into the West for one reason or another, those who settled and began to "civilize" the frontier truly tamed the continent. Asserts Roger Barr in *The American Frontier*, "As in earlier American frontiers, it was farmers, the last in the line of frontiersmen, who truly conquered the West. Dissatisfied by the conditions at home, lured by the promise of free land, and aided by new technology, they came by the thousands to the Great Plains beginning in the 1850s." Farmers had to learn new methods of farming; technological advances, such as John Deere's 1837 invention of the steel plow, made their work easier. Another invention, barbed wire (1874), allowed farmers to fence off their land to keep the growing numbers of livestock from trampling their crops.

Farming in the West was encouraged by the Homestead Act of 1862, which gave settlers up to 160 acres of free land if they settled on it and made improvements over a five-year span. The Timber Culture Act of 1873 granted an additional 160 acres to farmers who agreed to plant a portion of their land with trees. These acts drew many thousands of set-

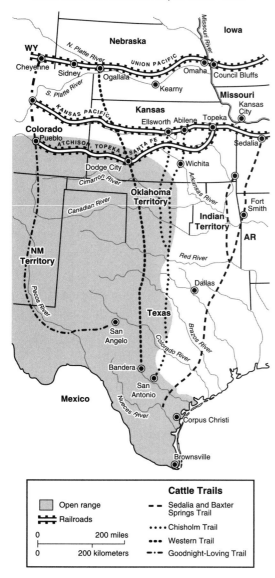

THE CATTLE KINGDOM, c. 1866–1887

Cattle Trails

Open range

Railroads

0   200 miles

0   200 kilometers

– – Sedalia and Baxter Springs Trail

•••• Chisholm Trail

•–• Western Trail

–•– Goodnight-Loving Trail

A map of cattle country in Texas shows the main trails used to get cattle from the open range to the railheads.
(Reproduced by permission of The Gale Group.)

tlers from the East and even from Europe into the wide-open spaces of the American West. Farming on the Plains was difficult, but by 1890 farmers had claimed more than 430 million acres of land—more land, writes Barr, "than all of their ancestors had claimed throughout American history." The biggest single land claim, known as the Oklahoma land rush, occurred on April 22, 1889, when in a single day some fifty thousand settlers claimed lands that were just opened to settlement.

Cattle ranching vied with farming as the dominant industry in the Plains, for ranchers found that they could graze vast herds of cattle on the open grasslands that had only years before been roamed by buffalo and American Indians. The construction of railroads meant that ranchers could get their cattle to slaughterhouses in the eastern states. As soon as Joseph McCoy established a railhead in Abilene, Kansas, in 1867, writes Barr, "the cattle industry was born. Between 1868 and 1871, nearly 1,500,000 cattle were driven from the Texas range north to Abilene and shipped east." The cattle boom did not last long, for increased competition among ranchers and between ranchers and farmers soon made cattle ranching less profitable.

As a settler in Texas, Elise Amalie Wærenskjold endured the hardships of pioneer life and rejoiced at the opportunities of life on the frontier. Her letters to friends and family in Norway paint a vivid picture of what life was like in Texas in the mid-1800s, when people were forging a new way of life and communities were just getting started.

Things to remember while reading the excerpt from "A Lady Grows Old in Texas":

- The following excerpt is from a chapter of *Land of Their Own* called "A Lady Grows Old in Texas." The chapter reprints a series of translated letters that Elise Amalie Wærenskjold wrote to family living in Norway. The excerpt includes letters written between 1852 and 1870.

- A mass migration from Norway to the United States began in the 1820s when the *Restoration* traveled to the United States.

- Before emigrating, Elise Amalie Wærenskjold edited the *Norway and America* magazine from 1846 to 1847.

- Wærenskjold settled in Texas in 1847.

Excerpt from "A Lady Grows Old in Texas"

Most people are Methodists

December 27, 1852. I should like to have various kinds of fruit stones and seeds sent over here to be planted. We have many good things in Norway that are lacking here; but it is not the fault of the land, for we could hardly expect to harvest what we have never sowed. Such a simple thing as ale I haven't been able to get up till now because of a lack of yeast; but since the last emigrants brought yeast with them, almost all of us have now brewed ale for Christmas, and it has never tasted so good to me as now. I haven't tasted a glass of wine in four years. If I could get fruit, I would certainly have wine and [fruit] juice too. It is certain that when one is suffering from fever thirst, one misses refreshing drinks, especially since cold water is looked upon as harmful....

*Last summer there was quite an unusual amount of sickness here. We were spared for a long time, but then Wilhelm got the fever, and since there was no **quinine** in the store or anywhere else in the neighborhood, he couldn't break it. Anne, the maid, had to do part of his work, so she got it too, and then when I was left alone, Otto and I got it also. After a few days had passed, however, we were lucky enough to get some quinine. It is wonderful how quickly*

Quinine: A drug used to treat malaria.

Women Homesteaders

Most women traveled westward with their families or followed their husbands, who had struck out ahead of them. Yet not every woman followed a man. The American West offered women more independence and more opportunities than were available to them in the East. The Homestead Act was open to women as well as men. While fewer women traveled west than men did, several hardy souls took advantage of the opportunities available to them. A single woman could claim her own land if she could dig a well, build a house, and plow at least twenty acres to grow crops for five consecutive years. The first applicant to file a claim for land in Gage County, Nebraska, was a woman. Under three different land acts, four sisters secured almost two thousand acres of their own in Nebraska. Lizzie Chrisman filed the sisters' first claim in Custer County in 1887. The next year Lutie Chrisman filed another. Jennie Ruth and Hattie filed in 1892 when they came of age.

In the West, women could vote, hold public office, and serve on juries before women in the East. The Wyoming Territory granted women these rights in 1869. A year later in South Pass City, Wyoming, Esther Morris became the first female justice of the peace in the United States.

and surely one can break the fever with quinine. In the shops it was soon sold out to the doctors, and so the Norwegians got little. The result was that nine people died, most of whom surely could have been saved if they had had this remedy....

My husband had sent out an invitation to people to pledge an annual contribution for a Norwegian Lutheran minister, and in a half-day something over $70 was pledged by only half of the settlement's inhabitants, so it seemed likely that the matter would progress satisfactorily, but these many deaths have so depressed most of the people that the matter has come to a complete standstill for a while. We are now expecting Gjestvang and ten or eleven families from Hedemark. If they should settle down here it is possible that something may come of it. There are all kinds of religions here, as you no doubt know, but most people are Methodists. They hold various kinds of meetings, of which their camp meetings deserve to be noted. They are held preferably in the fall and last for several days, when a number of ministers preach day and night, baptize adults as well as children, perform marriage ceremonies, and administer the holy sacraments. People assemble then from many miles around; some live in wagons, some in tents, and some in lodging houses that have been erected at the place where the camp meetings are held. There is no church there, but an open shed serves as such; into it some benches are brought which are perfectly in keeping with the building. People bring food with them in abundance and are most hospitable.

There is nothing unusual about their sermons or hymns, or their baptism or the sacrament of the Lord's Supper, which are administered about as with us; but in the after-

Cowboys herding cattle on horseback. Cattle ranching boomed in North America between 1868 and 1871. *(© Horace Bristol/Corbis. Reproduced by permission.)*

noon all the men go to one side and all the women to another for private prayer. There they alternate song and prayer, which one of the women says in a very loud voice. During these long and vehement prayers, they kneel at first, each in his own place, but gradually as they become more and more excited soon one, then another, will begin to scream and cry out, clap his hands, strike those standing nearest him, throw himself down on the ground, and on the whole act as one who is crazy or possessed by a devil. The others *press around the inspired ones and continue singing and praying. The same noise takes place in the evening after the sermon and after the minister's most zealous incitement. It seems as if they believed they could not get into heaven unless they took it by storm. There was no **edification** for me in this. Several of the Norwegians have abandoned their Lutheran faith. Andreas and Mads Vincentz have been baptized and have gone over to the Carmelites, Marie Grøgaard to the Episcopalians, Mother Staack to the Methodists, and her brother to the Baptists. I wish very much that we could soon get a good Lutheran minister.*

The Fourth of July was celebrated by the Norwegians in the settlement, one and all, and each person contributed either food or money. Wærenskjold gave half an ox and fifty cents. They gathered in the morning and continued celebrating a good twenty-four hours. They ate and drank lustily. A very few danced a little. Wærenskjold made a speech. As for me, I would rather have had nothing to do with the whole riotous affair, but such things are just what Wilhelm likes, especially when he can be at the head of the whole affair. Of what we are accustomed to call amusements I have few or none. My greatest joy is Otto, and then I also have a great satisfaction in seeing our various domestic animals thrive and multiply. Now you must soon send me a letter again. To get letters from Norway is one of my greatest pleasures, but with the exception of Gjestvang almost no one writes except when emigrants are coming; then we usually get a lot of newspapers too and a few books, which we read over and over until the next year when emigrants come again.

Cattle-breeding is our principal livelihood

January 6, 1857. You no doubt know that cattle-breeding is our principal means of livelihood. We do not plan to sell the cows, but only the steers until we can acquire about two hundred calves a year. This spring we can expect about seventy. Cows and calves are now $15 each, and a three-year old untrained ox costs the same. When it is trained for work, it costs much more. We have four mares, a horse, and a mule. The latter is unusually gentle and sure-footed. It is the children's and my riding horse. Niels sits in my lap and Otto behind me. We do have a four-wheeled carriage but very seldom use it.

We have sixty-two sheep, and this month and next we are expecting many lambs. I help clip the sheep, but I am not very good at it. I can clip only one sheep while the others clip two. Wilhelm can keep up with anyone. He is very quick at all kinds of work. I do not

Edification: Intellectual, spiritual, or moral improvement.

A pioneer woman gathers "buffalo chips" to fuel the fire.
(© Bettmann/Corbis. Reproduced by permission.)

know how many pigs we have, not because we have so many, but because pigs are so difficult to keep track of.

Since I hate liquor, it is a great joy to me that Wilhelm never tastes it. He has organized a temperance society in our settlement, and since that time the community has become so respectable and sober that it is a real pleasure. All of us Norwegians, about eighty persons counting young and old, can come together for a social gathering without having **strong drink**, but we do have coffee, ale, milk, and **mead**, and food in abundance at our gatherings.

In the older Norwegian settlement there is a disgusting amount of drinking, among both the Norwegians and the Americans. A young Norwegian boy shot himself as a result of his addiction to drink, and recently an American was stabbed to death by another American, likewise because of drunkenness. Drinking, quarreling, and fighting are common there. Yes, liquor destroys both body and soul.

Most difficult to get hired help

Strong drink: Liquor; alcoholic drinks made by distillation; the author differentiates these from fermented alcoholic drinks such as beer, ale, and mead.

Mead: An alcoholic beverage made of fermented honey and water.

June 9, 1869. You talk about peasants living as cottagers. Such conditions are unknown here where everybody, even the poorest Negro, is too independent to submit to such a state of dependence on others. It is even most difficult to get hired help for months at a time, since they who do not possess land of their own prefer to rent land. He who owns the land then has to supply buildings, working animals, tools, seeds; he also has to feed the animals and pay for the maintenance of the fences. For all this you get half the harvest. It is mainly freed Negro slaves who take land in this way. Many of them are lazy, cruel to the animals, or so careless with the tools that they cause you a lot of trouble. This year we have twenty-two acres of cotton, fourteen of corn, six of rye, and seven of wheat. The rye and the wheat have already been harvested. Plums and blackberries have been ripe for several weeks—is that not early? Otto has eight acres of cotton, and all he can harvest on that piece of land he is to have for himself. Niels's main job is to look after the cattle and the hogs. We have somewhere between two and three hundred hogs, and last winter we sold about $300 worth of hogs and bacon. We got $.05 a pound for live hogs and $.11 a pound for smoked bacon. We have also sold some oxen and ninety-three **wethers.** *Prices were $10 for a four-year-old ox and $1.50 for a wether. It used to be $3. In addition to this I sold turkeys last fall and got $25 for them, all told. Now that I have paid off my debts we are able to manage fairly well. I do not know as yet how things will work out with regard to the sum of money that is owing to me. It is an annoying affair.*

You can pick cotton from August to January

[This letter was most likely written in 1870, according to the editors of *Land of Their Choice.*] *Anyone who has little or nothing to start out with had best build a log house, since he can improve that as he goes along. But anyone who can afford to buy boards right away is wiser to build a frame or box house at once. I have a fairly large house (box) on the same estate where a Norwegian-German family is living now. This family has rented one of my fields. One of my chimneys is built of stone and the other of brick, and I have a kitchen range and a stove. For these stoves we only use iron pipes that go up through the roof.*

Most people also have a smokehouse for the smoking of meat and bacon, a granary, and a stable for the horses, all built of oak logs. The stable is then only for the horses you use every day or for the horses of guests who may stay overnight. Many horses are never kept in the stable and never fed; they find their own food all the year

Wethers: Castrated rams.

Sod House and Dugout

In the eastern territory, pioneers built wood-frame houses or log cabins. The Plains offered few trees for such luxuries, however. The first homesteaders who moved onto the Plains settled near rivers where trees grew, but latecomers had to use grass and mud to build their homes. Some dug caves into the side of hills and made sod bricks to enclose the opening. Homesteaders used oxen- or horse-drawn plows to cut the sod bricks, which were three-foot-long, four-inch-thick, two-and-a-half-foot-wide strips of soil and grass that weighed about fifty pounds each. These dugouts were usually temporary living arrangements for families. "A dugout with one window, a door, a stove, and several beds of straw cost less than $3 to build," according to A. S. Gintzler in *Rough and Ready Homesteaders.*

More permanent homes were also built of sod bricks. A large sod home would take five men three weeks and ten acres of sod to build, according to Dorothy Hinshaw Patent in *Homesteading: Settling America's Heartland.* Homesteaders stacked up sod brick walls and filled any gaps with mud. A flat roof was made of sod supported by wooden poles that lay across the top of the walls. Windows and floors were covered with buffalo hides.

These cheap, earthen homes remained warm in the winter and cool in the summer; they withstood strong winds and didn't burn in prairie fires. However, they were not resistant to heavy rains. Although the Plains were dry for most of the year, rains would sometimes soak roofs, making waterfalls pour in from the ceiling. Water-laden homes would sometimes collapse and crush families.

More frequent problems came from pests. Sod homes and dugouts created cozy living quarters for snakes, mice, flies, and grasshoppers. Without glass windows, wooden floors, or doors, homesteaders could do nothing but accept life with their animal, reptile, and insect neighbors.

round. I also have a kind of house for my sheep (completely open to the south and east) and a chicken coop, but [these] *are an extravagance in Texas....*

The plowing preparatory to the planting of corn and cotton can be done at any time during the winter; they are planted in rows with about three feet between the rows. The corn is planted from the end of February to May, though the beginning of March is the best time. The cotton is planted from April 10 to May 10. After both of these plants have come up, a furrow is plowed at either side of the plants, and then the weeds and some of the cotton plants are hoed away.

A frontier family in front of their sod house in Nicodemus, Kansas. Sod houses were much more practical to build in parts of the frontier where timber wasn't readily available.
(Denver Public Library-Wester Collection. Reproduced by permission.)

Fodder: Food.

After this the whole middle area of the field is plowed up once more and is gone over again with the hoe, and the field is then ready to be harvested. At the second hoeing all the corn and cotton which is in excess of the desired quantity is removed. The corn plant grows up with a very tall stem with broad leaves and usually two ears. In August the leaves are picked off, dried, and used as **fodder** for the horses. During the plowing period the working horses are fed with corn and fodder (leaves of corn) and sometimes also with oats.

The cotton plant grows to be quite tall, too, but it branches out more, like a tree, and has large yellow flowers which turn red before they are shed. On the same plant you may often see both yellow and red flowers. The cotton is picked off when the ripe seed capsule opens, and the seed is then separated from the fibers of cotton in a cotton gin. You can pick cotton from August to Christmas, yes, even in January. It is easy work that pays well, from $.50 to $1 per one hundred pounds; and a person can pick from one hundred to three hundred pounds a day, depending on the skill of the picker and the quality of the cotton. You can mow as much hay as you please out on the prairie, which is *open to everybody. But the Americans do not want to take that trouble, and if you cannot mow the hay yourself, you are unable to hire anyone to do it for you....* [Blegen, pp. 323–6, 333, 338–40]

What happened next . . .

Elise Amalie Wærenskjold lived in Texas until her death in 1895 at age eighty-one. She wrote extensively throughout her life, publishing various articles in Norwegian American newspapers and magazines, including a history of the Norwegian colony in Texas in the late 1860s.

When Wærenskjold lived in Texas, she reported that its population was about one million, including twelve to fourteen hundred Norwegians. She lauded the state's excellent climate for growing crops, noting that crops "require only a quarter of the labor that one has to expend on them in the climate of my native country." Her descriptions of the natural resources and the availability of land enticed many people to emigrate from Norway to the United States. Her letters—and similar letters from other emigrants—spread the word that the United States was the land of opportunity.

Did you know . . .

- The U.S. population increased from slightly more than seventeen million in 1840 to thirty-eight million in 1860.

- The population of the western states and territories (including present-day Arizona, California, Colorado, Idaho, Montana, Nevada, New Mexico, Oregon, Washington, Wyoming, and Utah) in 1850 was 179,000 and grew to 3,134,000 by 1890.

- Controversy over the improper and unfair use of barbed-wire fencing provoked arguments over who had the right to use public lands for grazing cattle in Texas and other western states. After erecting miles of fencing around public lands, the largest cattle-raising companies tried to secure leases to graze their animals on the federal lands. By 1883, those opposed to fencing the open range lands had begun cutting barbed fences in a protest that became known as the Fence Cutter's War.

• Legislation regulating how and where fences could be erected on or near public lands curbed the fence cutting in Texas in 1884, and similar legislation soon eased tensions in other states. The impact of the laws was impressive; they ended the Fence Cutter's War less than a year after it started and reinforced the patterns of ranching introduced by barbed-wire fencing. Nevertheless, the conflict was so divisive and devastating that fence cutting remained a felony in Texas at the end of the twentieth century.

• When President Franklin Delano Roosevelt (1882–1945) withdrew the remainder of the public land from private settlement in 1935, some 285 million acres had been homesteaded.

Consider the following . . .

• What did Wærenskjold have to give up to move to America?

• Did Wærenskjold think the hardships of homesteading were worth the trouble?

• What did Wærenskjold think of the various religions she witnessed in Texas?

• What was Wærenskjold's opinion of other homesteaders?

For More Information

Barr, Roger. *The American Frontier.* San Diego: Lucent Books, 1996.

Blegen, Theodore C., ed. *Land of Their Choice: The Immigrants Write Home.* Minneapolis: University of Minnesota Press, 1955.

Gates, Paul W. *Fifty Million Acres Conflicts over Kansas Land Policy, 1854–1890.* Ithaca, NY: Cornell University Press, 1954.

Gintzler, A. S. *Rough and Ready Homesteaders.* New York: John Muir Publications, 1994.

Hibbard, Benjamin H. *A History of the Public Land Policies.* New York: Macmillan Company, 1924.

Ottoson, Howard W. *Land Use Policy and Problems in the United States.* Lincoln: University of Nebraska Press, 1963.

Patent, Dorothy Hinshaw. *Homesteading: Settling America's Heartland.* New York: Walker and Company, 1998.

Robbins, Roy M. *Our Landed Heritage The Public Domain, 1776–1936.* Princeton, NJ: Princeton University Press, 1942.

Settling the West. Edited by the editors of Time-Life Books. Alexandria, VA: Time-Life Books, 1996.

The Cowboy Life

4

When most people think of the American West, they think of cowboys. Historian Walter P. Webb described this heroic image in *The Great Plains*:

> There is something romantic about him. He lives on horseback as do the Bedouins [members of nomadic desert tribes in Africa]; he fights on horseback, as did the knights of chivalry; he goes armed with a strange new weapon which he uses ambidextrously and precisely; he swears like a trooper, drinks like a fish, wears clothes like an actor, and fights like a devil. He is gracious to ladies, reserved toward strangers, generous to his friends and brutal to his enemies. He is a cowboy, a typical Westerner.

This stereotype of the cowboy is the West's most recognizable contribution to our national mythology. But what was the cowboy's life really like? And what about the women who also lived in the cattle country of the West? This chapter presents the tales of two real cowboys and a cowgirl.

Cattle country

In reality the era of the cowboy only lasted a few decades, from just after the Civil War (1861–65) to about 1890. Before the Civil War, many Texans owned cattle but few got rich from it. After the Civil War, however, rising beef prices in the northeastern regions of the country created a new demand for cheap meat and railroads that were built during the Civil War made it possible to ship beef from the Midwest. Suddenly cattle that were worth four dollars in Texas were worth forty dollars if they could be brought to northern markets. The only problem facing cattle ranchers was how to get the cattle to market. Their answer was the cattle drive, in which cowboys drove thousands of cattle northward to railheads (the end point of a railway line) in Kansas. From there the cattle could be shipped east and much money could be made. This is how the cattle boom began.

For two decades, cowboys drove cattle from ranches in Texas, Wyoming, Montana, Colorado, New Mexico, Idaho, and other western states to a variety of railheads. The cattle were then shipped east for slaughter and sale in eastern cities. All across the western regions, ranchers hired tough young men to ride out onto the range (open, unfenced grasslands) and bring all the cattle marked with the rancher's brand back to the ranch to ready them for the drive.

Cattle drives were lead by a trail boss, whose job it was to hire the other cowboys for the drive, plan the route (making sure they would have sources for water), locate campsites, and lead his cattle north. One cowboy was hired for every 250 to 300 head of cattle; this meant that a typical herd of 2,000 to 3,000 longhorns would require eight to twelve cowboys. The cowboys looked after the animals on the trail, kept them moving along the trail, and tried to prevent them from breaking into a stampede. The cook, usually an older cowboy, often called the Old Lady, was one of the most important members of a cattle drive crew. A good cook kept the cowboys happy with good "grub," tended wounds, and took care of other domestic duties. He was the second-highest-paid member of the crew behind the trail boss. The lowest-paid member of the crew was the wrangler, a younger cowboy who looked after the herd of workhorses.

A herd on trail moved about ten miles a day. Leading the way was the trail boss and the Old Lady with his wagon. To the side of the herd rode most of the cowboys, who kept wandering cattle from separating from the rest of the herd. Bringing up the rear, and eating the dust of several thousand shuffling cattle, were the drag men. Cowboys joked that the drag was where a cowboy learned to curse.

Driving a herd of cattle across prairies was hard, dangerous work, for the terrain was difficult and the cattle could get spooked and stampede at any time. The difficulties increased when the cowboys crossed lands controlled by hostile Native American tribes or patrolled by cattle rustlers (thieves who stole cattle). Despite such problems, many of the cowboys found real pleasure in the independence and camaraderie of life on the trail, not to mention the rip-roaring fun they had once they arrived in town. With pockets full of money and eager for excitement, cowboys helped create the Wild West that is celebrated in films and fiction.

After 1885 a number of factors led to the end of the cowboy era. The increased settlement of Kansas led to the closing of the major cattle towns, including Abilene and Dodge City, and expanding railroad lines meant that ranchers didn't have to drive their cattle to faraway railheads. Huge blizzards that struck the plains in 1886 and 1887 killed off cattle by the thousands in the northern plains, proving that cattle couldn't just be left to fend for themselves. Finally, farmers claimed more western land, and ranchers were forced to purchase and fence land for their cattle. Men who were once cowboys now became mere farmhands, but the legend of the cowboy lives

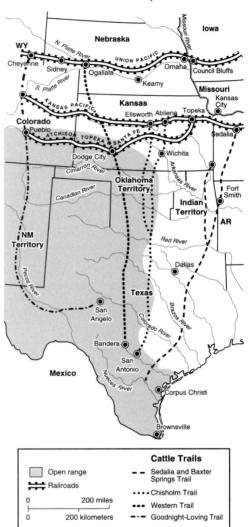

THE CATTLE KINGDOM, c. 1866–1887

Cattle Trails

Open range

Railroads

0   200 miles

0   200 kilometers

‒ ‒ Sedalia and Baxter Springs Trail

•••• Chisholm Trail

••• Western Trail

‒•‒ Goodnight-Loving Trail

Map of the cattle country in Texas shows the main trails used by cowboys.
(Reproduced by permission of The Gale Group.)

on in novels, films, and television shows that celebrate the tough and fiercely independent American cowboy.

The accounts of real cowboys and one cowgirl excerpted below provide evidence that will let you judge the accuracy of the cowboy legend. Nat Love became a cowboy at a young age and wrote about his colorful adventures as he traveled across the Great Plains. Because Love was one of a very few African Americans to record their experiences on the range, his ***The Life and Adventures of Nat Love, Better Known in the Cattle Country as "Deadwood Dick"*** has been of great interest to historians, though many have been disappointed at how little Love's race seemed to matter to him. E. C. "Teddy Blue" Abbott also became a cowboy at a young age. Although he never achieved the fame of Nat Love, his autobiography, ***We Pointed Them North: Recollections of a Cowpuncher,*** gives a detailed account of a cowboy's life. In *No Life for a Lady*, Agnes Morley Cleaveland offers her unique perspective as a woman who tended a ranch in southwestern New Mexico late in the nineteenth century.

Nat Love

Excerpt from **The Life and Adventures of Nat Love, Better Known in the Cattle Country as "Deadwood Dick"**
Originally published in 1907

The cowboy is considered the hero of the American West. A tough, straight-talking man who spent long days on the range driving cattle to market, the cowboy maintained a sense of honor and decency and was often perceived as a protector of women. Like the knights of the Middle Ages, this American cowboy is a myth—only a reflection of what people would like to think about the past. Real cowboys were more complex. Many, like Nat Love, were rowdy, fun-loving men unlikely to be pointed out as role models to anyone. And as an African American, Nat Love does not fit the cowboy stereotype portrayed in old movies. Love's story indicates that the cowboy life may have been quite different than what we usually imagine.

Love's memoirs are filled with fantastic stories of his adventures. He tells of his winning the name "Deadwood Dick" in a shooting contest that pitted him against the most famous cowboys in the West, and of his capture and later escape from a band of Indians. "Horses were shot out from under me, men killed around me, but always I escaped with a trifling wound at the worst," recalled Love. The excerpts from *The Life and Adventures of Nat Love, Better Known in the Cattle*

Nat Love.
(Courtesy of the Denver Public Library.)

Country as "Deadwood Dick" relate his cowboy training and several of his more colorful adventures.

Things to remember while reading the excerpt from *The Life and Adventures of Nat Love*:

- Nat Love was only fifteen when he left home and headed west to become a cowboy.

- Nat Love was one of several cowboys who claim to have been "Deadwood Dick," the winner of a famous shooting contest.

- Some readers have doubted the truth of Love's stories. Do you find elements of his stories that are not trustworthy? What makes them troublesome? How might you confirm their accuracy?

- Readers of Love's account have marveled that he never speaks openly about any racism he encountered.

- Historian Kenneth Wiggins Porter, quoted in Jack Weston's *The Real American Cowboy,* asserts that in Texas black cowboys "frequently enjoyed greater opportunities for a dignified life than anywhere else in the United States. They worked, ate, slept, played, and on occasion fought, side by side with their white comrades, and their ability and courage won respect, even admiration."

- Love is no humanitarian: when he talks about Indians "made good" in battle, he means they were killed. Readers have often been struck by his harsh opinions about Mexicans and Indians, especially since Love himself must have encountered racial discrimination.

Excerpt from
The Life and Adventures of Nat Love

CHAPTER VI: THE WORLD IS BEFORE ME. I JOIN THE TEXAS COWBOYS. RED RIVER DICK. MY FIRST OUTFIT. MY FIRST INDIAN FIGHT. I LEARN TO USE MY GUN.

It was on the tenth day of February, 1869, that I left the old home, near Nashville, Tennessee. I was at that time about fifteen years old, and though while young in years the hard work and farm life had made me strong and hearty, much beyond my years, and I had full confidence in myself as being able to take care of myself and making my way.

I at once struck out for Kansas of which I had heard something. And believing it was a good place in which to seek employment. It was in the west, and it was the great west I wanted to see, and so by walking and occasional lifts from farmers going my way and taking advantage of every thing that promised to assist me on my way, I eventually brought up at Dodge City, Kansas, which at that time was a typical frontier city, with a great many saloons, dance halls, and gambling houses, and very little of anything else. When I arrived the town was full of cow boys from the surrounding ranches, and from Texas and other parts of the west. As Kansas was a great cattle center and market, the wild cow boy, prancing horses of which I was very fond, and the wild life generally, all had their attractions for me, and I decided to try for a place with them. Although it seemed to me I had met with a bad outfit, at least some of them, going around among them I watched my chances to get to speak with them, as I wanted to find some one whom I thought would give me a civil answer to the questions I wanted to ask, but they all seemed too wild around town, so the next day I went out where they were in camp.

Approaching a party who were eating their breakfast, I got to speak with them. They asked me to have some breakfast with them, which invitation I gladly accepted. During the meal I got a chance to ask them many questions. They proved to be a Texas outfit, who had just come up with a herd of cattle and having delivered them they were preparing to return. There were several colored cow boys among them, and good ones too. After breakfast I asked the camp boss for a job as cow boy. He asked me if I could ride a wild horse. I said "yes sir." He said if you can I will give you a job. So he spoke to one of the colored cow boys called Bronco Jim, and told him to go out and rope old Good Eye, saddle him and put me on his back. Bronco Jim gave me a few pointers and told me to look out for the horse was especially bad on pitching. I told Jim I was a good rider and not afraid of him. I thought I had rode pitching horses before, but from the time I mounted old Good Eye I knew I had not learned what pitching was. This proved the worst horse to ride I had ever mounted in my life, but I stayed with him and the cow boys were the most surprised outfit you ever saw, as they had taken me for a **tenderfoot**, pure and simple. After the horse got tired and I dismounted the boss said he would give me a job and pay me $30.00 per month and more later on. He asked what my name was and I answered Nat Love, he said to the boys we will call him Red River Dick. I went by this name for a long time.

The boss took me to the city and got my outfit, which consisted of a new saddle, bridle and spurs, chaps, a pair of blankets and a fine 45 Colt revolver. Now that the business which brought them to Dodge City was concluded, preparations were made to start out for the Pan Handle country in Texas to the home ranch. The outfit of which I was now a member was called the Duval outfit, and their brand was known as the Pig Pen brand. I worked with this outfit for over three years. On this trip there were only about fifteen of us riders, all excepting myself were hardy, experienced men, always ready for anything that might turn up, but they were as jolly a set of fellows as [one] could find in a long journey. There now being nothing to keep us longer in Dodge City, we prepared for the return journey, and left the next day over the old Dodge and Sun City lonesome trail, on a journey which was to prove the most eventful of my life up to now.

A few miles out we encountered some of the hardest hail storms I ever saw, causing discomfort to man and beast, but I had no notion of getting discouraged but I resolved to be always ready for any call that might be made on me, of whatever nature it might be, and those with whom I have lived and worked will tell you I have kept that resolve. Not far from Dodge City on our way home we encountered a band of the old Victoria tribe of Indians and had a sharp fight.

These Indians were nearly always [harassing] travelers and traders and the stock men of that part of the country, and were very troublesome. In this band we encountered there were about a hundred painted **bucks** all **well mounted**. When we saw the Indians they

Tenderfoot: Someone not tough enough for life on the range.

Bucks: Slang for Indian men.

Well mounted: They had good horses.

Nat Love

The youngest of three children, Nat Love was born in a slave cabin in Davidson County, Tennessee, in 1854. His father, Sampson, was foreman of field hands on the Robert Love plantation, and his mother worked in the kitchen. Although formal education was against the law for slaves, his father taught him to read and write. After the Civil War, Sampson Love rented twenty acres and struggled to make a living as a sharecropper. He died in 1868, leaving his two sons, Nat and Jordan, to support the family.

To supplement his income from sharecropping (a system in which a poor farmer gives up a portion of his crops in exchange for the use of land), Nat Love took a variety of odd jobs, one of which—breaking colts for a neighbor—helped to prepare him for life on the range. Yet the limited opportunities for an African American youth in post–Civil War Tennessee frustrated the restless young man. When an uncle returned to the family farm, Love took the opportunity to leave. On February 10, 1869, the fifteen-year-old set off on foot for Kansas and the Wild West, in search of better opportunities and adventure.

Soon after he arrived in Dodge City, Kansas—known as the "cowboy capi-tal" of the West—Love landed a job as a cowpuncher (a slang term for cowboy) with the Sam Duval outfit, based at a ranch on the Palo Duro River in northern Texas. According to Love's memoirs, he was one of a number of black cowboys in the company. He won the confidence and admiration of his peers by breaking the wildest bronco in the outfit. During his three years with the Duval outfit, he participated in dozens of cattle drives from Texas to Kansas and beyond. In the process, he learned to handle a gun, and before long he had become a sharpshooter. By the 1870s Love's skills as a cowboy landed him the position of "chief brand reader" for the prosperous Pete Gallinger Company, a position that left him wholly responsible for the identification and care of the company's livestock during round-ups on the open range.

By the end of the 1880s, railroads were crossing the western ranges and the plains were crowded with the covered wagons of pioneers heading for their new homesteads. The cowboy way of life was rapidly fading. In 1890 Love left the range and applied for a job as a Pullman porter on the new cross-country trains. Love died in Los Angeles, California, in 1921.

were coming after us yelling like demons. As we were not expecting Indians at this particular time, we were taken somewhat by surprise.

We only had fifteen men in our outfit, but nothing daunted we stood our ground and fought the Indians to a stand. One of the boys was shot off his horse and killed near me. The Indians got his horse, bridle and saddle. During this fight we lost all but six of our horses, our entire packing outfit and our extra saddle horses, which the Indians stampeded, then rounded them up after the fight and drove them off. And as we only had six horses left us, we were unable to follow them, although we had the satisfaction of knowing we had **made several good Indians** out of bad ones.

This was my first Indian fight and likewise the first Indians I had ever seen. When I saw them coming after us and heard their blood curdling yell, I lost all courage and thought my time had come to die. I was too badly scared to run, some of the boys told me to use my gun and shoot for all I was worth. Now I had just got my outfit and had never shot off a gun in my life, but their words brought me back to earth and seeing they were all using their guns in a way that showed they were used to it, I **unlimbered my artillery** and after the first shot I lost all fear and fought like a veteran.

We soon **routed** the Indians and they left, taking with them nearly all we had, and we were powerless to pursue them. We were compelled to finish our journey home almost on foot, as there were only six horses left to fourteen of us. Our friend and companion who was shot in the fight, we buried on the plains, wrapped in his blanket with stones piled over his grave. After this engagement with the Indians I seemed to lose all sense as to what fear was and thereafter during my whole life on the range I never experienced the least feeling of fear, no matter how trying the ordeal or how desperate my position....

....[It was] absolutely necessary for a cowboy to understand his gun and know **how to place its contents** where it would do the most good, therefore I in common with my other companions never lost an opportunity to practice with my 45 Colts and the opportunities were not lacking by any means and so in time I became fairly **proficient** and able in most cases to hit a barn door providing the door was not too far away, and was steadily improving in this as I was in experience and knowledge of the other branches of the business which I had chosen as my life's work and which I had begun to like so well, because while the life was hard and in some ways **exacting**, yet it was free and wild and contained the elements of danger which my nature craved and which began to manifest itself when I was a **pugnacious** youngster on the old plantation in our rock battles and the breaking of the wild horses. I gloried in the danger, and the wild and free life of the plains, the new country I was continually traversing, and the many new scenes and incidents continually arising in the life of a rough rider....

Made several good Indians: Cowboys said they made an Indian good by killing him, so this is Love's way of saying they killed several Indians.

Unlimbered my artillery: Opened fire.

Routed: Drove out.

How to place its contents: Where to aim the bullets.

Proficient: Skilled.

Exacting: Demanding, difficult.

Pugnacious: Combative or belligerent.

EN ROUTE TO WYOMING. THE INDIANS DEMAND TOLL. THE FIGHT. A BUFFALO STAMPEDE. TRAGIC DEATH OF CAL. SURCEY. AN EVENTFUL TRIP.

After getting the cattle together down on the Rio Grande and both man and beast had got somewhat rested up, we started the herd north. They were to be delivered to a man by the name of Mitchell, whose ranch was located along the Powder river, up in

Dodge City, Kansas, in the 1880s.

(Corbis-Bettmann. Reproduced by permission.)

The Cowboy Life: Nat Love | 155

northern Wyoming. It was a long distance to drive cattle from Old Mexico to northern Wyoming, but to us it was nothing extraordinary as we were often called on to make even greater distances, as the railroads were not so common then as now, and transportation by rail was very little resorted to and except when beef cattle were sent to the far east, they were always transported on the hoof overland. Our route lay through southern Texas, Indian Territory, Kansas and Nebraska, to the Shoshone mountains in northern Wyoming. We had on this trip five hundred head of mostly four year old longhorn steers. We did not have much trouble with them until we struck Indian Territory. On nearing the first Indian reservation, we were stopped by a large body of Indian bucks who said we could not pass through their country unless we gave them a steer for the privilege. Now as we were following the regular Government trail which was a free public highway, it did not strike us as justifiable to pay our way, accordingly our boss flatly refused to give the Indians a steer, remarking that we needed all the cattle we had and proposed to keep them, but he would not mind giving them something much warmer if they interfered with us. This ultimatum of our boss had the effect of starting trouble right there. We went into camp at the edge of the Indian country. All around us was the tall blue grass of that region which in places was higher than a horse, affording an ideal hiding place for the Indians. As we expected an attack from the Indians, the boss arranged strong watches to keep a keen lookout. We had no sooner finished making camp when the Indians showed up, and charged us with a yell or rather a series of yells, I for one had got well used to the blood curdling yells of the Indians and they did not scare us in the least. We were all ready for them and after a short but sharp fight the Indians withdrew and every thing became quiet, but us cow boys were not such guys as to be fooled by the seeming quietness. We knew it was only the calm before the storm, and we prepared ourselves accordingly, but we were all dead tired and it was necessary that we secure as much rest as possible, so the low watch turned in to rest until midnight, when they were to relieve the upper watch, in whose hands the safety of the camp was placed till that time. Every man slept with his boots on and his gun near his hand. We had been sleeping several hours, but it seemed to me only a few minutes when the danger signal was given. Immediately every man was on his feet, gun in hand and ready for business. The Indians had secured reinforcements and after dividing in two bands, one band hid in the tall grass in order to pick us off and shoot us as we attempted to hold our cattle, while the other band proceeded to stampede the herd, but fortunately

there were enough of us to prevent the herd from stringing out on us.... Back and forward, through the tall grass, the large herd charged, the Indians being kept too busy keeping out of their way to have much time to bother with us. This kept up until daylight, but long before that time we came to the conclusion that this was the worst herd of cattle to stampede we ever struck, they seemed perfectly crazy even after the last Indian had disappeared. We were unable to account for the strange actions of the cattle until daylight, when the mystery was a mystery no longer. The Indians in

Cowboys awakening their relief watch. The men would take turns staying up with the herd, keeping a lookout for anything that might spook the cattle and for cattle thieves.
(Corbis-Bettmann. Reproduced by permission.)

*large numbers had hid in the tall grass for the purpose of shooting us from ambush and being on foot they were unable to get out of the way of the herd as it stampeded through the grass, the result was that scores of the painted savages were trampled under the hoofs of the maddened cattle, and in the early gray dawn of the approaching day we witnessed a horrible sight, the Indians were all cut to pieces, their heads, limbs, trunk and blankets all being ground up in an inseparable mass, as if they had been through a sausage machine. The sight was all the more horrible as we did not know the Indians were hidden in the grass during the night, but their presence there accounted for the strange actions of the herd during the night. We suffered no loss or damage except the loss of our rest, which we sorely needed as we were all pretty well **played out.** However, we thought it advisable to move our herd on to a more desirable and safe camping place, not that we greatly feared any more trouble from the Indians, not soon at any rate, but only to be better prepared and in better shape to put up a fight if attacked. The second night we camped on the open plain where the grass was not so high and where the camp could be better guarded. After eating our supper and placing the usual watch the men again turned in, expecting this time to get a good night's rest. It was my turn to take the first watch and with the other boys, who were to watch with me, we took up **advantageous positions** on the lookout. Everything soon became still, the night was dark and sultry. It was getting along toward midnight when all at once we became aware of a roaring noise in the north like thunder, slowly growing louder as it approached, and I said to the boys that it must be a buffalo stampede. We immediately gave the alarm and started for our herd to get them out of the way of the buffalo, but we soon found that despite our utmost efforts we would be unable to get them out of the way, so we came to the conclusion to meet them with our guns and try and turn the buffalo from our direction if possible, and prevent them from going through our herd. Accordingly all hands rode to meet the oncoming stampede, **pouring volley after volley** into the almost solid mass of rushing beasts, but they paid no more attention to us than they would have paid to a lot of boys with pea shooters. On they came, a maddened, plunging, snorting, bellowing mass of horns and hoofs. One of our companions, a young fellow by the name of Cal Surcey, who was riding a young horse, here began to have trouble in controlling his mount and before any of us could reach him his horse bolted right in front of the herd of buffalo and **in a trice** the horse and rider went down and the whole herd passed over them. After the herd had passed*

Played out: Exhausted; out of energy.

Advantageous positions: Positions from which they had a good view of the surrounding area.

Pouring volley after volley: Shooting their guns.

In a trice: Quickly; within a few seconds.

Westward Expansion: Primary Sources

we could only find a few scraps of poor Cal's clothing, and the horse he had been riding was reduced to the size of a jack rabbit. The buffalo went through our herd killing five head and crippling many others, and scattering them all over the plain. This was the year that the great buffalo slaughter commenced and such stampedes were common then. It seemed to me that as soon as we got out of one trouble we got into another on this trip. But we did not get discouraged, but only wondered what would happen next. We did not

Cowboys in a storm trying to control a stampede. Painting by Frederic Remington. This was one of the most important and most dangerous of the cowboys' jobs. *(Corbis-Bettmann. Reproduced by permission.)*

The Cowboy Life: Nat Love | 159

care much for ourselves, as we were always ready and in most cases anxious for a brush with the Indians, or for the other dangers of the trail, as they only went to relieve the dull **monotony** of life behind the herd. But these cattle were entrusted to our care and every one represented money, good hard cash. So we did not relish in the least having them stampeded by the Indians or run over by the buffaloes. If casualties kept up at this rate, there would not be very many cattle to deliver in Wyoming by the time we got there. After the buffalo stampede we rounded up our scattered herd and went into camp for a couple of days' rest before proceeding on our journey north. The tragic death of Cal Surcey had a very depressing effect on all of us as he was a boy well liked by us all, and it was hard to think that we could not even give him a Christian burial. We left his remains trampled into the dust of the prairie and his fate caused even the most hardened of us to shudder as we contemplated it.... [The cowboys made the rest of their journey and delivered the herd to Mitchell in Wyoming having lost only five cattle.]

To the cow boy accustomed to riding long distances, life in the saddle ceases to be tiresome. It is only the dull monotony of following a large herd of cattle on the trail day after day that tires the rider and makes him long for something to turn up in the way of excitement. It does not matter what it is just so it is excitement of some kind. This the cow boy finds in dare-devil riding, shooting, roping and such sports when he is not engaged in fighting Indians or protecting his herds from the organized bands of white cattle thieves that infested the cattle country in those days. It was about this time that I hired to Bill Montgomery for a time to assist in taking a band of nine hundred head of horses to Dodge City. The journey out was without incident, on arriving at Dodge City we sold the horses for a good price returning to the old ranch in Arizona by the way of the old lone and lonesome Dodge City trail. While en route home on this trail we had a sharp fight with the Indians. When I saw them coming I shouted to my companions, "We will battle them to hell!" Soon we heard their yells as they charged us at full speed. We met them with a hot fire from our **winchesters**, but as they were in such large numbers we saw that we could not stop them that way and it soon developed into a hand to hand fight. My saddle horse was shot from under me; at about the same time my partner James Holley was killed, shot through the heart. I caught Holley's horse and continued the fight until it became evident that the Indians were too much for us, then it became a question of running or being scalped. We thought it best to run as we did not think

Monotony: Sameness.

Winchesters: Rifles.

we could very well spare any hair at that particular time, any way we mostly preferred to have our hair cut in the regular way by a competent barber, not that the Indians would charge us too much, they would have probably done the job for nothing, but we didn't want to trouble them, and we did not grudge the price of a hair cut any way, so we put spurs to our horses and they soon carried us out of danger. Nearly every one of us were wounded in this fight but Holley was the only man killed on our side though a few of the Indians were **made better** as the result of it. We heard afterwards that Holley was scalped and his body filled with arrows by the red devils. This was only one of the many similar fights we were constantly having with the Indians and the cattle thieves of that part of the country. They were so common that it was not considered worth mentioning except when we lost a man, as on this occasion. This was the only trouble we had on this trip of any importance and we soon arrived at the Montgomery ranch in Texas where after a few days rest with the boys, resting up, I made tracks in the direction of my own crib in Arizona....

Cowboys roping steer. Quieter moments on the trail allowed cowboys to practice their daredevil riding, shooting, and roping.
(Archive Photos, Inc. Reproduced by permission.)

Made better: Killed, in cowboy slang.

CHAPTER XI: A BUFFALO HUNT. I LOSE MY LARIAT AND SAD-
DLE. I ORDER A DRINK FOR MYSELF AND MY HORSE. A CLOSE
PLACE IN OLD MEXICO.

....[After going on a buffalo hunt with a group of cowboys
from the home ranch] *we were sent down in Old Mexico to get a
herd of horses, that our boss had bought from the Mexicans in the
southwestern part of Old Mexico. We made the journey out all right
without special incident, but after we had got the horses out on the
trail, headed north I was possessed with a desire to show off and I
thought surprise the staid old* **greasers** *on whom we of the northern
cattle country looked with contempt. So accordingly I left the boys
to continue with the herd, while I made for the nearest saloon,
which happened to be located in one of the low mud houses of that
country, with a wide door and clay floor. As the door was standing
open, and looked so inviting I did not want to go to the trouble of
dismounting so urging my horse forward, I rode in the saloon, first
however, scattering with a few random shots the respectable sized
crowd of dirty Mexicans hanging around as I was in no humor to
pay for the drinks for such a motley gathering. Riding up to the bar,
I ordered keller for myself and a generous measure of pulky for my
horse, both popular Mexican drinks.*

*The fat wobbling greaser who was behind the bar looked scared,
but he proceeded to serve us with as much grace as he could command. My forty-five colt which I proceeded to reload, acting as a per-
suader. Hearing a commotion outside I realized that I was surrounded.
The crowd of Mexican bums had not appreciated my kindly greeting
as I rode up and it seems did not take kindly to being scattered by bullets. And not realizing that I could have killed them all, just as easy as I
scattered them, and seeing there was but two of us—I and my horse—
they had summoned sufficient courage to come back and seek revenge. There was a good sized crowd of them, every one with some
kind of* **shooting iron**, *and I saw at once that they meant business. I
hated to have to hurt some of them but I could see I would have to or
be taken myself, and perhaps strung up to ornament a telegraph pole.
This* **pleasant experience** *I had no especial wish to try, so putting spurs
to my horse I dashed out of the saloon, then knocking a man over with
every bullet from my Colts I cut for the open country, followed by several volleys from the angry Mexicans' pop guns.*

*The only harm their bullets did, however, was to wound my
horse in the hip, not seriously, however, and he carried me quickly
out of range. I expected to be pursued, however, as I had no doubt I*

Greasers: An offensive term
used to refer to Mexicans.

Shooting iron: Gun.

Pleasant experience: Love is
referring sarcastically to being
hung.

had done for some of those whom I knocked over, so made straight for the Rio Grande river riding day and night until I sighted that welcome stream and on the other side I knew I was safe. [Love, pp. 40–3, 44–5, 58–63, 64–5, 73–7]

What happened next . . .

After the mid-1880s a variety of conditions made the cowboy obsolete. A series of blizzards in 1886 and 1887 killed off thousands of cattle; rail lines extended into cattle country, making the cattle drives unnecessary; and the growth of farms—with their barbed-wire fences—closed off open range land. With the cowboy era over, in 1890 Nat Love left the range and applied for a job as a Pullman porter on the new cross-country trains. Pullmans were luxurious railroad passenger cars that offered passengers one of the most comfortable modes of travel available at the time. Unlike many other railroad jobs, Pullman service offered a certain degree of independence and dignity. It was, at the time, one of the best jobs available to African American men.

Love approached his work with pride and enthusiasm, determined to become the best Pullman porter in the country. As Philip Durham and Everett L. Jones remarked in *The Negro Cowboys,* "the qualities which made him a successful cowboy for 20 years made him, in the 1890s, a successful porter. He gloried in the people he met and the tips he earned. He gave no indication that he felt his change from the life of a cowboy to the life of a porter was anything other than the result of the changing times.... He had, he claimed, ridden into the West on horseback, ridden throughout the rangeland as Deadwood Dick and then ridden into the twentieth century on a train." Love wrote his memoirs in 1907 and died in 1921.

Did you know . . .

• The Texas longhorn was a mixed breed created when British cattle brought west by Texans met up with wild

Spanish cattle. The result was a tough, durable animal that could handle the most difficult environment.

- The first cowboys were called vaqueros (pronounced vah-kair-ohs). They were generally Indians who tended cattle for Spanish ranchers in California and present-day Texas in the late 1700s.

- In less than two decades, more than six million steers and cows were moved north along the main cattle trails.

- The four main trails on which cowboys led cattle north to the railheads were the Chisholm, the Shawnee, the Western, and the Goodnight-Loving.

- Twenty-five percent of the cowboys participating in cattle drives between 1866 and 1895 were African American.

Consider the following . . .

- How does this excerpt support or challenge your views about cowboys?

- Can you trust that this author is telling the truth? Why, or why not?

- Love speaks very harshly about Mexicans and Indians. Is this surprising to you? Why?

For More Information

Cromwell, Arthur, ed. *The Black Frontier.* Lincoln: University of Nebraska Television, 1970.

Dary, David. *Seeking Pleasure in the Old West.* New York: Knopf, 1995.

Durham, Philip, and Everett L. Jones. *The Negro Cowboys.* Lincoln: University of Nebraska Press, 1965.

Dykstra, Robert R. *The Cattle Towns.* New York: Knopf, 1968.

Felton, Harold W. *Nat Love, Negro Cowboy.* New York: Dodd Mead, 1969.

Granfield, Linda. *Cowboy: An Album.* New York: Ticknor & Fields, 1994.

Katz, William Loren. *The Black West: A Documentary and Pictorial History.* New York: Doubleday, 1971.

Landau, Elaine. *Cowboys.* New York: Franklin Watts, 1990.

Love, Nat. *The Life and Adventures of Nat Love; Better Known in the Cattle Country as "Deadwood Dick."* 1907. Reprint, Lincoln: University of Nebraska Press, 1995.

Monaghan, Jay. *The Book of the American West*. New York: Bonanza Books, 1963.

Place, Marian T. *American Cattle Trails East & West*. New York: Holt, Rinehart and Winston, 1967.

Rosa, Joseph G. *The Taming of the West: Age of the Gunfighter, Men and Weapons on the Frontier, 1840–1900*. New York: Smithmark, 1993.

Savage, Jeff. *Cowboys and Cow Towns of the Wild West*. Springfield, NJ: Enslow, 1995.

Savage, W. Sherman. *Blacks in the West*. Westport, CT: Greenwood Press, 1976.

Seidman, Laurence I. *Once in the Saddle: The Cowboy's Frontier, 1866–1896*. New York: Facts on File, 1990.

Steckmesser, Kent Ladd. *The Western Hero in History and Legend*. Norman: University of Oklahoma Press, 1997.

Weston, Jack. *The Real American Cowboy*. New York: Schocken Books, 1985.

Yount, Lisa. *Frontier of Freedom: African Americans in the West*. New York: Facts on File, 1997.

E. C. "Teddy Blue" Abbott

Excerpt from We Pointed Them North:
Recollections of a Cowpuncher
Originally published in 1939
By E. C. "Teddy Blue" Abbott and Helena Huntington Smith

E.C. "Teddy Blue" Abbott was by all accounts a regular cowboy who had worked on the range in the 1870s and 1880s. Abbott was "discovered" by a journalist named Helena Huntington Smith, who had read an interview with Abbott in a Montana newspaper. She began to meet with him and soon became convinced that his stories needed to be documented. Working with the aging cowboy in 1937 and 1938, Smith wrote as quickly as Abbott talked, preserving the tone and excitement of his stories.

On December 17, 1860, Abbott was born in Norfolk, England. His family moved to the United States when he was a baby and settled near Lincoln, Nebraska, where his father became a farmer. Abbott's father, who he described as "overbearing and tyrannical," wanted Abbott to join him in working the farm, but the young man had other ideas. He was enthralled with the cowboys who passed through Lincoln and by the age of twelve had left school to look after his father's herd of cattle. Though he was not yet living the life of a cowboy, he knew that someday he would. The excerpt from Abbott's autobiography begins when he was fourteen and just about to start his career as a cowboy.

Things to remember while reading the excerpt from *We Pointed Them North*:

- Teddy Blue Abbott drove cattle on the Western Trail, which stretched from San Antonio, Texas, to Miles City, Montana, with important stops at Dodge City, Kansas, and Ogallala, Nebraska.

- Teddy Blue Abbott told his stories to Helena Huntington Smith when he was in his late seventies. Smith swore that he never mixed up his stories and that every fact she checked on turned out to be true.

- Like Nat Love, Abbott became a cowboy in his mid-teens.

Excerpt from We Pointed Them North

From 1874 to 1877 I was taking care of my father's cattle, and after awhile the neighbors began putting cattle with me, paying me a dollar fifty a head for six months. I herded them in the daytime and penned them at night, and for the first time in my life I could rustle a little cash. In 1875 I made twenty-nine dollars that way, and my brother Harry and I had one hell of a time. We bought a bottle of whisky, shot out the lights on the street corners, and run our horses through the streets of Lincoln whooping and yelling like Cheyenne Indians on the warpath. We'd have gone to jail sure if some of Gus Walker's trail men had not been with us. They got the blame, as everything was laid to the Texas men, but they left next day for Texas and so it all blew over. This was my first experience standing up to the bar buying drinks for the boys, and I sure felt big.

That summer, I remember, Ace Harmon, who was one of John T. Lytle's trail bosses and a god to me, said: "In a year or two Teddy will be a real cowboy." And I growed three inches and gained ten pounds that night....

From the time I was fourteen and staying out with the cattle most all the time, I got to be more and more independent. The boys took turns staying out there with me, but Lincoln was only twelve miles from camp, and when we had a little money, one of us would slip off to town on his pony, leaving the other one on herd. We'd *hang around the saloons, listening to those men and getting filled up with talk about gunfights and killings. One time I remember I was in a saloon, and I heard a fellow talking about the Yankees. He said: "I was coming down the road and I met a damn blue-bellied **abolitionist**, and I **paunched** him. And he laid there in the brush and belched like a beef for three days, and then he died in fits. The bastard!"*

*He told that before a whole crowd of men. I don't know that he ever done it. But that was the way he talked to get a fight. Those early-day Texans was full of that stuff. Most of them that came up with the trail herds, being from Texas and Southerners to start with, was **on the side of the South**, and oh, but **they were bitter.** That was how a lot of them got killed, because they were filled full of the old dope about the war and they wouldn't let an abolitionist arrest them. The marshals in those cow towns on the trail were usually Northern men, and the Southerners wouldn't go back to Texas and hear people say: "He's a hell of a fellow. He let a Yankee lock him up." Down home one Texas Ranger could arrest the lot of them, but up North you'd have to kill them first.*

I couldn't even guess how many was killed that way on the trail. There was several killed at every one of those shipping points in Kansas, but you get different people telling the same story over and over again and the number is bound to be exaggerated. Besides, not all that were killed were cowboys; a lot of saloon men and tinhorn gamblers bit the dust. While I saw several shooting scrapes in saloons and sporting houses, I never saw a man shot dead, though some died afterwards.

*But in the **seventies** they were a hard bunch, and I believe it was partly on account of what they came from. Down in Texas in the early days every man had to have his six-shooter always ready, every house kept a shotgun loaded with buckshot, because they were always looking for a raid by Mexicans or Comanche Indians. What is more, I guess half the people in Texas in the seventies had moved out there on the frontier from the Southern states and from the rebel armies, and was the type that did not want any restraints.*

But there is one thing I would like to get straight. I punched cows from '71 on, and I never yet saw a cowboy with two guns. I mean two six-shooters. Wild Bill carried two guns and so did some of those other city marshals, like Bat Masterson, but they were professional gunmen themselves, not cowpunchers. The others that carried two guns were Wes Hardin and Bill Longley and Clay Allison and them desperadoes. But a cowboy with two guns is all movie stuff,

Abolitionist: A supporter of freeing enslaved African Americans.

Paunched: Shot him in the stomach.

On the side of the South: In favor of slavery, Northerners wanted to end slavery in the United States; it was this issue that led to the Civil War.

They were bitter: The Southerners were bitter because they lost the Civil War.

Seventies: 1870s.

*and so is this business of a gun on each hip. The kind of fellows that did carry two would carry one in the **scabbard** and a hide-out gun down under their arm.*

*There was other people besides cowboys in Nebraska in the seventies, but they was not the kind that could influence a boy. The settlers were very religious and narrow-minded. I remember once, me and Harry went fishing on Sunday and caught a big catfish. One of the neighbors saw it and had us arrested, and Father had to pay a five-dollar fine. Most of the settlers had been Union soldiers and did not like Texas people, **and their love was returned plenty.***

About this time, 1876, when I had that picture taken, the one with the cigar in my mouth. I had a bottle of whisky in the other hand, but it doesn't show, because I had a fight with the other fellow in the picture and tore off his half of it. I was drunk when the picture was made, and I guess I wanted the world to know it. I was sixteen then and dead tough. Oh, God, I was tough. I had a terrible reputation, and I was sure proud of it. I'll never forget the time I walked home with a nice girl. Her people were English, some of those cart-horse-bred English that my father looked down on, and she had walked up to our house to visit with the girls and stayed to supper. I took her home afterwards. It was only about half a mile. Her family just tore her to pieces. They saw to it she never went out with me again.

And I was really dangerous. A kid is more dangerous than a man because he's so sensitive about his personal courage. He's just itching to shoot somebody in order to prove himself. I did shoot a man once. I was only sixteen, and drunk. A bunch of us left town on a dead run, shooting at the gas lamps. I was in the lead and the town marshal was right in front of me with his gun in his hand calling, "Halt! Halt! Throw 'em up!" And I throwed 'em up all right, right in his face. I always had that idea in my head—"Shoot your way out." I did not go to town for a long time afterwards, but he never knew who shot him, because it was dark enough so he could not see. He was a saloon man's marshal anyway and they wanted our trade, so did not do much about it. That was how us cowboys got away with a lot of such stunts. Besides, the bullet went through his shoulder and he was only sick a few days and then back on the job. But they say he never tried to get in front of running horses again....

But I was worse than ever afterwards. I remember about this time there was a big banker in this Nebraska country who had been a gambler, and he had straightened out and wanted to marry a decent girl. So he began courting one of my sisters and one day he

Scabbard: A sheath; a side holster.

And their love was returned plenty: The Texans didn't like the settlers from the North either.

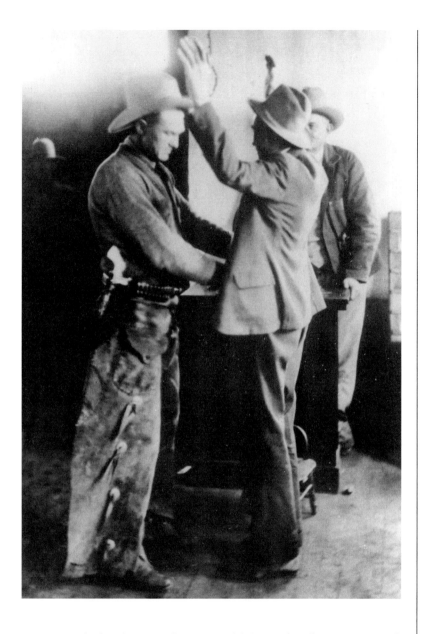

A Texas Ranger patting down a man in a saloon in Kilgore, Texas. In the 1860s and 1870s the cattle towns of Texas had become famous for their lawlessness.
(Corbis/Underwood & Underwood. Reproduced by permission.)

came to take her buggy riding. I wouldn't see anything wrong with it now. But I came up and told them both to get out of that buggy or I'd shoot them out of it, and I would have. I was insulted because my sister was going around with a gambler. I wasn't going to have my sister talked about—and all that kind of thing.

To show you what kids can be, I had a fight with my brother Harry when I was twelve years old and he was fourteen. We tried to cut each other with knives and we made a pretty good job of it too. He had rode one of my ponies. I thought I was a cowpuncher, and it's a deadly insult to a cowpuncher to ride one of his horses without his permission. We got out our jackknives and flew at each other like a pair of little tigers. He cut me all over the hands, and I cut his chin—I was aiming at his throat. Little damned fools. And that night we slept together as though nothing had happened....

[Harry's] death was what made an **infidel** *of me. I asked my mother if God could have kept him from dying, and she said, yes, God was all-powerful and could have prevented it if he had wished. So I said: "I'll never go in one of your damn churches again." And I never have. That family stuffed me full of all that religious bull when I was a kid, but I never had any more use for it after I was growed, and in that I was like the rest of the cowpunchers. Ninety per cent of them was infidels. The life they led had a lot to do with that. After you come in contact with nature, you get all that stuff knocked out of you— praying to God for aid, divine* **Providence***, and so on—because it don't work. You could pray all you damn pleased, but it wouldn't get you water where there wasn't water. Talk about trusting in Providence, hell, if I'd trusted in Providence I'd have starved to death.*

But the settlers would all get in their churches Sundays, and that **exhorter** *would be hollering hell-fire and brimstone so you could hear him a mile. We'd all go to hell, the way they looked at it. If they were right there was no hope for me. You know you ride around alone at night, looking at the stars, and you get to thinking of those things.*

Most of southeastern Nebraska and the whole state west of Lincoln was open range when we got there in '71, but about 1876 a flock of settlers took the country, and after that there was only a few places where you could hold cattle. Father was lucky. There was a lot of rough country adjoining **him** *that did not get settled till '79 or '80, and he run cattle until then, but afterwards he went to farming with the rest of them. That was how I came to leave home for good when I was eighteen. I was back for visits afterwards, because I wanted to see my mother, but except for those visits my family and I went separate ways, and they stayed separate forever after. My father was all for farming by that time, and all my brothers turned out farmers except one, and he ended up the worst of the lot—a sheepman and a Republican.*

But I stayed with the cattle and went north with them. You see, environment—that's a big word for me, but I got onto it—does everything for a boy. I was with Texas cowpunchers from the time I

Infidel: Person with no religious beliefs.

Providence: Guidance from God.

Exhorter: Preacher.

Him: Abbott's father's land.

was eleven years old. And then my father expected to make a farmer of me after that! It couldn't be done.

The summer of 1878 I ran a herd of beef for some men in Lincoln, and I took them up on Cheese Creek—that was the last open range in that country. They limited me to 500 head so the cattle would do well, but they paid me twenty-five cents a head a month, and for four months I got $125 a month out of it. That was big money for a boy in those days, when the usual wages ran as low as $10, and believe me I thought I was smart. In the fall these fellows sold their cattle to feeders in the eastern part of the state and I took them down there, driving them right through the streets of Lincoln. Then I went home. After I got home my father said to me one night: "You can take old Morgan and Kit and Charlie and plow the west ridge tomorrow."

Like hell I'd plow the west ridge. And when he woke up next morning, Teddy was gone....

[The] trip up the trail in '79 was my second, but in a way it was the first that counted, because I was only a button the other time. I

A saloon in Telluride, Colorado. Saloons, gambling houses, and dance halls were prevalent in Wild West towns. Cowboys especially enjoyed frequenting these establishments after many months of hard work on the trail.
(Corbis-Bettmann. Reproduced by permission.)

wasn't nineteen years old when I come up the trail with the Olive herd, but don't let that fool you. I was a man in my own estimation and a man in fact. I was no kid with the outfit but a top cowhand, doing a top hand's work, and there is nothing so wonderful about that. All I'd ever thought about was being a good cowhand. I'd been listening to these Texas men and watching them and studying the disposition of cattle ever since I was eleven years old.

Even in years I was no younger than a lot of them. The average age of cowboys then, I suppose, was twenty-three or four. Except for some of the bosses there was very few thirty-year-old men on the trail. I heard a story once about a school teacher who asked one of these old Texas cow dogs to tell her all about how he punched cows on the trail. She said: "Oh, Mister So-and-So, didn't the boys used to have a lot of fun riding their ponies?"

He said: "Madam, there wasn't any boys or ponies. They was all horses and men."

Well, they had to be, to stand the life they led. Look at the chances they took and the kind of riding they done, all the time, over rough country. Even in the daytime those deep **coulees** could open up all at once in front of you, before you had a chance to see where you were going, and at night it was something awful if you'd stop to think about it, which none of them ever did. If a storm come and the cattle started running—you'd hear that low rumbling noise along the ground and the men on herd wouldn't need to come in and tell you, you'd know—then you'd jump for your horse and get out there in the lead, trying to head them and get them into a **mill** before they scattered to hell and gone. It was riding at a dead run in the dark, with cut banks and prairie dog holes all around you, not knowing if the next jump would land you in a shallow grave....

One day a man walked in the saloon carrying a big glass jar with a live rattlesnake in it. He wanted to sell it. Frank says: "Hell, no, they see snakes soon enough."

But the man kept arguing with him. He says: "It's big money for you if you'll buy it. Now I'll bet the drinks for the house there ain't a man here that can hold his finger on that glass and keep it there when the snake strikes."

To show you what a bonehead I was, I took him up. It was thick glass and I knew damn well the snake couldn't bite me, so I put my finger on it. The snake struck, and away come my finger. I

Coulees: Deep gulches or ravines.

Mill: To move in a circle.

got mad and made up my mind I would hold my finger on that glass or bust. It cost me seventeen dollars before I quit, but since then I've never bucked the other fellow's game and it has saved me a lot of money.

Frank bought the snake and he sure made money on it. It was lots of fun to get some sucker that thought he was long on nerve to go against it; no one ever could. But one night a bunch of cowboys came in and I knew some of them. They all tried the snake and failed, and one of them got mad and busted the glass with his six-shooter, and the snake got out and they had to kill it.

That was a big night in more ways than one. We all got well lit up and went to a hot show on Blake Street. The play I think was called "Poor Nell"; anyway, a burglar beats his wife to death on the stage. After he had knocked her down he taken hold of her hair and beat her head on the floor, and every time he struck her head he would stamp his foot. It sounded like her head hitting the floor, but it wasn't her head at all. I was sober enough to know that. But

Cowboys around the chuck wagon. These young men would drive cattle five hundred to eight hundred miles and often saw only each other for weeks on end. *(Corbis-Bettmann. Reproduced by permission.)*

some of them weren't. Bill Roden, one of the cowboys, had went to sleep but the noise woke him up, and the first thing he saw was the man beating the woman's head on the floor. We sat right in front, and he gave one jump onto the stage and busted the fellow on the head with his six-gun before he remembered where he was. The woman got up and began to cuss him, all hell broke loose, somebody pulled Bill off the stage, they called for the police, the boys shot out the lights, and everybody broke their necks getting away from there. They all run to Bailey's corral where the horses were and got away before the police knew who to arrest. I made a sneak down an alley to Frank's place, got what few dollars I had, and left town on foot....

*Lots of cowpunchers were killed by lightning, and that is history. I was knocked off my horse by it twice. The first time I saw a ball of fire coming toward me and felt something strike me on the head. When I came to, I was lying under old Pete and the rain was pouring down on my face. The second time I was trying to get under a railroad bridge when it hit me, and I came to in the ditch. The cattle were always restless when there was a storm at night, even if it was a long way off, and that was when any little thing would start a **run.***

Lots of times I have ridden around the herd, with lightning playing and thunder muttering in the distance, when the air was so full of electricity that I would see it flashing on the horns of the cattle, and there would be balls of it on the horse's ears and even on my mustache, little balls about the size of a pea. I suppose it was static electricity, the same as when you shake a blanket on a winter night in a dark room.

But when you add it all up, I believe the worst hardship we had on the trail was loss of sleep. There was never enough sleep. Our day wouldn't end till about nine o'clock, when we grazed the herd onto the bed ground. And after that every man in the outfit except the boss and horse wrangler and cook would have to stand two hours' night guard. Suppose my guard was twelve to two. I would stake my night horse, unroll my bed, pull off my boots, and crawl in at nine, get about three hours' sleep, and then ride two hours. Then I would come off guard and get to sleep another hour and a half, till the cook yelled, "Roll out," at half past three. So I would get maybe five hours' sleep when the weather was nice and everything smooth and pretty, with cowboys singing under the stars. If it wasn't so nice, you'd be lucky to sleep an hour. But the wagon rolled on in the

Run: Stampede.

morning just the same. [Abbott and Smith, pp. 22–3, 26–30, 35–6, 45–7, 66–7]

What happened next . . .

Teddy Blue Abbott's entire life wasn't as wild as his early years as a cowboy. By the 1880s, in fact, few cowboys were finding work on cattle drives. Rail lines had stretched into cattle country, so cattle drives simply weren't necessary any longer. More and more cattle were being raised in fenced pastures, putting cowboys out of work. Abbott moved to Montana, where cattle were still tended on the open range. In the late 1880s the love of a woman led him to settle down. Abbott married Mary Stuart in 1889.

"I took a homestead," wrote Abbott, "kept milk cows and raised a garden, though I still rode and kept cattle, and the truth is that after I was married, I rode much harder and longer hours than I ever done for forty dollars a month." Abbott was like many cowboys who settled down, took advantage of the opportunity to buy cheap land, and built small farms. Abbott became something of a legend in Montana for his fascinating stories of the cowboy era, and Helena Huntington Smith helped him record his memories in 1939. Abbott died just a few days after *We Pointed Them North* was published.

Did you know . . .

- Most cowboys were from the South, and many still nursed a grudge against all Northerners for the South's defeat in the Civil War.

- The life of a cowboy was hard and dangerous. Battles with Indians, prairie fires, breakneck chases across unfamiliar territory, and drunken fights in cowboy towns—all took their toll on the cowboy.

- On the open range, the cattle of many different ranchers mixed together. Cowboys identified their cattle by brands, distinctive marks burned into the hide when the animals were young.

- The cattle boom lasted only twenty-five years, from about 1866 to 1890. During that time some thirty-five thousand cowboys rode the range.

Consider the following . . .

- How does this excerpt support or challenge your views about cowboys?

- Can you trust that this author is telling the truth? Why, or why not?

For More Information

Abbott, E. C. ("Teddy Blue"), and Helena Huntington Smith. *We Pointed Them North: Recollections of a Cowpuncher.* Norman: University of Oklahoma Press, 1939.

Dary, David. *Seeking Pleasure in the Old West.* New York: Knopf, 1995.

Dykstra, Robert R. *The Cattle Towns.* New York: Knopf, 1968.

Granfield, Linda. *Cowboy: An Album.* New York: Ticknor & Fields, 1994.

Landau, Elaine. *Cowboys.* New York: Franklin Watts, 1990.

Monaghan, Jay. *The Book of the American West.* New York: Bonanza Books, 1963.

Place, Marian T. *American Cattle Trails East & West.* New York: Holt, Rinehart and Winston, 1967.

Rosa, Joseph G. *The Taming of the West: Age of the Gunfighter, Men and Weapons on the Frontier, 1840–1900.* New York: Smithmark, 1993.

Savage, Jeff. *Cowboys and Cow Towns of the Wild West.* Springfield, NJ: Enslow, 1995.

Seidman, Laurence I. *Once in the Saddle: The Cowboy's Frontier, 1866–1896.* New York: Facts on File, 1990.

Steckmesser, Kent Ladd. *The Western Hero in History and Legend.* Norman: University of Oklahoma Press, 1965.

Agnes Morley Cleaveland

Excerpt from No Life for a Lady
Originally published in 1941

In the 1800s cattle drives were considered men's work. But that didn't mean that women didn't play an important role in the cattle boom of the late nineteenth century. In fact, some of the infamous female figures in the West were as romanticized as their male counterparts. Horse thief and cattle rustler Belle Starr was widely known as the female Jesse James, and Calamity Jane was as celebrated as Wild Bill Hickok for her exploits with a gun. In the rowdy cattle towns that popped up across Kansas, dance hall girls and prostitutes were very colorful figures. However, most women—like most cowboys—led more ordinary lives than the legends indicate. Ranchers' wives worked alongside their husbands to build the ranches that were the bases for cattle drives. On small farms and ranches in the Far West, women often had to do much of the same work as men, as well as cook and take care of the children.

Agnes Morley Cleaveland was not a cowboy, but she was as close as a woman came to being a real cowgirl. Born Agnes Morley in 1874 to a renowned railroad engineer who owned plots of land throughout the West, Miss Agnes, as she was known on the ranch, grew up in the high desert country of southwestern New Mexico, near the village of Magdalena. Her parents worried about bringing up their daughter in the rough and turbulent atmosphere of the West, but, as her father said to her mother, "Well, Ada, we've put our hands to this plow. We can't turn around in the middle of the furrow. I've got to build the Santa Fe [railroad]." Cleaveland was sent east during the school year to attend boarding schools, but she returned every summer to the family ranch in Datil Canyon. It was there that she learned to ride and tend cattle.

When their parents passed away, Agnes and her brother Ray were left in charge of the ranch, which they ran together until Agnes married and moved to California in 1899. Cleaveland recorded her memories of growing up on and running the ranch in *No Life for a Lady,* a detailed account of a woman's life in one of the most remote and desolate parts of the American West. Though her stories are not quite as colorful or as dramatic as those told by Teddy Blue Abbott and Nat Love, they also speak of ceaseless labor, dangerous exploits—and romance. Cleaveland's account makes it clear that while women may have been protected by the cowboy's code of chivalry (a code of bravery, courtesy, honor, and gallantry toward women), women did plenty of hard work themselves and played an important part in the taming of the West.

Things to remember while reading the excerpt from *No Life for a Lady*:

- *No Life for a Lady* is a very rare account of a woman's experiences as a cowgirl. Little is known about how many women may have had such experiences.

- Women often found success and independence opening businesses—laundries, restaurants, and so on—in the small towns that sprang up throughout the West.

- In the early mining settlements in California and Colorado men outnumbered women nine or ten to one.

A cowgirl on horseback. As a rule, women didn't ride on the trails with cowboys; Agnes Morley Cleaveland grew up on a ranch in the Wild West and was as close as a woman came to being a real cowgirl.
(Corbis-Bettmann. Reproduced by permission.)

Excerpt from No Life for a Lady

"Frontier Chivalry"

As a class, certainly, the men of our frontier were chivalrous in their attitude toward women. It may be that when people live in a less highly organized state of society, and everybody is under the same pressure of external circumstances in order to keep alive, the sex issue of itself recedes. Or, it may be that evilly-disposed men were less likely to go unhanged. Women, because of their very scarcity, were undoubtedly more valued and their own men correspondingly more fierce in their protection. Anyway, the **crimes with which my youth was conversant** seem to me to have been cleaner crimes than the sex horrors of today. Gun fights between men, or even horse-stealing, carried with them something of sportsmanship, which, while not making them praiseworthy, at least removed them from the realm of rank cowardice.

In all the years of my youth I never knew a case of assault, and the frequently heard statement that a "good" woman was always safe seems to have been historically true. Only once did I feel even vaguely ill at ease when I found myself alone with any man, stranger or not. Even on this one occasion my emotion was less fear than cold wrath.

It was shortly after Gray Dick [her favorite horse] was taken. I had stationed myself for several weeks at one of the outlying camps to take care of our remaining horses in the big pasture which had been built there. (We always "built pasture" rather than fences. Incidentally, the fences often cost more than the land.)

One afternoon a trail herd with half a dozen men in charge passed my cabin. The men all came in for a drink of water and, of course, discovered that as frequently happened I was alone and had been alone for several weeks. The boss-owner of the small outfit inquired about leasing the pasture to let his cattle "rest up and put on a little weight." When I refused, he took his outfit on, but in half an hour he was back, alone, and in the house before I realized it, doors being seldom closed and never locked.

Assuming that he had come back to discuss the lease matter again, I motioned him to a chair and sat down myself on a cot across the room. It was only a moment before he came over and sat down beside me.

I was saying, "I'm sure we don't want to lease the pasture; we need it for our own horses," when he reached over and ran his cupped hand down the length of my braided hair. And that was in the category of forbidden things. There was not that easy attitude toward the laying on of hands that exists today. Instinct, however, on this occasion warned me that there were explosive possibilities in a wrong move, and that my role must be casualness.

"Yore hair'd make a dandy **cinch**," he said, with banal attempt at humor.

Crimes with which my youth was conversant: Crimes committed by her generation, in their youth.

"Wouldn't it?" Ostensibly I fell in with the jest, and with a laugh arose and crossed over to a side table, upon which lay my own small thirty-two. I thrust it into my belt and returned to my place beside him. "No," I said, "I'm sure we don't want to lease the pasture."

The man looked at me, his eyes slightly narrowed, and then he rose to his feet with an assumption of casualness equal to my own. "Good afternoon to you," he said. "I never let no woman take a shot at me"—and was gone.

This was the closest approach to having to "fight for my honor" that ever confronted me in the hundreds of instances when I was alone with men, singly or in groups.

One incident in particular shows to what lengths most men, even of the roughest sort, carried chivalry; I used it once in a published story with a story-teller's license, but I want to relate it here without the hampering requirement of "a beginning, a body, and an ending." One Monday in late summer when I went for the mail, my mount was Chico, a young mustang of boundless endurance and bad disposition.

As a young woman living in the West, Agnes Morley Cleaveland was something of a rarity. In early settlements in the West, men usually outnumbered women nine or ten to one. *(Archive Photos, Inc. Reproduced by permission.)*

Cinch: A rope used to tie a saddle on a horse.

The Cowboy Life: Agnes Morley Cleaveland | 183

The mail was later than usual and Chico became restive from standing for hours at a hitching-rack. When the stage finally arrived, well after dark, it brought with it the county sheriff. I was trying to tie my mail-sack to the saddle-strings and having trouble with the snorting and pawing Chico when the sheriff came out to help me.

"Going up the **cañon** alone?" he said. I thought I detected an odd quality in his voice. "Hadn't you better wait till daylight?"

I assured him that I could not, that I had often made the trip alone after nightfall, and what was there to be afraid of, anyhow?

"Mebbe yore right," he conceded, I thought reluctantly, and held Chico's bit while I mounted. For once I did "start off at full gallop." I couldn't help myself. Chico had had enough of that hitching-rack and he was going home. It was several miles before I got him quieted down to an impatient high trot.

We had just topped the brow of a hill, where the trail skirted around the fenced cañon bottom, when Chico snorted violently and stopped. In the trail just ahead, clearly outlined in the bright starlight of that high altitude, was another horseman. He, too, had stopped precipitately. I could hold Chico still but for a second. We came almost horse nose to horse nose before the man spoke.

"Good evening, miss?" with a sort of inquiring inflection on the "miss."

"Yes," I said. "Good evening."

"Nice evening," the man said, to which I echoed, "Nice evening."

He drew his horse out of the trail and waited for me to pass, Chico still champing his bits and pulling on the bridle reins.

An hour later the man lay dead, with the sheriff's bullet in his heart. He had made the mistake of trying to steal a fresh mount for himself from Baldwin's horse pasture instead of taking mine. A fresh mount was all he had needed to get himself and the gold which weighed down his saddlebags over the border into Mexico and safety. He threw away his chance, and his life with it, to protect a young girl from a bad fright.

Impersonal circumstances, however, were quite indifferent to such codes of honor: they took their toll without regard for chivalry.

Once, when I had stopped to "**noon**" on a trip to town and my team was feeding, I climbed back into the high seat of the wagon and picked up a book. I did not hear the silent footfall of a horse and was

Cañon: Canyon.

startled when one of the team snorted. I looked up to see a horseman beside the wagon. He was a Mexican, **swarthy** and **begrimed**.

He looked at me curiously.

"You all alone?" he asked in his own tongue. I told him I was.

I could read puzzlement in his face. Mexican girls did not go about alone, even in our country.

"Why you all alone?" he persisted.

"Have to," I told him.

This seemed to puzzle him all the more. He sat looking at me intently.

"You not afraid?" he asked finally.

"No."

"Why you not afraid?"

I reached under the edge of the Navajo blanket that covered the seat and pulled out my little thirty-two.

Noon: Take a midday break.

Swarthy: Dark-skinned.

Begrimed: Grimy; dirty.

He nodded approvingly.

"Bueno," he said, and rode on.

Another time I was alone at the ranch when Lon, a neighboring cowboy, came in and stayed for an early supper. During the meal a bat flew in at the open door and repeatedly circled close above my head. Now, bats will *tangle in long hair.*

When this bat's claw-tipped wings had repeatedly all but brushed the top of my head, I got up from the table and put on my Stetson.

"Why, Miss Agnes!" Lon exclaimed in pained surprise. "This is the first time I ever seen you *scared.*"

"If that bat ever got tangled in my hair," I explained, "you'd have to cut my hair out in little chunks to get the bat out."

A look of horror came over his face.

"Oh, I'd never do it, Miss Agnes," he said, in the tone of one **rebuking sacrilege.** "I'd cut the *bat* out in little chunks."

After he had helped me wash dishes, we sat awhile by the open fireplace. He smoked in silence a moment and then said: "Sitting here like this reminds me of the story of Johnny Gollymike. Ever hear tell of him?"

I looked at my visitor **askance.**

"Johnny Gollymike!"

"Y'see," said Lon, with elaborate innocence, "Johnny Gollymike was sorta like you. Not scared of nothin'—that is, almost *nothin'.* So some fellers told him they bet he was scared of **ha'nts.**

Johnny said he wasn't, neither. Well, **the'** was a **ha'nted** house near-by and Johnny said as how he'd go stay in it all night all by hisself. He went to the house and built him up a fire in the fireplace, and when it was just twelve o'clock, the time the ha'nt **allus** come, Johnny rolled hisself a **cigareet.**

He looked around, and **thar** a-settin' on the bench beside him was the ha'nt, a-rollin' hisself a cigareet, too.

"'Nice smoke you and me's havin' together,' says the ha'nt, and Johnny Gollymike went away from there. He took out like a jack-rabbit with a coyote after him. When he was plumb give out, he set down on a log **a-blowin'** like a windbroke horse, and there a-settin' alongside him on the log was the ha'nt, a-blowin' like a wind-broke ha'nt horse, too.

Bueno: Good.

Rebuking: Scolding.

Sacrilege: Something that offends sacred beliefs.

Askance: Doubtfully.

Ha'nts: Haunts, or ghosts.

The': There.

Ha'nted: Haunted.

Allus: Always.

Cigareet: Cigarette.

Thar: There.

"'Nice footrace you 'n' me had,' sez the ha'nt.

"'It sure was,' says Johnny, 'but pardner, it wasn't nothin' to the one we're goin' to have right now.'"

While I was deciding whether or not this was the place to laugh, Lon picked up his hat.

"Well, I guess I better be gettin' along like Johnny Gollymike." Chivalrous exit from a **tête-à-tête**, that!

I'll call this one Tod—good a name as any.

All summer long, Tod had hunted his **peripatetic** but **wholly mythical horses** in our end of Datil Cañon. He was also regular about being at the post office on Mondays ready to ride home with me. He came bringing gifts, usually a quarter of beef, in a sack carried on the saddle in front of him. **Saddletrees** were not then the present-day short, squatty affairs with swell forks, but were long enough in the seat to accommodate many kinds of things besides the rider, including babies, as many a ranch woman can testify.

But during all of this summer when Tod rode with me we talked of—well, I suppose it was horses. Maybe we mentioned cows, but it was horses about which most conversation revolved.

Finally, the last Monday before I must go back to school arrived. Tod rode home with me as he had done every Monday of the summer. But now he did not have anything to say. Once he slapped my pony's neck with the ends of his own bridle reins as if giving release to some unspoken feeling, but other than that we rode side by side in complete silence. I think I was afraid to start a conversation lest it take a turn which I dreaded.

At last we were in sight of the house. I remember that the last afterglow of the sun lay on its bleaching shingles, giving them a silvery sheen. Tod drew his horse to a stop.

"Miss Agnes," he said, "yo're leavin' tomorrow. No tellin' what things'll be like when you come back, so I just got to tell you I got mighty fond of you this summer."

There it was. My face must have shown dismay, but before I could choose words that I hoped would be kind, Tod had gathered in his bridle reins.

"It's all right, Miss Agnes," he said simply. "Don't fret yoreself about me. I'll git over it."

A-blowin': Breathing heavy.

Tête-à-tête: A private conversation between two persons.

Peripatetic: Traveling on foot; wandering.

Wholly mythical horses: Tod pretended that his horses had wandered over to the end of Cleaveland's family's land as an excuse to visit with Cleaveland.

Saddletrees: The frame of a saddle.

Cowgirls in Pasadena, California, in 1917.
(UPI/Corbis-Bettmann. Reproduced by permission.)

Gallant gentleman, I salute you! I remember you long after I have forgotten others who swore to high heaven they'd never get over it, and promptly did.

*I did not go back to my Philadelphia school which I had left at Easter time, so confident of returning soon—Philadelphia seemed much too far away: and since we had friends in **Ann Arbor** I finished high school there.*

But at Ann Arbor as at Philadelphia life had very little reality for me. I worked hard, but everything except the ranch was unimportant to me. The next summer found me joyfully getting off at the Magdalena railroad station. [Cleaveland, pp. 139–45]

Ann Arbor: A town in Michigan.

What happened next . . .

       After her parents died, Agnes Morley Cleaveland ran the family ranch with her younger brother, Ray Morley, until she married and moved away to California with her husband. Cleaveland became a part-time journalist, but she returned frequently to the New Mexico ranching land that she described so lovingly in her book. Ray Morley became one of the biggest ranchers in Catron County, New Mexico, buying up adjacent ranch land and tending large herds of cattle. After New Mexico became a state in 1912, the federal government contained much of the Morley land within the boundaries of what is now the Cibola National Forest. Unhappy at having to obey rangers' requests that he take down his barbed-wire fence, Morley waged a long and losing battle against the Forest Service. Morley eventually sold the ranch land.

Did you know . . .

- New Mexico did not become a state until 1912.

- In 1836 Narcissa Whitman and Eliza Spalding, two Protestant missionaries, became the first white women to cross the Rocky Mountains.

- Women won the right to vote in four western states before 1900, well before women in eastern states did.

For More Information

Armitage, Susan and Elizabeth Jameson, eds. *The Women's West.* Norman: University of Oklahoma Press, 1987.

Armitage, Susan, Ruth B. Moynihan, and Christine Fischer Dichamp, eds. *So Much to Be Done: Women Settlers on the Mining and Ranching Frontier.* Lincoln: University of Nebraska Press, 1990.

Brown, Dee. *The Gentle Tamers: Women of the Old Wild West.* New York: Bantam Books, 1974.

Cleaveland, Agnes Morley. *No Life for a Lady.* Boston: Houghton Mifflin, 1941.

Jeffrey, Julie Roy. *Frontier Women.* New York: Hill & Wang, 1979.

Levy, JoAnn. *They Saw the Elephant: Women in the California Gold Rush.* Hamden, CT: Archon Books, 1990.

Myres, Sandra L. *Westering Women and the Frontier Experience, 1800–1915.* Albuquerque: University of New Mexico Press, 1982.

Reiter, Joan Swallow, et al. *The Old West: The Women.* New York: Time-Life Books, 1978.

Schlissel, Lillian. *Women's Diaries of the Westward Journey.* New York: Schocken Books, 1981.

Stratton, Joanna L. *Pioneer Women: Voices from the Kansas Frontier.* New York: Simon and Schuster, 1981.

West, Elliott. *Growing Up with the Country: Childhood on the Far Western Frontier.* Albuquerque: University of New Mexico Press, 1989.

The Gold Rush

5

The discovery of gold in the Sacramento Valley of northern California, inland from the San Francisco Bay, in 1848 marked the beginning of one of the most dramatic periods in American history. The day James Marshall's eye was caught by a shiny object in the bottom of a ditch while he managed the construction of a sawmill for his boss John Sutter would be recounted again and again as news of the discovery spread around the world. Soon thousands of adventurers would migrate to California, searching for their own fortunes.

The California gold rush lasted just a few years, but it dramatically changed the future of the state and the nation. Of the thousands who migrated to California with hopes of instant riches, only a few struck it big in the gold fields. Many more built new lives providing services in the rapidly growing city of San Francisco. Others died on the arduous journey west or—if they were Native American, African American, Chinese, or Hispanic—faced discrimination as white settlers took control of the state. The gold rush changed California from a sparsely populated Mexican territory to a rapidly growing state within a decade.

When gold was first discovered in 1848, many people dropped everything to search for their own fortune. However, some established Californians were skeptical. Editor of the *California Star,* Edward Cleveland Kemble had read the accounts of gold in the hills but he doubted the abundance of it. Kemble was one of the first to travel to Sutter's Mill to verify the rumors; his memoirs, **Reminiscences of Early San Francisco 1847–48** recorded the skepticism of longtime settlers as well as the tension between those who knew where the gold was and those who were searching for it.

Although thousands of people from all over the country struck out for California, their journey was not easy. Diaries of the overland travelers related the hardships of trekking across the country and the elation or disappointment of travelers when they finally reached the mines. Elisha Douglass Perkins was one of the thousands who hoped to "strike it rich." The journal Perkins kept between May 1849 and February 1850 was published in 1967 as **Gold Rush Diary: Being the Journal of Elisha Douglass Perkins on the Overland Trail in the Spring and Summer of 1849.** It describes his two-thousand-mile journey to the mines and the few months he spent digging in chilly riverbeds, searching to find a strong vein of gold.

The gold rush horrified the native populations, who had never considered the sparkling mineral in their rivers to be of any great worth. The frenzied excitement of the gold miners is usually presented as an example of the adventurous spirit of frontier settlers. Letters and diaries describe the thrill of the journey toward fortune and, more often than not, the disappointment of failure. But the rapid influx of miners and other settlers into California had serious consequences fo the Native Americans there. Pushed off their land and denied basic human rights, Indians struggled to cope with the thousands of newcomers. Newspaper articles from the period record the mistreatment of the native population and the growing hostility between whites and Indians in the mid-1800s. By 1870, the devastation was done; the Indian population had plummeted to one-sixth its size before the gold rush. Life in California was forever changed. The gold rush had created a thriving state and the resulting population growth had devastated the Native American way of life. Several excerpts from *"Exterminate Them" Written Accounts of the Murder, Rape, and Slavery of Native Americans During the California Gold Rush, 1848–1868* illustrate both sides: the exuberance of the new settlers and the reactions of the Indians.

Edward Kemble

Excerpt from **Reminiscences of Early San Francisco 1847–48**

First published in the *Sacramento Daily Union* in 1873
Reprinted in *A World Transformed:*
Firsthand Accounts of
***California Before the Gold Rush*, 1999**
Edited by Joshua Paddison

It took several months for people in San Francisco—barely one hundred miles away from Sutter's Mill—to hear of Marshall's discovery of gold on January 24, 1848. As the first news of gold trickled through the small California towns, some were skeptical. In San Francisco, a town of about five hundred people, settlers were busy setting up shops to support the growing farming communities; farming was considered the best economic opportunity in the territory at the time. However, as workers from Sutter's Mill began buying goods with gold dust, the rumors of gold in the hills of California were hard to deny.

The curious editor of the *California Star* newspaper, Edward Cleveland Kemble, wanted to know if the rumors were true. He joined the first party to leave San Francisco for the gold mines. In 1873, Kemble published a rare perspective about the beginning of the gold rush in a series of articles for the *Sacramento Daily Union*. His reports highlight the skepticism of the party and the difficulty in finding gold. His account also provides a unique perspective on the relations between Indians and miners.

Things to remember while reading the excerpt from *Reminiscences of Early San Francisco 1847–48*:

- In early 1847, the population of California was recorded as five hundred Californians and "foreigners"—Americans, English, Kanakas (native Hawaiians), and others.

- California became a U.S. territory on January 13, 1847.

- When gold was discovered on the American River, northern California was already known for its abundant mineral resources. People had already been digging for silver, quicksilver, coal, iron, copper, sulfur, salt, and black lead.

Excerpt from Reminiscences of Early San Francisco 1847–48

*We didn't believe in it; we didn't profess to believe in it! The first party to the gold mines was not **a party to** any such miserable fraud as we believed the pretended gold discoveries to be. They would have told you—and it was true—that they were not going to look for gold; they had not lost any gold—and if Captain Sutter's mill hands on the **American Fork** had found gold, they ought to be allowed to keep it....*

*The first party that left San Francisco to go to the gold mines consisted of Major Pierson B. Reading, George McKinstry, Jr., and the editor [Kemble] of the little paper already mentioned; time of year, the last week in March or the first in April [1848]; **conveyance**, Leidesdorff's "launch" or schooner, the Rainbow. Major Reading, the accomplished gentleman, the adventurous pioneer, the amateur trapper and hunter, and the gallant soldier, will be remembered by all the old Californians. McKinstry was a pleasant writer and companion and was employed at Sutter's Fort in keeping the hospitable captain's books and accounts. The editor of the Star was a youth, not out of his teens, a printer and pioneer, who had served in the campaign in the south under **Frémont**....*

This was the party, and the vessel in which they embarked was admirably suited to the occasion—full of the suggestions of failure.

A party to: A part of.

American Fork: Part of the American River in California.

Conveyance: Mode of travel.

Frémont: John C. Frémont.

The *Rainbow was one of those morning illuminations at which "sailors take warning"; it had not bright promise to be fulfilled. It was the hull of the little* Sitka, *the pioneer steamboat on the bay, from which the boiler and engine had been removed— the shell of the grub from which the butterfly had departed....*

One trip up the Sacramento in those weary days and nights of schooner navigation—of flapping sails and "ashen breezes" by day, and flapjacks and ashcakes and embattled hosts of mosquitoes along the banks at night—was so much like another, and either one or the other so uninviting of repetition that even the reproduction of the incidents of such a one as I am narrating seems undesirable. The party were from five to seven days on the journey. At "old Schwartz," on the river, a few miles below the **embarcadero** *of Sutter's Fort (present site of Sacramento) they stopped to have a feast of salmon....*

Overland Mail Route To

CALIFORNIA

SIX DAYS TO SACRAMENTO

CONNECTING WITH THE DAILY STAGE

To all interior mining towns in Northern California and Southern Oregon.

Travelers Avoid Risk of Ocean Travel

Passing through the HEART OF OREGON, embracing the most BEAUTIFUL, BOLD, GRAND and Picturesque Scenery on the Continent. The highest snow-capped mountains, Mt. HOOD, Mt. SHASTA and others, deepest ravines and most beautiful valleys.

OREGON STAGE COACH LINE

Stages stop over one night at Jacksonville and Eureka for passengers to rest. Passengers will be permitted to lay over at any point and resume their seats at pleasure within one month.

FARE THROUGH, FIFTY DOLLARS

Ticket Office at Arrigoni's Hotel, Portland

The Rainbow *made her landing in fine style, all ill omens having failed on the trip, and Major Reading's little Indian body servant, who had accompanied him from San Francisco, ran up to the fort to* **apprise** *Captain Sutter of the arrival. Soon there were saddle horses led by an Indian* **vaquero** *galloping through the trees to be placed at the disposal of the major for the conveyance of the party to the fort. The setting sun was throwing a flood of mellow light beneath the arching branches, brightening the silver shafts of the cottonwood and turning to molten gold the miniature lakes spread out on every side....*

The next morning after their arrival, the gold hunters (still disclaiming such a title, however) resumed their journey. During the evening spent with Captain Sutter they had not been specially enlightened in regard to the discoveries. If Captain Sutter was a believer in their importance, he managed to hide it from his friends more successfully than the artless old gentleman concealed anything before or since. [James] Marshall's enthusiasm appeared rather to amuse than convince him, though he was troubled at the shape

As news of gold in California spread, business opportunities increased in the territory. This advertisement offers information on traveling to California via stagecoach. *(Archive Photos, Inc. Reproduced by permission.)*

Embarcadero: Wharf, pier, dock.

Apprise: Inform, to give notice to.

Vaquero: Cowboy.

matters had taken at the mill. Work had been suspended on account of high water, and the men did not even appear disposed to engage in logging while the mill lay idle. Out of his anxiety for the fate of the mill, rather than interest in the new discoveries, Captain Sutter consented to take one of the party to the gold mines. He had been there once before, in the previous month, when Marshall, wild with excitement, had dragged him **thither** to behold the future scene of the world's wonder—a few grains of dull-looking metal stopped in the quill of some mountain bird was the first remittance of gold made from the mines of California.

There was, then, Captain Sutter, Major Reading, McKinstry, and the editor aforesaid—with two Indian "boys," Antonio and José, favorites of the captain, to look after the horses and make camp—and the party started at an early hour, because it was not expected to reach the mill before the next day. Captain Sutter, singular as it may seem, is a very poor horseman. Rarely in those days did he ever venture on the back of a horse, riding a mule in preference. On this occasion he was mounted on a favorite mule called Katy. Frequently that morning, in crossing marshy places or ascending slippery paths, the captain would fall to the rear and be heard in low tones of earnest **expostulation** with his mule: "Now, den, Katy—de **oder** foot! God bless me, Katy—de oder foot, child!"

Little of interest occurred during the day's ride, except that Major Reading, carrying a small hammer, frequently rode out from the trail to break off bits of rock, and once or twice he thought he had found traces of silver....

Straight before them, seeming so very near in the **transparent atmosphere** of that early morning, rose in solemn majesty the **hoary heads** of the Sierras.... A wild, wild group of mountains intervened, and then the beautiful **vale** of Coloma, nestling at their feet, cleft by the cold, rushing waters of the American. The hills that stand around it are clad with dense forests of evergreen. From the nearest summits, the pine and redwood rear high their sturdy crests motionless and without a murmur, or the song of a bird from their branches. The course of the river is lost to the eye in the dense growth of forest—we can scarcely catch at this distance the sound of its white, flashing waters. Only one sign of life, and that is a thin, blue column of smoke ascending dreamily from the depths of the vale, marking the locality of the lumbermen's camp.

Down the hill we rode, single file, with jingling Spanish spurs and bridle-bit, shaping our course for the camp without regard to

Thither: To or toward that place; in that direction.

Expostulation: To reason with a person in an effort to dissuade or correct.

Oder: Other.

Transparent atmosphere: Clear skies.

Hoary: Old, white with age.

Heads: Mountain peaks.

Vale: A valley, often coursed by a stream.

the meanderings of the trail. The sun was well up in the heavens, but the eastern slopes of the mountains lay buried in the shadows. The major, on his iron-gray steed, led the way, glancing right and left from under his broad-brimmed hat for silver signs, while the captain, on his mule, brought up the rear, picking his steps with anxious care, grasping the **pummel** of the saddle and dropping a word of earnest expostulation now and then to Katy. The chill air of the valley steals around us, and the roar of the rapids rises upon our ears.

Gold was discovered at Sutter's Mill in California in 1848, starting the great California gold rush.
(© Bettmann/Corbis. Reproduced by permission.)

Pummel: Spelled *pommel*; the upper front part of a saddle.

The Gold Rush: Edward Kemble

199

On a beach of land near the base of the long hill that we are descending, under majestic, spreading trees, we spy the camp of Marshall and his companions. It is a rude **bivouac** in the open air, with blankets, smoke-blackened kettles and tins, and **provender** sacks and boxes strewed all around, as though the men were on a march. The morning meal had been consumed, and the lumbering crew (they would have passed for a "lumbering" set most anywhere) were sitting or sprawling on the ground about the smoldering fire. They hardly returned our greeting as we rode up. It was apparent from the first moment we came in sight, we were unwelcome guests. We had not been slow to perceive in the words and looks that were exchanged before we came within hearing that the object of our visit was well understood and would receive no aid or encouragement from Marshall and his friends.

We unsaddled our beasts, and while Captain Sutter and Marshall started off by themselves, the major and the rest of the party endeavored to gain a little information respecting the gold discovery from the other lumbermen. Opening oysters with a wooden toothpick would have been an easy task compared to that job. One of the fellows "allowed" he didn't "go much on its being gold, anyway." Another guessed Marshall was a "little mite cracked" on the subject. In answer to the direct question where the gold was found, the reply was, "Oh, anywhere along the race or down by the river, where you've a mind to try for it." Which was true enough, as it afterwards appeared, but intended to be a very smart and evasive answer. Marshall, when afterwards asked to designate the precise locality where he first discovered the gold, took a large chip and, without speaking, made two scratches upon it with the point of a knife with which he had been moodily whittling, and then struck the blade in where the lines intersected, jerking out only the word "thar," and going on with his whittling without **deigning** any further explanation. No wonder men said Marshall was crazy. But he was not crazy; he was only eccentric, and just now he was acting a part.

Whew! It was getting warm as the sun began to send his rays vertically into the valley. There was not a breath of air. The major proposed that we should try our luck gold mining "along the race or the river or anywhere." So, borrowing an Indian basket, one of those handsome, water-tight utensils, woven of grass and ornamented with the gay plumage of the scarlet-winged **chenate** —a household vessel very common in those days—we walked down to the nearest point of the mill race. The major filled the basket with earth and

Bivouac: A temporary encampment often in an unsheltered area.

Provender: Dry food, such as hay, used as feed for livestock.

Deigning: Condescending to offer.

Chenate: A kind of bird.

Westward Expansion: Primary Sources

commenced the **laborious** process of washing for gold after the fashion of the **placer miners** in southern California. It was a new operation to the lookers on—probably Reading himself had never tried his hand at it before. It was very slow—we looked in vain for a sign of gold when the black sand was reached. "Try again," said the major, cheerily, proceeding to refill the basket. Higher rose the sun and hotter fell his beams on boulder and stream. The mill stood idle and deserted a few hundred yards below us. We began to look around for a shade. The major bent his back to his work.

Slowly, we walked down to the mill. Everything appeared unfinished or finished in haste, and a mechanic would have called it a bad job the moment his eye fell on the work. The dam was overflowed; the water had backed up into the race and nearly surrounded the mill. We saw no traces of gold-digging, nor could we find where men had washed their gold. Some Indians appeared on the other side. They were on their way up to the camp to talk with their friend, Captain Sutter, whose arrival in the valley they seem to have ascertained by a sort of instinct.

We left the river and wandered back into the woods, leaving the major twirling and dipping his basket while we slowly directed our steps by a shaded path to the camp. The **churlish** and inhospitable crew of lumbermen had gone out to **make a feint** of logging, or some other labor, for Captain Sutter's satisfaction. Our Indian boys prepared a lunch, and soon the Indians dropped in, one by one, and after a friendly salutation, sat down and eyed us in silence. Sutter came up and there was a grand handshaking, and now from another quarter, "remote, unfriended, melancholy, slow," approaches the sole representative of the mining interest in our party. He is greeted with a quiet "what success, major?" and replies, "not enough to buy a drink," which would be literally less than the value of a **Spanish real** in gold. There could be no reality in such gold discoveries as these. So we dropped the subject for the time being, and the editor of the Star noted in his memorandum book, as a subject for his next week's paper, the practical result of a test made of the gold-producing qualities of the soil at the alleged gold mines, and wrote overall, in emphatic character, "humbug."

That evening, when the cold dews began to descend, we heaped up the lumbermen's fire with logs and turned to our Indian visitors, each of whom had been provided with his supper and a present, and asked them what they knew about gold in these mountains. They replied that they knew much about it—that it was very

Laborious: Labor intensive.

Placer miners: Those who obtained minerals from placers (gravel deposits) by washing or dredging the site to release the minerals.

Churlish: Rude.

Make a feint: To pretend.

Spanish real: A silver coin.

Edward Kemble

Edward Cleveland Kemble was one of the first American settlers to come to California. He was born in Troy, New York, in 1828. His father, John, was the editor and owner of the *Troy Northern Budget*. As a teenager, Edward apprenticed in the print shop for Samuel Brannan's newspaper, *The Prophet*.

At eighteen, Kemble arrived in California with Samuel Brannan on the *Brooklyn* on July 31, 1846. He soon signed up to fight with the U.S. Army in the Mexican-American War (1846–48) to secure California for the United States. During the war, he was able to meet and ride into battle with John Frémont, one of the men Kemble admired and whose writings had inspired the young man to come to California. After the war, he returned to San Francisco. Brannan placed Kemble in charge of his newspaper, the *California Star*. Kemble would remain at the helm of the newspaper through a merger with *The Californian* to create the *Alta California*, the first daily paper in San Francisco.

Elicited: Brought or drew out.

Padres: Fathers, priests.

Proselytes: New converts to a religion.

Prosecuted: Practice; carried on.

Denounced: Condemned openly as being evil or reprehensible.

bad. As this seemed to confirm the editor of the Star *in his opinion, he was naturally desirous to know more. So Captain Sutter, through one of his boys acting as interpreter and turning it into Spanish,* **elicited** *the surprising fact that the existence of the gold had been known to the Indians for many generations, and that it was considered by them as owned and guarded by evil spirits. There was a lake, said the chief speaker, not far from here, where there is plenty of this bad medicine, but it is guarded by a fearful animal. The Indian described him as a species of dragon, which had an unpleasant appetite for human flesh and would devour all who came into his domains for gold.*

The Indians appeared to know nothing of the value of the yellow metal, and the conclusion we reached after hearing their statement was that the early mission **padres** *had obtained a knowledge of the gold mines and had warned their Indian* **proselytes** *not to tamper with them, intending to develop these mines with Indian labor someday. Such a knowledge certainly existed among the Franciscans who founded the California missions, and it may be that gold mining was carried on by them in a small way by means of Indians. The first mining regularly attempted after the discoveries of 1848 was* **prosecuted** *mainly by the aid of Indians. Until the dastardly outrage committed on a party of unoffending Indians by drunken Oregon desperados in the spring of this year, there was no difficulty in getting labor from these humble people. The shooting of half a dozen in cold blood, after they had been lured into camp on a pretense of friendship, drove the tribes into the mountains and provoked retaliations, which cost the lives of several innocent white men. This was the beginning of troubles between the red race and our own people in California. As usual, the whites were the cruel aggressors.*

The first party to the gold mines from San Francisco in 1848 returned as empty-handed as it had started, so far as the mere acquisition of gold was concerned. In the acquisition of knowledge it was more successful. The editor of the California Star, for example, had derived, as he believed, facts, which justified him in proclaiming the gold discoveries to be a delusion and a snare. Accordingly, the next issue of the paper after his arrival **denounced** the whole theory and alleged success as an arrant cheat and imposture. The

Miners panning for gold in California. The California gold rush, which began in 1848, hit its peak in 1849 and 1850.
(The Granger Collection, New York. Reproduced by permission.)

Stars *in their courses fought against the gold mines.* [Paddison, pp. 323, 324–331]

What happened next . . .

On May 12, 1848, two weeks after the party returned empty-handed to San Francisco, Samuel Brannan, the publisher of the *California Star,* paraded down the street waving a bottle of gold dust in his hand and yelling "Gold! Gold! Gold from the American River!" His testimony was enough to send many to the gold fields. Even the once skeptical Kemble closed the *Star* newspaper by June 14, writing "We have done. Let our word of parting be, *Hasta Luego.* "

Unfortunately, Kemble was unsuccessful in his search for gold and returned to the newspaper. He eventually became one of the most respected newspapermen in California, and at the end of his career he wrote a valuable history of California newspapers.

Did you know . . .

- Eighty thousand people arrived in California for the gold rush in 1849 and extracted approximately $10 million in gold from the Sacramento Valley.

- Shortly after James Marshall discovered gold at Sutter's Mill, New Mexicans began herding sheep to California to feed the miners.

- By 1854, three hundred thousand people had arrived in California for the gold rush.

Consider the following . . .

- How did the workers at Sutter's Mill respond to the party's inquiries?

- How did the Indians respond to the party's inquiries?

- What news did the party bring back with them to San Francisco?

For More Information

Holliday, J. S. *The World Rushed In: The California Gold Rush Experience, An Eyewitness Account of a Nation Heading West.* New York: Simon and Schuster, 1981.

Paddison, Joshua, ed. *A World Transformed: Firsthand Accounts of California Before the Gold Rush.* Berkeley, CA: Heyday Books, 1999.

White, Richard. *"It's Your Misfortune and None of My Own": A New History of the American West.* Norman: University of Oklahoma Press, 1991.

Elisha Douglass Perkins

Excerpt from Gold Rush Diary: Being the Journal of Elisha
Douglass Perkins on the Overland Trail
in the Spring and Summer of 1849
Written between May 1849 and February 1850
Published in 1967
Edited by Thomas D. Clark

In 1848 the discovery of gold in California created a wave
of excitement across America. The news of gold in California spread through the United States like wildfire, and the
migration to California increased. The *New York Herald* reported that "the great discovery of gold has thrown the
American people in a state of the wildest excitement. Gold
can be scooped up in pans at the rate of a pound of pure
dust a scoop. 'Ho! For California' is the cry everywhere."
Similar announcements appeared in newspapers across the
country.

By the summer of 1848 other westerners—Hawaiians, Oregonians, Mexicans, and Latin Americans—caught
wind of the discovery and set out for California. Late in
1848 the *Oregon Spectator* reported that "Almost the entire
male population has gone gold digging in California." In
July 1848, the number of gold seekers stood at two thousand; by October there were five thousand; and by year's
end they numbered eight thousand. Yet there were more to
come. Many of the first Californians to reach the gold
mines—known as the '48ers—wrote letters to eastern rela-

tives. These letters, filled with boasts of vast treasure troves, were often dismissed as rumors. The rumors were first confirmed in July when copies of Sam Brannan's special edition of the *California Star* reached Missouri. Other papers reprinted the story, creating a buzz in many cities throughout the eastern states. Still, many refused to believe the stories until they received some official confirmation. That confirmation came on December 5, 1848, when President James K. Polk told Congress that "the accounts of the abundance of gold in that territory are of such extraordinary character as would scarcely command belief were they not corroborated by authentic reports of officers in the public service." Polk's message left no room for doubt: there was gold in California.

Many people succumbed to the desire to "strike it rich" and set off over land or sea to California. One such person was Elisha Douglass Perkins. His diary tells of experiences that were typical for many people who braved the overland trails in search of gold. Perkins conveys the excitement of the time and the strong sense of boundless possibilities, but he also describes the reality of his situation with vivid detail.

The Marietta Gold Hunters

Perkins was intrigued by the prospect of earning his fortune in the gold mines of California. To fuel his interest, he read the first edition of Edwin Bryant's *What I Saw in California,* the best-selling account of John C. Frémont's western explorations, and a couple of the popular guidebooks to the overland trail. The possibilities seemed worth the risk. With five other men, Perkins soon formed the "Marietta Gold Hunters." By May 8, 1849, the Marietta Gold Hunters had assembled two wagons full of supplies and departed for St. Louis, where they transferred to the Missouri River steamer *Highland Mary II* and continued on to St. Joseph, the main point of departure for the overland trails. In St. Joseph they purchased mules and horses to make the trip. As he had done on his previous journeys, Perkins recorded his daily travels. His diary provides an accurate picture of the conditions of overland travel and the excitement of the time.

Things to remember while reading the excerpt from *Gold Rush Diary*:

- Perkins was one of many diarists who recorded their experiences on the overland trail. The accuracy of his account has been verified against other diaries. J. Elza Armstrong, John Banks, J. Goldsborough Bruff, David DeWolfe, Elijah Farnham, and Charles Glass Gray were among the diarists traveling a day ahead or a few days behind Perkins, who recorded similar experiences. Taken as a whole these accounts paint a vivid picture of the way the gold rush experience shaped lives.

- Two of Perkins's traveling companions, Samuel E. Cross and Zebulon Chesebro, crossed the trail in eighty-five days—almost record time—by following Edwin Bryant's advice to limit their supplies to the bare necessities and move along the trail quickly.

A wagon train heading west. Thousands migrated to California during the gold rush in hopes of striking it rich.
(Archive Photos, Inc. Reproduced by permission.)

• Throughout the diary Perkins misspells words that can be understood if sounded out.

Excerpt from Gold Rush Diary

May 9–May 21, 1849.... *Having decided upon undertaking a journey across the Plains by way of the South Pass of the Rocky Mtns. to the far famed valley of the Sacramento, I left my pleasant home & dear friends in Marietta, Ohio—on steamboat DeWitt Clinton—Wed. May 9, 1849, in company with five good fellows. S.E. Cross, Z.L. Chesebro, Jos. L. Stephens, J.L. Huntington & J.Q.A. Cunningham. Our trip down the Ohio & up to St. Louis was without incident worthy of record. The scenery of these rivers has been over & over again described every one has heard of their rapidly growing cities & towns. In St. Louis we met with an abundance of that scourge of the world the* **cholera,** *but were ourselves preserved from any personal acquaintance with it....*

At Jefferson City we saw a most melancholy monument of the ravages of the cholera in the steamer Monroe. *This vessel left St. Louis last week with about 100 cabin passengers & 50* **deck,** *all well, at the mouth of the Missouri the Cabin passengers began to be* **attacked** *& before reaching Jefferson City 150 miles—70 of them died; at the city the boat was deserted & all fled for their lives. Of the 100 passengers only* three *are now living & well!...*

Tuesday May 29. *Struck our tent this morning and packed it with the saddles* **&c,** *on our pack mules, harnessed up our team & by 12 oclock were ready to move. Doct Riggs not being ready we waited for him till 8 when we finally* **bid adieu** *to* **St. Joe** *& took up our line of march for the far distant gold region. Day hot & pleasant, Wind West.*

Our commencement was not very **flattering.** *We had hardly gone 1 mile when we came to a little hill, but very steep almost perpendicular, & there gave it two fair trials our mules could get only half way up when they would give in & commence backing down. There was no way but to unload so at it we went & after getting one wagon up the hill packed our goods up on our backs & loaded again. Twas about the hardest days work I ever did & gave us a very*

Cholera: An infectious disease of the small intestine that is characterized by profuse watery diarrhea, vomiting, muscle cramps, and severe dehydration.

Deck: Passengers who rode on the deck throughout the journey.

Attacked: Came down with cholera.

&c: Etc.

Bid adieu: Said goodbye.

St. Joe: St. Joseph, Missouri.

Flattering: Encouraging.

Elisha Douglass Perkins

Born on March 23, 1823, Perkins traveled a great deal as a youth as his father pursued various trades. Ultimately the family settled in Marietta, Ohio, where Perkins's father opened a drugstore. Since his father was a member of the professional class, the young Perkins had the luxury of attending an academy to prepare for college. He first studied in the Farmington Academy in Connecticut, but he found the winters too harsh and damaging to his health. He left school after three years to recover his health in Illinois. After his recovery, Perkins joined his family in Ohio and went back to school. He worked with his father in the drugstore and even invented an alcohol-fired steam engine that turned mixers and pounders. On May 11, 1847, Perkins married Harriett Eliza Hildreth.

His father's drugstore proved too small to support Perkins, his wife, and soon-to-be-born baby, so Perkins struggled to find a suitable career. In 1848 he traveled to New Orleans and Florida in hopes of finding a good place to set up his own drugstore, but he returned discouraged. Shortly after his return, however, the Marietta *Intelligencer* reported the discovery of gold in California and the opportunities in the western territory. Soon people were discussing the possibilities of digging fortunes out of the hills in California. By February, the yearning for gold and the belief that it was really available inspired several Ohioans to form gold-hunting companies to organize and prepare for the overland journey to the gold fields.

fair insight into our future. Out of this scrape we went on without trouble to the ferry, four miles where we arrived about sundown & finding we could not get acrossed camped....

Friday June 1. *Morning clear & pleasant. Woke up feeling very dizzy & weak & on attempting to rise was very sick at my stomach. Sent for Doct Riggs who said I must take some **calomel** & morphine & left some powders. Had a bed made up in the wagon & all being ready was helped into it & we started at 8 oclock. As we left it clouded up & a drizzling rain fell which continued at intervals **thro** the day. The jolting of the heavy wagon did me no good & my sickness increased, but I said nothing & took my powders every two hours.... In afternoon owing to some bad & dangerous places in the road was obliged to get out & crawl along myself for a short distance.*

....Distance today 20 miles. Here we first saw wild Indians, a small portion of the Sacs being in the vicinity, who came galloping round us,

Calomel: A white or brown compound used to evacuate the bowels.

Thro: Misspelling of *through*.

& with their fine horses & red blankets made quite an imposing & military appearance. They dismounted & threw themselves flat on the ground to watch our proceedings, leaving their horses to graze at their pleasure. In general they were a fine looking set of men & rather exceeded any previously formed opinion of the tribe of Black Hawk the Prophet. The mission at his place have some 30 to 40 Indian youth whom they are educating & some of our boys went up & took supper with them. They represented them as being very orderly & well behaved & at the supper table everything was like clock work....

Met today two or three returning Emigrants on horseback & they undertook to deposit our letters at St. Jos. for which we were very grateful. Said they turned back because they wanted to, a reason which there is no arguing against.

Wednesday July 11. Morn clear & warm, breeze East. Wind has changed at last & the disagreeable west wind, raising such clouds of dust has left us. I hope never to return....

*When we left the frontier we were told great stories about the selfishness & want of feeling among the Emigrants that the hardships and uncertainties of the journey had soured what "milk of human kindness" they might have possessed. I wish to bear my testimony against this slander. Never have I seen so much hospitality & good feeling anywhere exhibited as since I have been on this route. Let any stranger visit a camp no matter who or where, & the best of everything is brought out, he is fed, & **caressed** almost universally. If at meal time the best pieces are put on his plate & if the train has any luxuries they are placed before him. Nor have I seen any man in trouble, deserted, without all the assistance they could render. There are of course individual exceptions to all this, & such men are known to almost every train following. One fellow left an old man on the road without money or provisions. He was picked up & **brot** along by the next train, & I have not overtaken or fallen in with any companies yet but in course of conversation had something to say about this affair. "They would like to catch the fellow out alone." Some "would give him five hundred lashes." "We damn him Id go in for hanging him up to the first tree" &c....*

Having determined to pack from this place. I have spent this afternoon in making pack saddles arranging provisions &c. I shall take only 90 lbs each of bread & meat, being allowance for 60 days though the mountaineers tell me I might go through in 40. Once started I shall push on with all possible expedition. My cart I turn over to Cross & Co as being far superior to their own....

Caressed: Treated kindly.

Brot: Misspelling of *brought.*

Sutter's: Sutter's Mill was the first place gold was discovered in California.

Capt: Captain.

Monday July 23.... *Our reflections on "passing the Pass" are rather of an agreeable nature. We are now considerably more than half-way through our journey, with fine road & grass most of the remainder & down hill. From here to* **Sutter's** *is something less than 800 miles, & I hope to make it in 30 days....*

With most persons the first part of the journey is expected to be very pleasant. They intend to hunt, fish or have plenty of provisions some luxuries & perhaps enjoy themselves much. From now, however, stern perseverance without regard to personal comfort is necessary. Your provisions are reduced to hard crackers & bacon. No more game of consequence to find animals pretty well worn down & yourself considerably tired of your undertaking & you have nothing cheerful to look forward to but the getting through. The temptation is great to find some cool shady place to waste time in listless idleness. Many are so dallying now & most of these with ox teams too, & I am much mistaken if they do not have to pay for their comfort now by spending the winter in the mountains. How many have provisions to keep them in case they are compelled to do so I know not but vast quantities have been thrown away....

Friday August 3.... *Counted seventeen dead oxen today. Being out of the alkaline region pretty much, I have neglected keeping account of dead cattle, we however pass usually from 5 to 12 every day. How much further this will continue I cannot tell. Probably however more or less will be seen all the way to California "given out" for some reason or other....*

Monday August 27.... *A very fair hoax was played off this afternoon opposite our camp by the* **Capt** *of the Cherokee train which was some two or three miles back. He had been forward to look for grass & was returning when he met at our camp several trains*

Pile of stones marking a pioneer grave along the Oregon Trail.
(© James L. Amos/Corbis. Reproduced by permission.)

The Gold Rush: Elisha Douglass Perkins | 213

Men resting on the prairie, taking what could be a costly break during their overland trek. Travelers had to keep moving if they wanted to make it over the mountains before snow began to fall.
(Archive Photos, Inc. Reproduced by permission.)

which had stopped for water & was Being dressed in half Indian costumes, with buckskin pants, moccasins &c, & rather dark complexion, he was taken for a French mountaineer, of who there are numbers through this country, & was immediately beset by a crowd of Emigrants anxious to learn the latest news from the "diggings." In answer to their inquiries he told them that he was just from California having left Sutters just three weeks ago yesterday, that Gold was plenty, and one fellow asking him how much a man could dig in a day he replied that "a man not used to very hard work but pretty industrious could easily get 500$ per day," "Ah," says the questioner rubbing his hands with a great deal of satisfaction, "thank God I've been brot up to hard work all my life." After a number more such yarns he left them as he was in a great hurry to reach Green River. To discuss the wealth in prospect & knots of them could be heard for two hours talking over the good news & disputing about what "the mountaineer" said & what he did not say. Everything of course becoming more & more exaggerated the more it was repeated. We happen to know the Capt as we had passed his train & the whole *thing was exceedingly rich & afforded us great amusement to watch the excited looks & gestures of the eager dupes, & hear their different versions of "the news" to new comers.*

*Wednesday Sept 12.... At 4 p.m. we emerged from the **canon** into what is called the Mist Valley, a beautiful level plain covered with fine grass, some 10 miles across & formed by the widening of the mountain ranges. Through this valley the river winds after leaving the gorge on the other side, its course marked by a line of cotton woods & willows. Soon after entering the valley we took a trail leaving the road to the right & supposing it to be a "cutoff" as the road wound round a belt of marsh which crosses the valley nearby at right angles with the river. We followed this trail around the base of the fills & soon found ourselves going off quite in a **contrary** direction to the course of the road, & the marsh on our right was entirely uncrossable a perfect **quagmire**. There was nothing to do but go back some 3 miles or follow the path & see the End of the Adventure & the latter we decided to do, & adventure indeed it nearly proved to us. About 5½ we came upon an Indian fishing nets [sic] of willow twigs being set in the creek which wound through the marsh, & their camping place among the rocks close by having fresh ashes in its fire place, everything indicated their recent presence & gave promise of their speedy return.*

*This then was our "Cutoff" a trail which the Indians carried their fish to dispose of to trains. It was too late for us to return or better our condition. So we unpacked & picketed our mules in the magnificent & untouched grass which surrounded us & quietly cooked our supper hoping the **"Varmints"** would not discover us but very apprehensive lest they should. Guns & pistols have received special attention this evening & we have made every preparation to defend ourselves should the Indians resent this inroad upon their domains....*

Wednesday Sept 26. Morn clear warm. Wind E. Night warm. Start 8. Met a mile from camp the first of the Government relief parties, & learned that some hundred thousand had been appropriated to be dispensed for the relief of those Emigrants whose late start or loss of cattle renders it doubtful whether they will pass the Nevada before winter. Hundreds of such there are as I know having passed multitudes who must now be 600 miles behind, & other parties will be joyfully hailed on their errand of mercy. Pity but the Government treasures could always be appropriated to a good purpose, in relieving misery instead of causing it.

Arrived at Vernon a small town at the junction of Feather & Sacramento Rivers, at 9 a.m. & first beheld the stream whose name

Canon: Canyon.

Contrary: Opposite.

Quagmire: Soft land that sinks underfoot.

Varmints: Pests; troublesome people; Perkins is referring to Native Americans.

& fame are known all over the world & whose golden sands seduced me from all I hold dear into the wilderness. At this place the Sacramento is a clear still beautiful River about 1/4 or 1/3 of a mile across, the banks lined with oaks & various vines & bushes, willows &c. Its valley of the beauty of which we have heard & read so much, is a vast waste plain covered with a scanty wiry grass, with occasional marshes in patches of trees.

Never was there such misrepresentation as about this country, both as to the futility, fertility or capability of cultivation, & richness of the mines, & all that a few men might make fortunes. Among the Emigrants you will hear Bryant, Frémont, Robinson & others whose published accounts were the chief inducement to many to leave their comfortable home, cussed up & down, & loaded with all kinds of **opprobrious** names. They have all amassed fortunes off of the Emigration they have induced. This valley presents few attractions to any one who has lived in the states. No beautiful forests, or rich meadows but very few singing birds, Except Owls, & these abound. There are some Elk in the plains & any quantity of wolves, also in the sloughs great numbers of cranes, geese, ducks &c, but every one without exception is disappointed both in the appearance of the country & the richness of vegetable or mineral productions.

We crossed the river at Vernon & a little town opposite called Frémont. I saw just below Frémont a sight cheering to my eyes, in the shape of vessels, schooners &c, which navigate this far up, with various cargoes at enormous prices. I felt as if we were once more within the pale of civilization & our desert journey was indeed at an end. Traveled down the Sacramento & encamped at 4. Distance 16 miles. Day hot, wind S.W.

Thursday Sept 27.... At 4 we turned to the left through the timber & came suddenly upon the banks of the River at the ferry & directly opposite the far-famed & busy Sacramento City, with its vessels & cloth houses & all the scenes & sounds of civilized life, Oh, how rejoiced we were at the prospect! & what a comfort there was in the anticipation of letters to be received & friends met, & many made!

Crossed the ferry for which we paid the last 50 cents that could be scraped together, & took our way up the river through the streets, feeling a little awkward in our dirty & ragged prairie costumes, & encamped just in the edge of the city on the American River, under some large sycamores & overhanging vines, & here we are at last, at the end or our long & tedious journey, & having for the last time thrown off our packs & turned our mules out to graze. We laid our-

Opprobrious: Scornful, abusive.

selves down in the shade to luxuriate in the glowing thought. No more desert to cross & no more thirst on those deserts, no more getting up at daylight to swallow a cracker & pack up for a tedious days tramp through the heavy sand & in the hot sun. No more fear for the safety of the mules & ourselves & doubts as to our getting through, &c &c. Here we are at last through without a cent in our pockets, but here money can be made & we are in no danger of starvation, however I must see what I can hear of "Doc" [an earlier traveling companion] *& whether letters are to be had & try to dispose of "Dav"* [his mule] *or "make a raise" some way, as our last flour goes into tonights baking....*

On review of our journey & its incidents now that it is all over & our sufferings & privations at an end, I would not have it differ in any respect from what it was, we saw everything of frontier traveling that could be seen & struck the life in all its varieties, with wagon, packs & on foot, & the harder the times we had the pleasanter the retrospect, by contrast....

November 1. Well here we are in the gold mines of California, & mining has been tried "& found wanting!" We left **Sac.** *City October 18, with our provisions &c in Chapins wagons en route for the Cosumne River distant some 28 or 30 miles & arrived here the 21. We are about S.E. from the city, in a rolling country & on a small rapid stream tumbling over a rocky bed. The appearance of the country through which we passed was somewhat better than that down the Sac. River, as we saw it, but yet I have not been in any part of the "beautiful valley" of which we used to hear. On locating here we immediately went to work making "washers." Doc & John being somewhat "under the weather" I did nearly all the work on the mine alone. I cut down a pine tree, cut it off the proper length peeled & cut down one side & with axe &* **adz** *hollowed it out till I reduced it to about $\frac{1}{2}$ inch in thickness by nearly two days of hard labor & blistering of hands &c, & another day put in the "ripples" dash screen &c & took it down to the rocky bar where we are to commence our fortunes! & since have worked away like a trooper, rain or shine, with but indifferent success.*

The first three days Doc took hold with pick & shovel we excavated a hole about 4 feet deep & made in that time about 2.00! Here Doc broke down & was taken sick & John being about recruited he commenced with me in another place & we have made something everyday, the highest 11.00 lowest 3 each. This wont do & we shall probably leave soon for richer diggings next week. Tis terrible

Sac.: Sacramento.

Adz: A tool used to shape wood.

hard work, & such a backache as we have every night! We are below the bed of the creek & have to bale out water from our "hole" every hour, & work in the mud & wet at its bottom.

I am pretty well satisfied that fortunes in Cal. as anywhere else, with some exceptions, take time *& hard work to get, & I must go home with out mine I'm afraid, as I would hardly lead this kind of life 5 years for any fortune, & I certainly would not be separated from H. [Harriett] that length of time....*

Thursday Nov. *Still in our camp on the Cosumne & poor as the "diggings" have proved are likely to remain here all winter. The rains have set in in earnest & teams cannot travel. Chapins teams went to town for our provisions & sundries & are stuck fast about 5 miles from here, not able to move a step. I fear we may have difficulty in getting anything to eat. Doc has finally left us for good, & will probably go home in the next steamer, couldn't stand the hard work & went to town last week. His leaving puts the finishing stroke to my list of disappointments "& now I'm all alone." Shall have to give up my expectations of accumulating sufficient to carry me home in the spring & be thankful if I get enough to pay my expenses this winter. Well I'm here & must take the country as I find it....*

Saturday Feb 28. *Have just returned from an expedition round the richest of the mines of which we have heard to see about our summers digging, & find however that all the rich accounts dwindle down as you approach their location into the success of some few lucky ones & am satisfied by my trip that the gold is pretty equally distributed through the country, & a man had better settle down somewhere & work steadily for what he can get & trust to chance for striking a rich hole.*

I went through Weaverton, Hangtown, Georgetown, where the Oregon men did so well & came back by way of Colloma & Sutter's Mill & stopped to see the famous place where the first discovery was made—the news of which had set the American world crazy. The mill stands on the American river, is surrounded by immense & almost perpendicular hills, & the discovery of gold was made in the mill race some hundred or more yards below the mill. The race was dug by Indians employed by Sutter with white superintendants over them. One of the Indians in excavating picked up a lump of something yellow—metallic & heavy which was examined by the superintendant & finally taken to Mrs. Weimar wife of one of the white men. This lady boiled the lump in strong lye for two hours without tarnishing it at all. It was then sent to San Francisco analyzed & ex-

amined & pronounced to be fine gold & hence spread the news like wild fire which has filled the wilderness of California with enterprising Yankees.

The spring seems to have at last set in with beautiful weather & we are beginning to think of moving & shall probably move over into Matheney's Creek next week. We have had two heavy falls of snow since December & the tops of the high hills are still covered. One snow fell over two feet deep.

From the top of a peak ½ of a mile back of our cabin can be seen the Sierra Nevada range, white as snow itself, completely covered, shrubbery & all, distant from 30 to 50 miles East. While westward can be seen the valley of the Sacramento, with its boundary ranges of Cascade Mountains on the Pacific & the bay & entrance to San Francisco distant about 140 miles & the eye can follow the valley N.W. up some 200 miles. The view is Extensive & magnificent. During the late pleasant weather John & myself have been working in some of the little ravines & have made something over 100 dollars—better than nothing, though small wages. —End— [Clark, pp. 2, 12, 16–17, 60–2, 74–5, 87, 109–10, 124–5, 138–9, 142, 147–9, 150, 153–4]

What happened next . . .

Elisha Douglass Perkins's life was filled with failure. California was not the land of opportunity he had hoped for when he read about it in Ohio. In the end, Perkins found no fortune in gold. His trek across the country left him mourning the death of his traveling companions and regretting his inability to support his faithful wife. Disillusioned by his mining efforts, he quit looking for gold in 1850 and became the captain of a steamer, only to contract dysentery and to die virtually penniless in 1852. Though Elisha Douglass Perkins never made an important contribution to the development of the West, his faithful journal entries provide us with one of the clearest pictures of the trials and tribulations experienced by many of the overland travelers seeking their fortunes in gold.

Did you know . . .

- People from more than seventy countries rushed to California in search of gold.

- Cholera claimed the lives of thousands who attempted to cross the overland trails. It could sometimes kill people in a matter of hours.

- Once people gathered the easy-to-find gold, many stayed in California to farm or engage in other industry for a living.

- Big mining companies continued to search for gold with sophisticated equipment after individual prospectors gave up.

Consider the following . . .

- Is Perkins an especially optimistic person?

- How does Perkins deal with difficulties on the trail?

- What cheers Perkins or gives him relief?

- How does Perkins feel about his peers?

For More Information

Altman, Linda Jacobs. *The California Gold Rush in American History.* Springfield, NJ: Enslow Publishers, 1997.

Clark, Thomas D., ed. *Gold Rush Diary: Being the Journal of Elisha Douglass Perkins on the Overland Trail in the Spring and Summer of 1849.* Lexington: University of Kentucky Press, 1967.

Van Steenwyk, Elizabeth. *The California Gold Rush: West with the Forty-Niners.* New York: Franklin Watts, 1991.

Native Americans and the California Gold Rush

Excerpts from Exterminate Them: Written Accounts
of the Murder, Rape, and Slavery of Native Americans
During the California Gold Rush, 1848–1868
Edited by Clifford E. Trafzer and Joel R. Hyer
Published in 1999

With its mild climate, its vast and fertile interior valleys, and an abundance of game, the region we now know as California once supported a large native population. Historians estimate that before contact with the Europeans some three hundred thousand native people lived in the territory known as California. These Indians organized themselves into more than one hundred different tribes. Each of these groups had distinct cultures and traditions, and all benefited from an environment that provided them with the best diet of any native population.

Blessed with ample land and food, California's indigenous peoples found little reason to come into conflict with one another. This peaceful life began to change in 1769, when Spanish missionaries arrived on the California coast and set out to convert the native population to Christianity. The Spanish sought to extend their empire northward into California. They began building missions (church-based districts), pueblos (villages), and presidios (forts) in the southern territory around San Diego extending all the way to San Francisco Bay. The primary goal of the Spanish missionaries who occupied the twenty-one missions in California was to convert the natives to Christianity. According to Father Francisco Palou, "We rejoiced to find so many pagans upon whom the light of our holy faith was about to dawn." Dawn it did, as missionaries baptized nearly fifty-four thousand Indians in the first decades of their work. By the turn of the century they had gathered nearly the entire population of native Californians south of San Francisco Bay into their missions.

It was the missionaries who truly changed Indian life. Not only did they convert the natives to Christianity; they also sought to convert them to a European way of life. Neophytes (newly baptized Indians) were taught a variety of skills in the missions. They learned to be weavers, brick makers, farmers, and vaqueros (cattle drivers, or cowboys). But they did so against their will, becoming slaves to their supposed saviors. The baptized Indians could not leave the missions, and they were severely disciplined for misbehavior.

Other Indians living in remote mountain valleys had little contact with the Spaniards. Yet for the majority of the Indians, abuse at the hands of missionaries and diseases brought by the Spaniards destroyed their way of life. Of the sixteen thousand Indians baptized by missionaries in their first decade, more than nine thousand died. By 1817, 90 percent of the mission Indians had died due to disease or abuse.

In 1821 Mexico declared its independence from Spain. In 1834 the Mexican government ended the dominance of the missions and granted large tracts of land to the Californios (descendants of the original Spanish settlers). The Indians received little from the breakup of the missions and remained subject to the control of the wealthy landowners.

When California became part of the United States in 1847 and less than one thousand Americans lived there, the native inhabitants could not have foreseen the impending destruction of their way of life. The influx of eighty thousand miners in 1849 alone provided a small glimpse of the change that was about to occur. As hundreds of thousands of emigrants arrived, the Indians became terribly hostile to the miners, and trouble stirred in the hills of California. By the end of

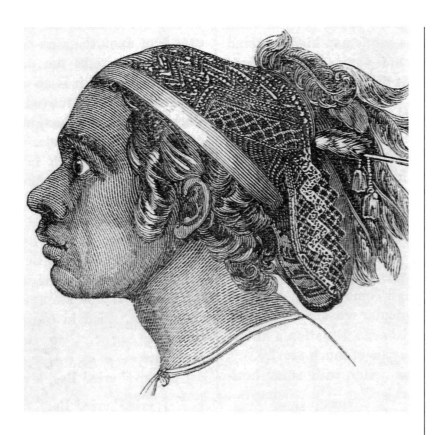

A native Californian, c. 1852.
(© Corbis. Reproduced by permission.)

the gold rush, the entire Indian population was devastated—it had declined to just thirty thousand people, down from three hundred thousand before European contact.

Newspaper accounts and government documents detail the hostile interactions of Indians and whites. Although these accounts are limited to the white perspective, some newspaper journalists were sympathetic to the Indians' plight and advocated more humane solutions to what was often referred to as "the Indian problem." The following excerpts provide examples of the interactions between Indians and whites that eventually led to the utter destruction of most Indian tribes in California.

Things to remember while reading the excerpts from *Exterminate Them*:

- Most whites, even those sympathetic to the plight of Native Americans, considered themselves better or more civilized than Indians and were very condescending toward Native Americans.

• The conflicts between Indians and whites helped many people recognize the need for governmental regulations of white and Indian interaction.

• Some people believed war with the Indians could have been avoided.

• Whites often created stereotypes of the Indian character that justified many of their treatment of the Indians.

• The first two articles are sympathetic to the Native Americans. The last two describe the stirrings of war between the whites and the Native Americans.

Daily Alta California, *January 18, 1849*
Sacramento City. Jan. 4th, 1849

*Yesterday we were all **agog** with a report which came in, that some wagoners, (some eight), were fighting with some Indians at the fork of the road between **here** and the "dry diggings, [sic]" three or four miles this side of the log cabin at the "Green Spa." Some say a wagon broke down, and that while one of the **teamsters** went to get help or another wagon, the other stopped to guard the broken one—that some Indians came about and a fight arose—that the other teamster and some other men came up, and a general fight took place—that the Indians ran, and that the Indians had stolen an ox, and that the whites wished to punish them. The proof that they stole the ox, is, that his tracks were found leading to the rancheria, but were not found going away from it.*

*To-day when I came in from work, I found the people all astir, in consequence of an express having arrived from Leidsdorff's ranch, saying some Indians had been to a camp near, and driven off eight white men, (Oregonians.) Everybody who could raise a horse turned out to go to their **relief** —They were just returning. They said the excitement was caused by the following circumstances:*

Yesterday an old Indian, well known in this neighborhood, and who had a good character came to a camp of Oregonians, and one

Agog: Intensely interested.

Here: Sacramento City.

Teamsters: People who drove the team of horses or mules that pulled the wagons.

Relief: Rescue.

of them claimed one of his horses. The Indian said he had bought the horse from a white man, and did not like to give him up.... The white man persisted that he was his horse, and took him away from him. The Indian was enraged, and rode off, making use of expressions which were not agreeable to the Oregonian, and he took up his rifle and shot him. The Indian's horse went home, his saddle covered in blood, but without his rider. Today, some time, armed Indians came to the camp of, or met some eight Oregonians, and the latter knowing the occurrence of yesterday, presumed *they had come to take revenge, and gave them battle, and were* **whipped.** One of them came in to the Fort and told his story, and the whole garrison turned out to their rescue, but when they returned, having heard other stories, they were pretty generally sorry the Indians had not whipped them worse.

Notice was given, that to-night there would be a meeting to take into consideration the propriety of organising [sic] a provisional government. [Trafzerand Hyer, pp.36–7]

Downing the Nigh Leader by Frederic Remington depicts the conflict that existed between settlers and Native Americans. Both groups felt they had legitimate rights to live on western lands. *(© Hulton Getty/ Liaison Agency. Reproduced by permission.)*

Whipped: Beaten.

Daily Alta California, *January 15, 1851*
Our Indian Difficulties

It is to be hoped that the **temperate** *and reasonable address of the Indian Agents, which we published yesterday, may have weight with the public, and induce that* **forbearance** *and moderation which the importance of the matter demands. Not only do we hope that the miners and people generally will pause and let reason and justice guide their conduct toward the ignorant starving savages, but that our legislators and all those who hold public and high trust will use their influence to prevent the* **effusion** *of blood. It is not for the benefit of our State, viewed even in a* **pecuniary** *light, to annihilate these poor creatures. But there are reasons infinitely beyond all estimated dollars and cents, all prospects of profitable business or possessions, which should guide our councils and conduct. There is a question of justice, of humanity, of right, of religion. They are the original possessors of the soil. Here are all the associations of their lives. Here are their traditions. The trees which we cut down are the volumes of their unwritten histories. The mountain-tops are their temples; the running streams which we turn aside for gold have been the store-houses of their food, their fisheries by us destroyed and their supplies cut off.*

The wild game, which gave them food we have driven from the valleys, the very graves of their **sires** *have been dug down for the glittering gold which lay beneath. The reckless of our people have not stopped at these* **inevitable** *results. They have abused and outraged the confidence and friendship of the trusting Indians, robbed and murdered them without* **compunction***, and, in short, perpetrated all those outrages against humanity, and decency, and justice, which have entailed upon the American public nearly every war which has turned red with Indian blood the green vallies [sic] from the Pequod and Narragansett nations, all the way through the continent, which we have taken from them, to the sand-bordered homes of the Yumas, and the oaten hills of the Clear Lake tribes.*

Is it not time to pause and inquire if might is right in this matter? We make war upon them and annihilate them. But is that the best policy? Is it humane? Is it polite? It is [sic] Christian? We answer it is not. The Indian has his **vices***; it is to be regretted that the white man has many—ay, greater by far than these poor children of nature. And is it known, too, that they have lived on the most friendly terms with us until oppression has broken all the bonds between the races?*

Temperate: Mild or moderate.

Forbearance: Patience.

Effusion: Flowing.

Pecuniary: Concerning money.

Sires: Forefathers.

Inevitable: Unavoidable.

Compunction: Second thought or guilt.

Vices: Moral vices.

Debauched: Seduced; had sexual relations with.

We have driven them to the wall. We have pushed them from the valleys where their arrows procured their meat, from the rivers where they caught their fish, we have destroyed their oak orchards; we have cut down or burned their wheat which was the seed of the wild grass; have slaughtered the men and **debauched** the women. And now the **atonement** is to be, utter destruction! Can God look down upon such cruelty, and bless the people guilty of the outrage? We therefore call once more for the moderation of council and moderation in action. Our agents are already upon the mission. Let all good citizens give a helping hand. Let us avoid if within the bounds of possibility, an Indian war. Such a calamity would not alone be one to the Indians. It will cost the lives of many valuable citizens. And should it end in the total destruction of the Indian tribes, it would be at a cost of treasure and blood horrible to contemplate, for which there could be no adequate return, and would be a result over which the **Philanthropist**, the Christian, and every true hearted man would mourn as the last great sin of national injustice, violence, and oppression. [Trafzer and Hyer, pp. 37–8]

An American Indian lies on the ground uttering the "last war-whoop." A few American newspapers tried to raise awareness that the decimation of the Native Americans' land, sources of food, and other resources had driven the Indians to attack whites and to steal food and supplies.
(© Hulton Getty/ Liaison Agency. Reproduced by permission.)

Atonement: Reconciliation, or reparation made for a wrong.

Philanthropist: Charitable person.

Daily Alta California, *January 21, 1851*
Our Indian Relations

*The bickerings between the Indians and whites, which at first, with an ordinary degree of tact and ability, tempered with justice, might have been silenced, and subsequent difficulties been avoided, have at length reached a point when very effective measures must be pursued, or the districts bordering upon the range of the mountain tribes be, if not depopulated, at least most **ruinously** checked in their progress. There is no doubt that the mountain tribes have at length assumed a hostile position, and are in sufficient numbers to **keep at bay** any weak parties of our people who may march against them. Being thoroughly acquainted with the mountain passes, they possess great advantages over most of the whites who are disposed to take part in the **foray** against them. Hunger and desperation are not likely to make them very **treatable**, and we, therefore, anticipate much trouble ere the present warlike demonstrations shall be quieted.*

The settlement of the whites in the plains and vallies [sic] has necessarily driven the game from the old grounds whence the Indians derived their supplies. Of course they attribute their threatened starvation to the presence of the whites, and reasoning as they have ever since our ancestors came into their country, they very naturally have come to the conclusion that if they could exterminate the whites the old condition of things would return. And that they can do so they fully believe. Meanwhile thefts and robberies have been committed by them and retaliations have followed. They have stolen horses and mules for food, the latter being considered by them most excellent. Thus things have been progressing until the attack upon the plundering of Savage's store and the murder of three of the four persons who were present. Since then, Savage having not met with success in his call upon the Governor for power to enlist volunteers, raised what men he could and gave battle, killing some thirty of the Indians. We have conversed with Judge Marvin, recently elected Superintendent of Public Instruction, and from him have learned many important particulars.

*He **represents** the Indians as numbering probably seven thousand, with **hostile determinations**, spread through the mountains between the waters of the Tuolumne and the head waters of the San Joaquin. They have intercommunications throughout the mountain passes, by which they will probably be able to concentrate the greater part of their force upon whatever point may be attacked by the Americans. Judge Marvin's opinion is that the Indians must be*

Ruinously: Harmfully.

Keep at bay: Hold off.

Foray: Attack.

Treatable: Willing to discuss a treaty.

Represents: Describes.

Hostile determinations: Plans to attack.

Drubbed: Defeated.

pretty severely **drubbed** before they will so far respect our power as to keep any treaties they may agree to, if such can be entered into with them. One thing is very evident; there must be immediate action. Our commissioners must be active, or a long, bloody and costly war is inevitable. While we hesitate or lose time, the golden moment for pacification may forever be lost. Even since this article was commenced, news has arrived of another battle, the particulars of which the reader will find in another place.

"Digger" Indians, members of the southern branch of the Paiute tribe of California. They live in wickiups, shelters of stick and brush fastened to poles made from willow trees.
(© Hulton Getty/ Liaison Agency. Reproduced by permission.)

There can be no doubt that the Indian tribes of the mountains have been under-estimated by writers and others. **The gentlemen above referred to** says that he considers them as brave as the Mohawks or any other of the eastern tribes. It is truly lamentable that the U.S. government did not one year ago send out Commissioners to treat with them, authorised [sic] to **purchase extinguishment [sic] of their titles to the land** and agree upon annual **subsidies** sufficient to compensate them for the **relinquishment** of their lands, fisheries, &c. Had this been done, the Commissioner, by a **judicious** distribution of presents and punctual payment of all things promised, would undoubtedly have found little difficulty in placing the relation between the two races upon such a basis as would have been for the advantage of both. It looks now very doubtful whether the gentlemen of the commission will be able to secure peace before a severe lesson shall have been taught these belligerent tribes.

One of them was to leave last evening for Sonoma, to make a requisition for an escort of troops. They wish to try peaceable measures if they be **practicable.** It might be the wisest course to forward all the available force of the U.S. troops in the region of the difficulties, not so near as to prevent the appearance of peaceable intentions and measures on the part of the commission, which might prevent success; nor yet so far removed as to cause the loss of much time and **advantageous** opportunities in case the sword and the rifle alone have to become the agents of peace. We believe the commission fully competent with the aid of gentlemen well acquainted with the Indian character, who are ready to co-operate to settle the whole matter if it be possible without the last appeal. But if that be done it must be done quickly. The **Saxon** blood is up. And when it is so, like the rolling Mississippi, no slight **levee** will stay it within its channels. [Trafzer and Hyer, pp. 40–1]

Sacramento Union, February 3, 1855
Indian War

The accounts from the North indicate the **commencement** of a war of extermination against the Indians. The **latter** commenced the attack of the **Klamath**; but who can determine their provocation or the amount of **destitution** suffered before the hostile blow was struck.

The intrusion of the white man upon the Indian's hunting grounds has driven off the game and destroyed their fisheries. The consequence is, the Indians suffer every winter for **sustenance.**

The gentleman above referred to: Judge Marvin.

Purchase extinguishment of their titles to the land: Pay the Indians to give up their land.

Subsidies: Payments.

Relinquishment: Handing over.

Judicious: Sensible.

Practicable: Possible.

Advantageous: Beneficial.

Saxon: Anglo-Saxon; referring to whites.

Levee: An embankment or wall to stop a flood.

Commencement: Beginning.

Latter: The author is referring back to the Indians.

Klamath: Klamath River in northwestern California.

Destitution: Hardship.

Sustenance: Food and other supplies needed for survival.

Hunger and starvation follows them wherever they go. Is it, then, a matter of wonder that they become desperate and resort to stealing and killing? They are driven to steal or starve, and the Indian mode is to kill and then plunder.

The policy of our Government towards the Indians in this State is most miserable. Had reasonable care been exercised to see that they were provided with something to eat and wear in this State, no necessity would have presented itself for an indiscriminate slaughter of the race.

The fate of the Indian is fixed. He must be **annihilated** *by the advance of the white man; by the disease, and, to them, the evils of civilization. But the work should not have been commenced at so early a day by the deadly rifle.*

To show how the matter is viewed on the Klamath, we copy the following from the Crescent City Herald. *The people look upon it there as a war of extermination, and are killing all grown up males. A writer from Trinidad, under date of January 22d, says:*

I shall start the two Indians that came down with me tonight, and hope they may reach Crescent City in safety, although I think it exceedingly doubtful, as the whites are shooting them whenever an opportunity offers; for this reason I start them in the night, hoping they may be out of danger **ere** *morning. On the Klamath the Indians have killed six white men, and I understand some stock. From the Salmon down the whites are in arms, with determination, I believe if possible, to destroy all the grown up males, notwithstanding this meets with the opposition of some few who have favorite Indians amongst them. I doubt whether this discrimination should be made, as some who have been considered good have proved the most treacherous. I understand that the ferry of Mr. Boyce, as also that of Mr. Simms, has been cut away.* **Messrs.** *Norton and Beard have moved their families from Elk Camp to Trinidad; they were the only white females in that section that were exposed to the savages. I have no doubt there will be warm times on the Klamath for some weeks, as the Indians are numerous, well armed and determined to fight.* [Trafzer and Hyer, pp. 47–8]

Annihilated: Destroyed.

Ere: By.

Messrs.: Plural of Mr.

What happened next . . .

The gold rush lasted from 1848 to 1868 in California. During this time the Indian population declined rapidly as the enormous influx of white miners and settlers brought deadly diseases and started fatal conflicts. By 1870 the Indian population had decreased to about one-sixth its size before the gold rush. As the Indian population diminished, the white population grew.

Because of the strong lure of wealth, California was one of the most quickly populated territories in American history. Yet it also created a unique community, one established solely for the accumulation of individual wealth. Only after the miners quit the mines and turned to service jobs or farming did large numbers of women and children join the American population in California. As more and more women and children migrated to the territory, permanent institutions, including schools and civic organizations, were established.

The new white community in California discriminated against foreigners of any type. When California entered the union in 1850, it passed laws insisting that those who did not possess American citizenship must pay twenty-dollar monthly fees to work in the mines. While the law resulted in many Mexicans leaving the mines, the Chinese paid and stayed. Angered by the nonwhites who continued to search for gold, Americans resorted to threats and violence to frighten nonwhites from the mines.

Starting with the passage of California Statute Chapter 133 on April 22, 1850, the California legislature passed twenty laws restricting the rights of Native Americans in California. Their way of life irreparably damaged, their lands polluted and stolen, Native Americans had little recourse. The laws denied Indians the opportunity to testify against whites in court, prohibited them from practicing some of their traditions like burning the prairie grasses to find game, and provided for Native Americans' indentured servitude to whites. The native populations suffered greatly from their diminished positions. Disease and fighting reduced the Native American population of California from about 120,000 before the gold rush to about 20,000 by 1870. Despite the brevity of the gold rush, it was one of the most influential periods in American history because it inspired so many to migrate westward.

Did you know . . .

- California achieved statehood in 1850.

- In 1846 the Native American population in California was estimated to be at least 120,000.

- Between 1846 and 1848 about one hundred thousand Indians died from disease, malnutrition, enslavement, or murder, according to Clifford Trafzer and Joel Hyer in *Exterminate Them.*

- An Act for the Government and Protection of Indians passed in April 1850. This act and amendments made to it in 1860 detailed how Indians could become the indentured servants of whites.

- California laws did not discriminate against African Americans, although whites in California still did.

- California established a $1.5 million fund to reimburse volunteer militia units that worked to subdue hostile Indians.

- Federal commissioners—Redick McKee, George Barbour, and O. M. Wozencraft—negotiated eighteen treaties with California Indian groups in the 1850s. The U.S. Senate rejected all of these treaties.

- Indian reservations eventually included less than one-seventh of California land.

Consider the following . . .

- What were the prejudices of the journalists, and how did they shape their opinions?

- Why did the hostilities between the Indians and whites seem to be escalating toward war?

- There were several arguments for solving the "Indian problem." How did these sympathetic journalists propose to resolve the conflicts?

- How could Indians protect themselves from the influx of miners?

- How could emigrating Americans protect themselves from Indians?

For More Information

Heizer, Robert F. *The Destruction of California Indians.* Santa Barbara, CA: Peregrine Smith, 1974.

Heizer, Robert F., and Alan J. Almquist. *The Other Californians.* Berkeley, CA: University of California Press, 1971.

Ketchum, Liza. *The Gold Rush.* Boston: Little, Brown, 1996.

Schanzer, Rosalyn. *Gold Fever! Tales from the California Gold Rush.* Washington, D.C.: National Geographic Society, 1999.

Trafzer, Clifford E. *California's Indians and the Gold Rush.* Newcastle, CA: Sierra Oaks Publishing Company, 1989.

Trafzer, Clifford E., and Joel R. Hyer, eds. *"Exterminate Them": Written Accounts of the Murder, Rape, and Slavery of Native Americans During the California Gold Rush, 1848–1868.* East Lansing: Michigan State University Press, 1999.

The Closing of the Frontier

The conquest of the American frontier is one of the most exciting and dramatic stories in American history. Settling western lands required nearly a century of warfare and hardship as Americans fought the British and many Indian groups to lay claim to the West. The United States was born out of the Revolutionary War, which was fought in part to guarantee the rights of colonists to settle west of the Appalachian Mountains. Yet winning the war and declaring independence from England didn't automatically open the West to the Americans. For four decades after they declared their independence in 1776, Americans battled the British and a variety of Native American groups to take possession of the lands stretching west to the Mississippi River.

The Louisiana Purchase of 1803 and the American victory in the War of 1812 opened the continent to western expansion. The Louisiana Purchase nearly doubled the size of the United States, adding a vast expanse of territory that reached from the Mississippi River to the Rocky Mountains and from the Gulf of Mexico to the Canadian border. The

War of 1812 was fought between the United States and Britain over shipping rights to France, but also over control of the western regions of the United States. Although the United States had won its independence from Britain in 1783, the British continued keeping forces in the northwest regions of the United States. The British also encouraged and assisted Native Americans in attacking American settlers. When the Americans defeated the British in the War of 1812, the United States firmly established its intent to claim and control all of the territory up to the Mississippi River.

After the War of 1812, thousands of Americans migrated to the middle section of the country. Mass emigration to the farther west began in the 1830s, increased in the 1840s, and became a flood after the California gold rush, which began in 1848 and reached its peak between 1849 and 1850. Still, Americans faced many hardships as they attempted to claim western lands. The Mexican–American War (1846–1848) resolved American claims to the Southwest, but Americans fought with various Indian groups in the area well into the 1870s. It wasn't until the final defeat of Indian forces at Wounded Knee in 1890 that America could truly claim to have conquered the frontier.

As more than a century of struggle and conquest came to an end, America was settled from sea to shining sea; in fact, there were few areas left unexplored or unsettled. This westward expansion was the work of an entire nation: For every charismatic leader like Andrew Jackson or Daniel Boone, there were hundreds of unnamed settlers who were equally brave and determined to claim their place in a new land. Many of the most dramatic westward movements were not started as part of an overall vision or plan; instead, they were the result of independent pioneers striking out and pulling civilization along behind them. Yet how had this expansion affected the people who accomplished it and the nation itself? This was the question that Frederick Jackson Turner attempted to answer in his important essay, **"The Significance of the Frontier in American History."**

Frederick Jackson Turner

"The Significance of the Frontier in American History"

Excerpted from *The Frontier in American History*
Originally published in 1920

In 1893 a then little-known historian named Frederick Jackson Turner (1861–1932) delivered an address at the World Columbian Exposition in Chicago that changed the way Americans thought about the American character and the conquest of the West. For years, scholars and historians who had tried to explain the development of America emphasized the European influences on American culture. According to these scholars and historians, the explorers, the settlers, their material culture (the physical things they owned), their institutions, their beliefs and values—all had been forged in Europe. Yet such explanations ignored a decisive factor in the shaping of the American character, argued Turner. That factor was the frontier.

According to Turner, what separated Americans from Europeans was the constant availability of new land to the west. In his speech, Turner maintained that the frontier—that region just beyond or at the edge of a settled area—washed away all European influences and created a distinctive American character. Although settlers in America brought their European culture and beliefs with them, they found themselves confronting a radically new environment: new terrain, new

Frederick Jackson Turner.
(Reproduced from the Collections of the Library of Congress.)

plants and animals, new cultures, and new problems. Almost instantly, Turner maintained, Americans began to behave differently from Europeans: they began to think differently, express themselves differently, make different objects, and develop different institutions. In the end, they became much different from their European relatives and heritage.

In Turner's view, the frontier experience led to the emergence of a new people and nation, shaped by the experience of individuals pushing westward into free land. This steady westward movement brought progress and civilization to an uncivilized world, while at the same time creating individuals who were self-reliant, tough, and competent. Though the frontier was now gone, Turner believed that Americans could better confront their future by fully realizing the unique nature of their past.

Turner delivered the following speech at the World Columbian Exposition in Chicago in 1893. Because his audience consisted of fellow historians, Turner could assume that they understood what he was talking about and he left many things unexplained. Read the following excerpts from Turner's speech with these questions in mind: What are Turner's main points? Why does Turner think the frontier played such an important role in shaping American character? What kinds of things does he overlook in emphasizing the influence of the frontier? Do you agree with Turner?

Things to remember while reading "The Significance of the Frontier in American History":

• Many Americans thought that the presence of a frontier offered a "safety valve" that would allow for the release of

Frederick Jackson Turner

On November 14, 1861, Frederick Jackson Turner was born in Portage, Wisconsin. As the son of a local political figure, young Turner grew up with firsthand knowledge of party politics and a healthy respect for the ability to influence people with words and ideas. As a boy, Turner read widely; when he was only fifteen, he began to contribute to his father's newspaper in a section called Pencil and Scissors Department, where Turner printed quotations that had attracted his attention. The young Turner's obvious intellectual ability and interest did not mean that he became the stereotypical bookworm. On the contrary, when not reading his favorite author, Ralph Waldo Emerson, he could be found hunting and fishing with his father or engaging in the sort of activities that Mark Twain had imagined for Tom Sawyer.

Turner excelled as a student and graduated from Portage's only high school in June 1878. While attending the University of Wisconsin, Turner studied history and became a noted orator. In 1885 Turner joined the faculty of the University of Wisconsin to teach history. In 1893 the young professor was one of four professional historians who presented papers at the World Columbian Exposition in Chicago. Turner's paper, "The Significance of the Frontier in American History," began a revolution in the study of American history. Turner went on to build Wisconsin's history department into one of the best in the nation, and his ideas and many essays helped shape the writing of American history for the remainder of the century. Turner died on March 14, 1932.

pressures created by increasing population. They thought that whenever towns got too big people could simply move to the frontier.

• The study of American history was a new profession in the 1890s and was just beginning to gain respectability.

• The first census in the United States was conducted in 1790.

• By 1900 the United States had forty-five states and a population of seventy-six million. The next three states to join the union were Oklahoma (1907), New Mexico (1912), and Arizona (1912).

Excerpt from "The Significance of the Frontier in American History"

In a recent bulletin of the Superintendent of the Census for 1890 appear these significant words: "Up to and including 1880 the country had a frontier of settlement, but at present the unsettled area has been so broken into by isolated bodies of settlement that there can hardly be said to be a frontier line. In the discussion of its extent, its westward movement, etc., it can not, therefore, any longer have a place in the census reports." This brief official statement marks the closing of a great historic movement. Up to our own day American history has been in a large degree the history of the colonization of the Great West. The existence of an area of free land, its continuous recession, and the advance of American settlement westward, explain American development.

Behind institutions, behind constitutional forms and modifications, lie the vital forces that call these organs into life and shape them to meet changing conditions. The peculiarity of American institutions is the fact that they have been compelled to adapt themselves to the changes of an expanding people, to the changes involved in crossing a continent, in winning a wilderness, and in developing at each area of this progress out of the primitive economic and political conditions of the frontier into the complexity of city life. Said Calhoun in 1817, "We are great, and rapidly—I was about to say fearfully—growing!" So saying, he touched the distinguishing feature of American life. All peoples show development.... In the case of most nations, however, the development has occurred in a limited area; and if the nation has expanded it has met other growing peoples whom it has conquered. But in the case of the United States we have a different phenomenon. Limiting our attention to the Atlantic coast, we have the familiar phenomenon of the evolution of institutions in a limited area, such as the rise of representative government; the differentiation of simple colonial governments into complex organs; the progress from primitive industrial society, without division of labor, up to manufacturing civilization. But we have in addition to this a recurrence of the process of evolution in each western area reached in the process of expansion. Thus American development has exhibited not merely advance along a single line, but a

Recession: Withdrawing or going back.

Phenomenon: Occurrence or circumstance.

Representative government: A government in which representatives are elected by the citizens.

return to primitive conditions on a continually advancing frontier line, and a new development for that area. American social development has been continually beginning over again on the frontier. This *perennial* rebirth, this fluidity of American life, this expansion westward with its new opportunities, its continuous touch with the simplicity of primitive society, furnish the forces dominating American character. The true point of view in the history of this nation is not the Atlantic coast, it is the Great West. Even the slavery struggle, which is made so exclusive an object of attention by writers like Professor von Holst, occupies its important place in American history because of its relation to westward expansion.

In this advance, the frontier is the outer edge of the wave—the meeting point between savagery and civilization. Much has been written about the frontier from the point of view of border warfare and the chase, but as a field for the serious study of the economist and the historian it has been neglected.

The American frontier is sharply distinguished from the European frontier—a fortified boundary line running through dense populations. The most significant thing about the American frontier is, that it lies at the hither edge of free land. In the **census reports** it is treated as the margin of that settlement which has a density of two or more to the square mile. The term is an **elastic** one, and for our purposes does not need sharp definition. We shall consider the whole frontier belt, including the Indian country and the outer margin of the "settled area" of the census reports. This paper will make no attempt to treat the subject **exhaustively**; its aim is simply to call attention to the frontier as a fertile field for investigation, and to suggest some of the problems which arise in connection with it.

In the settlement of America we have to observe how European life entered the continent, and how America modified and developed that life and reacted on Europe. Our early history is the study of European **germs** developing in an American environment. Too exclusive attention has been paid by institutional students to the Germanic origins, too little to the American factors. The frontier is the line of most rapid and effective Americanization. The wilderness masters the colonist. It finds him a European in dress, industries, tools, modes of travel, and thought. It takes him from the railroad car and puts him in the birch canoe. It strips off the garments of civilization and arrays him in the hunting shirt and the moccasin. It puts him in the log cabin of the Cherokee and Iroquois and runs an Indian **palisade** around him. Before long he has gone to planting

Perennial: Constant; repeated regularly.

Census reports: Reports produced every ten years that offer a count of the nation's population.

Elastic: Flexible; can be defined many ways.

Exhaustively: At great length; completely; from all angles of the subject.

Germs: Seeds, or beginnings.

Palisade: A fence of pointed logs or sticks.

Reversion: Returning.

Terminal moraines: Deposits left by the withdrawal of a glacier.

Glaciations: Covering over with glaciers.

Partakes: Takes part or shares in.

Precipitated: Separated, as solids sink to the bottom of a liquid solution.

Disposition: Administration or control.

Public domain: Land or property that is available to everyone.

Intercourse: Communication.

Prim little townships of Sleswick: Turner is referring to the attempt of historians to explain American happenings by referring to European history.

Statutes: Laws.

Indian corn and plowing with a sharp stick; he shouts the war cry and takes the scalp in orthodox Indian fashion. In short, at the frontier the environment is at first too strong for the man. He must accept the conditions which it furnishes, or perish, and so he fits himself into the Indian clearings and follows the Indian trails. Little by little he transforms the wilderness but the outcome is not the old Europe, not simply the development of Germanic germs, any more than the first phenomenon was a case of **reversion** to the Germanic mark. The fact is, that here is a new product that is American. At first, the frontier was the Atlantic coast. It was the frontier of Europe in a very real sense. Moving westward, the frontier became more and more American. As successive **terminal moraines** resulting from successive **glaciations,** so each frontier leaves its traces behind it, and when it becomes a settled area the region still **partakes** of the frontier characteristics. Thus the advance of the frontier has meant a steady movement away from the influences of Europe, a steady growth of independence on American lines. And to study this advance, the men who grew up under these conditions, and the political, economic, and social results of it, is to study the really American part of our history....

From decade to decade distinct advances of the frontier occurred.... [Turner describes the slow advance of the frontier line from the crest of the Appalachian Mountains westward to the Mississippi River, then leaping across the nation to California, and slowly encroaching on the lands in between.]

In these successive frontiers we find natural boundary lines which have served to mark and to affect the characteristics of the frontiers, namely: the "fall line;" the Alleghany Mountains; the Mississippi; the Missouri where its direction approximates north and south; the line of the arid lands, approximately the ninety-ninth meridian; and the Rocky Mountains.... Each was won by a series of Indian wars.

At the Atlantic frontier one can study the germs of processes repeated at each successive frontier. We have the complex European life sharply **precipitated** by the wilderness into the simplicity of primitive conditions. The first frontier had to meet its Indian question, its question of the **disposition** of the **public domain**, of the means of **intercourse** with older settlements, of the extension of political organization, of religious and educational activity. And the settlement of these and similar questions for one frontier served as a guide for the next. The American student needs not go

to the *"prim little townships of Sleswick"* for illustrations of the law of continuity and development. For example, he may study the origin of our land policies in the colonial land policy; he may see how the system grew by adapting the **statutes** to the customs of the successive frontiers.... Each tier of new States has found in the older ones material for its constitutions. Each frontier has made similar contributions to American character, as will be discussed farther on....

The Rocky Mountains marked the western boundary of the United States and the edge of the American frontier in the mid-1800s.
(Archive Photos, Inc. Reproduced by permission.)

The Closing of the Frontier: Frederick Jackson Turner   245

Loria, the Italian economist, has urged the study of colonial life as an aid in understanding the states of European development, affirming that colonial settlement is for economic science what the mountain is for geology, bringing to light primitive **stratifications**. "America," he says, "has the key to the historical enigma which Europe has sought, for centuries in vain, and the land which has no history reveals luminously the course of universal history." There is much truth in this. The United States lies like a huge page in the history of society. Line by line as we read this continental page from West to East we find the record of **social evolution**. It begins with the Indian and the hunter; it goes on to tell of the disintegration of savagery by the entrance of the trader, the pathfinder of civilization; we read the **annals** of the **pastoral** stage in ranch life; the exploitation of the soil by the raising of unrotated crops of corn and wheat in sparsely settled farming communities; the intensive culture of the denser farm settlement; and finally the manufacturing organization with city and factory system. This page is familiar to the student of census statistics, but how little of it has been used by our historians. Particularly in eastern States this page is a **palimpsest**. What is now a manufacturing State was in an earlier decade an area of intensive farming. Earlier yet it had been a wheat area, and still earlier the "range" had attracted the cattle-herder. Thus Wisconsin, now developing manufacture, is a State with varied agricultural interests. But earlier it was given over to almost exclusive grain-raising, like North Dakota at the present time....

....The Atlantic frontier was **compounded** of fisherman, fur-trader, miner, cattle-raiser, and farmer. Excepting the fisherman, each type of industry was on the march toward the West, impelled by an irresistible attraction. Each passed in successive waves across the continent. Stand at **Cumberland Gap** and watch the procession of civilization, marching single file—the buffalo following the trail to the salt springs, the Indian, the fur-trader and hunter, the cattle-raiser, the pioneer farmer—and the frontier has passed by. Stand at **South Pass** in the Rockies a century later and see the same procession with wider intervals between. The unequal rate of advance compels us to distinguish the frontier into the trader's frontier, the rancher's frontier, or the miner's frontier, and the farmer's frontier. When the mines and the cow pens were still near the fall line the traders' pack trains were tinkling across the **Alleghanies**, and the French on the Great Lakes were fortifying their posts, alarmed by the British trader's birch canoe. When the trappers scaled the Rockies, the farmer was still near the mouth of the Missouri....

Stratifications: Layers.

Social evolution: A gradual and orderly progression from lack of civilization to civilization.

Annals: Records.

Pastoral: Based on livestock raising.

Palimpsest: A document recording many layers of past experiences.

Compounded: Made up of; included.

Cumberland Gap: A pass through the Cumberland Plateau or Cumberland Mountains in northeast Tennessee; used by Daniel Boone to settle in Kentucky.

South Pass: A pass through the Rocky Mountains located in Wyoming; South Pass was used extensively during westward emigration.

Alleghanies: The Alleghany Mountains, range of mountains in the Appalachian mountain system.

*The effect of the Indian frontier as a **consolidating agent** in our history is important.... This frontier stretched along the western border like a cord of union. The Indian was a common danger, demanding united action....* [Turner suggests that this common enemy forced many colonies and states to work in union to confront a common threat.] *In this connection may be mentioned the importance of the frontier ... as a military training school, keeping alive the power of resistance to aggression, and developing the stalwart and rugged qualities of the frontiersman....*

*Having now roughly outlined the various kinds of frontiers, and their modes of advance, chiefly from the point of view of the frontier itself, we may next inquire what were the influences on the East and on the Old World. A rapid **enumeration** of some of the more noteworthy effects is all that I have time for.*

*First, we note that the frontier promoted the formation of a **composite nationality** for the American people....* [Turner explains how those who moved into the frontier came from a variety of

A romantic representation of Americans settling and civilizing the West.
(Archive Photos, Inc. Reproduced by permission.)

Consolidating agent: An element that brings things together.

Enumeration: Listing.

backgrounds and not just from the more homogenous areas (areas where people come from the same backgrounds) of New England and the Deep South.]

In another way the advance of the frontier decreased our dependence on England. The coast ... lacked diversified industries, and was dependent on England for the bulk of its supplies....

Before long the frontier created a demand for merchants. As [the frontier] *retreated from the coast it became less and less possible for England to bring her supplies directly to the consumer's wharfs, and carry away staple crops, and staple crops began to give way to diversified agriculture for a time. The effect of this phase of the frontier action upon the northern section is perceived when we realize how the advance of the frontier aroused seaboard cities ... to engage in rivalry for what Washington called "the extensive and valuable trade of a rising empire."*

The legislation which most developed the powers of the national government, and played the largest part in its activity, was conditioned on the frontier.... The growth of **nationalism** *and the evolution of American political institutions were dependent on the advance of the frontier....*

....The pioneer needed the goods of the coast, and so the grand series of internal improvement and railroad legislation began, with potent nationalizing effects. Over **internal improvements** *occurred great debates, in which grave constitutional questions were discussed....* [Turner goes on to discuss the many ways that the growth of the frontier helped the national government define its role; Turner pays special attention to the acquisition and sale of land.]

It is safe to say that the legislation with regard to land, tariff, and internal improvements—the American system of the nationalizing Whig party—was conditioned on frontier ideas and needs....

But the most important effect of the frontier has been in the promotion of democracy here and in Europe. As has been indicated, the frontier is productive of individualism. Complex society is precipitated by the wilderness into a kind of primitive organization based on the family. The tendency is anti-social. It produces antipathy to control, and particularly to any direct control. The tax-gatherer is viewed as a representative of oppression. Prof. Osgood, in an able article, has pointed out that the frontier conditions prevalent in the colonies are important factors in the explanation of the American

Composite nationality: A nationality that was formed from the meetings of many different peoples who had to find common ground.

Nationalism: Devotion to the interests of a particular nation.

Internal improvements: Projects such as road, bridge, and railroad building that would aid internal trade.

Revolution, where individual liberty was sometimes confused with absence of all effective government. The same conditions aid in explaining the difficulty of instituting a strong government in the period of the confederacy. The frontier individualism has from the beginning promoted democracy....

The East has always feared the result of an unregulated advance of the frontier, and has tried to check and guide it. The English authorities would have checked settlement at the headwaters of the Atlantic tributaries and allowed the "savages to enjoy their deserts in quiet lest the peltry trade should decrease."...

But the English Government was not alone in its desire to limit the advance of the frontier and guide its destinies. [Turner relates the many ways in which the states tried to halt westward expansion.] *When the Oregon question was under debates, in 1824, Smyth, of Virginia, would draw an unchangeable line for the limits of the United States at the outer limit of the two tiers of States beyond the Mississippi, complaining that the seaboard States were being drained of the flower of their population by the bringing of too much land into market. Even Thomas Benton, the man of widest views of the destiny of the West, at this stage of his career declared that along the ridge of the Rocky mountains "the western limits of the Republic should be drawn, and the statue of the fabled god Terminus should be raised upon its highest peak, never to be thrown down." But the attempts to limit the boundaries, to restrict land sales and settlement, and to deprive the West of its share of political power were all in vain. Steadily the frontier of settlement advanced and carried with it individualism, democracy, and nationalism, and powerfully affected the East and the Old World....*

From the conditions of frontier life came **intellectual traits** of profound importance. The works of travelers along each frontier from colonial days onward describe certain common traits, and these traits have, while softening down, still persisted as survivals in the place of their origin, even when a higher social organization succeeded. The result is that to the frontier the American intellect owes its striking characteristics. That coarseness and strength combined with **acuteness** and inquisitiveness; that practical, inventive turn of mind, quick to find **expedients**; that masterful grasp of material things lacking in the artistic but powerful to effect great ends; that restless, nervous energy; that dominant individualism, working for good and for evil, and withal that buoyancy and exuberance

Intellectual traits: Ways of thinking.

Acuteness: Intensity.

Expedients: Something invented to fit an urgent need.

which comes with freedom—these are traits of the frontier, or traits called out elsewhere because of the existence of the frontier. Since the days when the fleet of Columbus sailed into the waters of the New World, America has been another name for opportunity, and the people of the United States have taken their tone from the **incessant** *expansion which has not only been open but has even been forced upon them. He would be a rash prophet who should assert that the expansive character of American life has now entirely ceased. Movement has been its dominant fact, and, unless this training has no effect upon a people, the American energy will continually demand a wider field for its exercise. But never again will such gifts of free land offer themselves. For a moment, at the frontier, the bonds of custom are broken and unrestraint is triumphant. There is not* **tabula rasa.** *The stubborn American environment is there with its* **imperious summons** *to accept its conditions; the inherited ways of doing things are also there; and yet, in spite of environment, and in spite of custom, each frontier did indeed furnish a new field of opportunity, a gate of escape from the bondage of the past; and freshness, and confidence, and scorn of older society, impatience of its restraints and its ideas, and indifference to its lessons, have accompanied the frontier. What the Mediterranean Sea was to the Greeks, breaking the bond of custom, offering new experiences, calling out new institutions and activities, that, and more, the ever retreating frontier has been to the United States directly, and to the nations of Europe more remotely. And now, four centuries from the discovery of America, at the end of a hundred years of life under the Constitution, the frontier has gone, and with its going has closed the first period of American history.* [Turner, pp. 1–4, 6, 9–12, 15, 22–5, 27, 30, 33–5, 37–8]

What happened next . . .

While Turner's speech reached only a small audience of his fellow historians, within a year it was published and almost immediately began to influence American historians. Turner had put forth a new "paradigm"—a basic model—that could explain America's past. Between 1830 and 1870, a little more than 2 percent of history textbooks cited the impor-

Incessant: Continual.

Tabula rasa: Blank slate; an area not yet formed by experience or impressions.

Imperious summons: Authoritative command.

tance of the West in shaping the American character, while the majority explained it in terms of European ancestry. After Turner's thesis became widely accepted, the frontier experience became a rich source for American historians to mine for clues into the American character. Between 1900 and 1925, 93 percent of the published student textbooks named the frontier as the most influential force in the nation's development, according to Paul O'Neil in *The End and the Myth*. Because it was such a big part of how history was taught in the United States, the Turner thesis inevitably had an effect on how Americans perceived themselves. We saw ourselves as a nation of frontiersmen and pioneers who hacked our way through the wilderness, built cozy communities, and brought progress and civilization to a once untamed continent.

By the middle of the twentieth century, many historians began to criticize what is often called the Turner thesis. They found several problems with Turner's thesis: It presents an overly optimistic (happy) view of western expansion that does not acknowledge the real difficulties involved in expansion; it ignores the cultures of Native Americans, explaining Indians only as an obstacle to white conquest; it ignores Spanish and French influences in the New World; it places undo emphasis on white achievements and makes the white conquest of the West seem both inevitable and entirely beneficial; and it ignores the influence of industrialization, immigration, and the rise of the city. By the 1960s, Turner's thesis had largely been discarded and replaced by theories that examine the complexity of interactions between a variety of white colonists and Indians, as well as the French, Spanish, and British. Moreover, the new western history, as it is called, emphasizes the role that women as well as governmental and secular organizations played in the development of the West. Although the new western historians have refined or overturned many of Turner's ideas, the basic idea that the frontier shaped the American character remains a significant concept.

Did you know . . .

- The frontier thesis became the most important and controversial interpretation in American history during the first three decades of the twentieth century.

- The census report's conclusion about the closing of the frontier helped encourage President Theodore Roosevelt (1858–1919) to begin setting aside public lands as national parks.

- Historians continue to argue about Turner's thesis more than one hundred years after it was first presented.

- Turner was known as a gifted orator, or public speaker. His speeches were said to electrify his audience.

- When Turner gave his speech about the frontier he had not yet finished a graduate degree in history and was just thirty-two years old.

Consider the following...

- Why does Turner think the frontier promotes democracy?

- Why does Turner think the East (England or the eastern states) wished to halt the advance of people onto the frontier?

- In what ways was Turner correct in depicting the frontier as the primary influence on American character? In what ways was he wrong?

- What did Turner overlook in forming his argument?

- Who are the heroes in Turner's explanation of American development? What people might be overlooked by his explanation?

- What role do women play in Turner's thesis?

- How would an environmentalist react to Turner's thesis? Is there a role for wilderness in Turner's view of the inevitable development of civilization?

For More Information

Bennett, James D. *Frederick Jackson Turner*. Boston: Twayne Publishers, 1975.

Benson, Lee. *Turner and Beard: American Historical Writing Reconsidered*. Glencoe, IL: Free Press, 1960.

Billington, Ray A. *Frederick Jackson Turner: Historian, Scholar, Teacher*. New York: Oxford University Press, 1973.

Carpenter, Ronald H. *The Eloquence of Frederick Jackson Turner.* San Marino, CA: Huntington Library, 1983.

Hofstadter, Richard. *The Progressive Historians: Turner, Beard, Parrington.* New York: Knopf, 1968.

Jacobs, Wilbur R. *The Historical World of Frederick Jackson Turner, with Selections from His Correspondence.* New Haven, CT: Yale University Press, 1968.

O'Neil, Paul. *The End and the Myth.* Alexandria, VA: Time-Life Books, 1979.

Taylor, George Rogers, ed. *The Turner Thesis: Concerning the Role of the Frontier in American History.* Boston: D.C. Heath, 1949.

Turner, Frederick Jackson. "The Significance of the Frontier in American History." *The Frontier in American History.* New York: Holt, 1920, pp. 1–38.

Where to Learn More

The following list of resources focuses on works appropriate for middle school or high school students. These sources offer broad coverage of the history of westward expansion. For additional resources on specific topics please see individual entries. Please note that the web site addresses, though verified prior to publication, are subject to change.

Books

Billington, Ray Allen. *Westward to the Pacific: An Overview of Westward Expansion.* St. Louis, MO: Jefferson National Expansion Historical Association, 1979.

Collins, James L. *Exploring the American West.* New York: Franklin Watts, 1989.

Edwards, Cheryl, ed. *Westward Expansion: Exploration and Settlement.* Lowell, MA: Discovery Enterprises, 1995.

Erdosh, George. *Food and Recipes of the Westward Expansion.* New York: PowerKids Press, 1997.

Faber, Harold. *From Sea to Sea: The Growth of the United States.* New York: Charles Scribner's Sons, 1967, 1992.

Mancall, Peter C., ed. *Westward Expansion, 1800–1860.* Detroit: Gale, 1999.

Milner, II, Clyde A., Carol A. O'Connor, and Martha A. Sandweiss, eds. *The Oxford History of the American West*. New York and Oxford: Oxford University Press, 1994.

Penner, Lucille Recht. *Westward Ho! The Story of the Pioneers*. New York: Random House, 1997.

Smith, Carter, ed. *The Conquest of the West: A Sourcebook on the American West*. Brookfield, CT: Millbrook Press, 1992.

Utley, Robert M., and Wilcomb E. Washburn. *Indian Wars*. Boston: Houghton Mifflin, 1987.

Waldman, Carl. *Atlas of the North American Indian*. New York: Facts on File, 1985.

Wexler, Alan, ed. *Atlas of Westward Expansion*. New York: Facts On File, 1995.

White, Richard. *"It's Your Misfortune and None of My Own": A New History of the American West*. Norman: University of Oklahoma Press, 1991.

Web sites

"American History Sources for Students: The Westward Movement." *Global Access to Educational Sources: A Cybrary for Middle School and Beyond*. [Online] http://www.geocities.com/Athens/Academy/6617/west.html (accessed August 21, 2000).

The American West. [Online] http://www.americanwest.com (accessed August 21, 2000).

Georgia College and State University. *Ina Dillard Russel Library Special Collections: Native American Resources*. [Online] http://library.gcsu.edu/~sc/resna.html (accessed August 21, 2000).

Internet Resources about Black Cowboys and Pioneers. [Online] http://danenet.wicip.org/lms/themes/cowboys.html (accessed August 21, 2000).

The West [Online] http://www.pbs.org/weta/thewest/ (accessed August 21, 2000).

"Which 'Old West' and Whose?" *American History 102: Civil War to the Present*. [Online] http://us.history.wisc.edu/hist102/lectures/lecture03.html (accessed August 21, 2000).

Index

Bold type indicates main documents and speaker profiles.

Illustrations are marked by (ill.).

FOR REFERENCE

Do Not Take From This Room

DATE DUE
